SOLAR SYSTEM

THE SUN, MERCURY, AND VENUS

REVISED EDITION

Linda T. Elkins-Tanton

Facts On File
An imprint of Infobase Publishing

To my husband, James Stuart Tanton

● ◐ ◑ ○ ○ ◑ ●

THE SUN, MERCURY, AND VENUS, Revised Edition

Copyright © 2011, 2006 by Linda T. Elkins-Tanton

Facts On File, Inc.
An imprint of Infobase Publishing
132 West 31st Street
New York NY 10001

Library of Congress Cataloging-in-Publication Data
Elkins-Tanton, Linda T.
    The sun, mercury, and venus / Linda T. Elkins-Tanton ; foreword, Maria T. Zuber—Rev. ed.
        p. cm.—(The solar system)
    Includes bibliographical references and index.
    ISBN 978-0-8160-7700-7
    1. Sun—Popular works 2. Mercury (Planet)—Popular works. 3. Venus (Planet)—Popular works. I. Title.
    QB521.4.E45 2011
523.7—dc22   2010002445

Facts On File books are available at special discounts when purchased in bulk quantities for businesses, associations, institutions, or sales promotions. Please call our Special Sales Department in New York at (212) 967-8800 or (800) 322-8755.

You can find Facts On File on the World Wide Web at http://www.factsonfile.com

Text design by Annie O'Donnell
Composition by Hermitage Publishing Services
Illustrations by Pat Meschino
Photo research by Elizabeth H. Oakes
Cover printed by Bang Printing, Brainerd, Minn.
Book printed and bound by Bang Printing, Brainerd, Minn.
Date printed: November 2010
Printed in the United States of America

10 9 8 7 6 5 4 3 2 1

Contents

foreword

While I was growing up, I got my thrills from simple things—one was the beauty of nature. I spent hours looking at mountains, the sky, lakes, et cetera, and always seeing something different. Another pleasure came from figuring out how things work and why things *are* the way they *are*. I remember constantly looking up things from why airplanes fly to why it rains to why there are seasons. Finally was the thrill of discovery. The excitement of finding or learning about something new—like when I found the Andromeda galaxy for the first time in a telescope—was a feeling that could not be beat.

Linda Elkins-Tanton's multivolume set of books about the solar system captures all of these attributes. Far beyond a laundry list of facts about the planets, the Solar System is a set that provides elegant descriptions of natural objects that celebrate their beauty, explains with extraordinary clarity the diverse processes that shaped them, and deftly conveys the thrill of space exploration. Most people, at one time or another, have come across astronomical images and marveled at complex and remarkable features that seemingly defy explanation. But as the philosopher Aristotle recognized, "Nature does nothing uselessly," and each discovery represents an opportunity to expand human understanding of natural worlds. To great effect, these books often read like a detective story, in which the 4.5-billion year history of the solar system is reconstructed by integrating simple concepts of chemistry, physics, geology, meteorology, oceanography, and even biology with computer simulations, laboratory analyses, and the data from the myriad of space missions.

Starting at the beginning, you will learn why it is pretty well understood that the solar system started as a vast, tenuous ball of gas and dust that flattened to a disk with most of the mass—the future Sun—at the center. Much less certain is the transition from a dusty disk to the configuration with the planets, moons, asteroids, and comets that we see today. An ironic contrast is the extraordinary detail in which we understand some phenomena, like how rapidly the planets formed, and how depressingly uncertain we are about others, like how bright the early Sun was.

Once the planets were in place, the story diverges into a multitude of fascinating subplots. The oldest planetary surfaces preserve the record of their violent bombardment history. Once dismissed as improbable events, we now know that the importance of planetary impacts cannot be overstated. One of the largest of these collisions, by a Mars-sized body into the Earth, was probably responsible for the formation of the Earth's Moon, and others may have contributed to extinction of species on Earth. The author masterfully explains in unifying context the many other planetary processes, such as volcanism, faulting, the release of water and other volatile elements from the interiors of the planets to form atmospheres and oceans, and the mixing of gases in the giant planets to drive their dynamic cloud patterns.

Of equal interest is the process of discovery that brought our understanding of the solar system to where it is today. While robotic explorers justifiably make headlines, much of our current knowledge has come from individuals who spent seemingly endless hours in the cold and dark observing the night skies or in labs performing painstakingly careful analyses on miniscule grains from space. Here, these stories of perseverance and skill receive the attention they so richly deserve.

Some of the most enjoyable aspects of these books are the numerous occasions in which simple but confounding questions are explained in such a straightforward manner that you literally feel like you knew it all along. How do you know what is inside a planetary body if you cannot see there? What makes solar system objects spherical as opposed to irregular in shape? What causes the complex, changing patterns at the top of Jupiter's atmosphere? How do we know what Saturn's rings are made of?

When it comes right down to it, all of us are inherently explorers. The urge to understand our place on Earth and the extraordinary worlds beyond is an attribute that makes us uniquely human. The discoveries so lucidly explained in these volumes are perhaps most remarkable in the sense that they represent only the tip of the iceberg of what yet remains to be discovered.

—Maria T. Zuber, Ph.D.
E. A. Griswold Professor of Geophysics
Head of the Department of Earth,
Atmospheric and Planetary Sciences
Massachusetts Institute of Technology
Cambridge, Massachusetts

Preface

On August 24, 2006, the International Astronomical Union (IAU) changed the face of the solar system by dictating that Pluto is no longer a planet. Though this announcement raised a small uproar in the public, it heralded a new era of how scientists perceive the universe. Our understanding of the solar system has changed so fundamentally that the original definition of *planet* requires profound revisions.

While it seems logical to determine the ranking of celestial bodies by size (planets largest, then moons, and finally asteroids), in reality that has little to do with the process. For example, Saturn's moon Titan is larger than the planet Mercury, and Charon, Pluto's moon, is almost as big as Pluto itself. Instead, scientists have created specific criteria to determine how an object is classed. However, as telescopes increase their range and computers process images with greater clarity, new information continually challenges the current understanding of the solar system.

As more distant bodies are discovered, better theories for their quantity and mass, their origins, and their relation to the rest of the solar system have been propounded. In 2005, a body bigger than Pluto was found and precipitated the argument: Was it the 10th planet or was, in fact, Pluto not even a planet itself? Because we have come to know that Pluto and its moon, Charon, orbit in a vast cloud of like objects, calling it a planet no longer made sense. And so, a new class of objects was born: the dwarf planets.

Every day, new data streams back to Earth from satellites and space missions. Early in 2004, scientists proved that standing liquid water once existed on Mars, just a month after a mission visited a comet and discovered that the material in its nucleus is as strong as some *rocks* and not the loose pile of ice and dust expected. The MESSENGER mission to Mercury, launched in 2004, has thus far completed three flybys and will enter Mercury orbit at 2011. The mission has already proven that Mercury's core is still molten, raising fundamental questions about processes of planetary evolution, and it has sent back to Earth intriguing information about the composition of Mercury's crust. Now the New Horizons mission is on its way to make the first visit to Pluto and the Kuiper belt. Information arrives from space observations and Earth-based experiments, and scientists attempt to explain what they see, producing a stream of new hypotheses about the formation and evolution of the solar system and all its parts.

The graph below shows the number of moons each planet has; large planets have more than small planets, and every year scientists discover new bodies orbiting the gas giant planets. Many bodies of substantial size orbit in the asteroid belt, or the Kuiper belt, and many sizable asteroids cross the orbits of planets as they make their way around the Sun. Some planets' moons are unstable and will in the near future (geologically speaking) make new ring systems as they crash into their hosts. Many moons, like Neptune's giant Triton, orbit their planets backward (clockwise when viewed from the North Pole, the opposite way that the planets orbit the Sun). Triton also has the coldest surface temperature of any

The mass of the planet appears to control the number of moons it has; the large outer planets have more moons than the smaller inner planets.

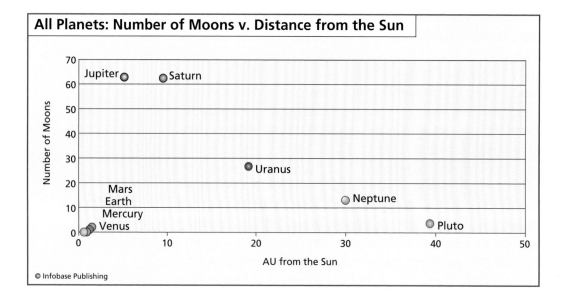

All Planets: Number of Moons v. Distance from the Sun

moon or planet, including Pluto, which is much farther from the Sun. The solar system is made of bodies in a continuum of sizes and ages, and every rule of thumb has an exception.

Perhaps more important, the solar system is not a static place. It continues to evolve—note the drastic climate changes we are experiencing on Earth as just one example—and our ability to observe it continues to evolve, as well. Just five planets visible to the naked eye were known to ancient peoples: Mercury, Venus, Mars, Jupiter, and Saturn. The Romans gave these planets the names they are still known by today. Mercury was named after their god Mercury, the fleet-footed messenger of the gods, because the planet Mercury seems especially swift when viewed from Earth. Venus was named for the beautiful goddess Venus, brighter than anything in the sky except the Sun and Moon. The planet Mars appears red even from Earth and so was named after Mars, the god of war. Jupiter is named for the king of the gods, the biggest and most powerful of all, and Saturn was named for Jupiter's father. The ancient Chinese and the ancient Jews recognized the planets as well, and the Maya (250–900 C.E., Mexico and environs) and Aztec (~1100–1700 C.E., Mexico and environs) knew Venus by the name Quetzalcoatl, after their god of good and light, who eventually also became their god of war.

Science is often driven forward by the development of new technology, allowing researchers to make measurements that were previously impossible. The dawn of the new age in astronomy and study of the solar system occurred in 1608, when Hans Lippenshey, a Dutch eyeglass-maker, attached a lens to each end of a hollow tube and thus created the first telescope. Galileo Galilei, born in Pisa, Italy, in 1564, made his first telescope in 1609 from Lippenshey's model. Galileo soon discovered that Venus has phases like the Moon does and that Saturn appeared to have "handles." These were the edges of Saturn's rings, though the telescope was not strong enough to resolve the rings correctly. In 1610, Galileo discovered four of Jupiter's moons, which are still called the Galilean satellites. These four moons were the proof that not every heavenly body orbited the Earth as Ptolemy, a Greek philosopher, had asserted around 140 C.E. Galileo's discovery was the beginning

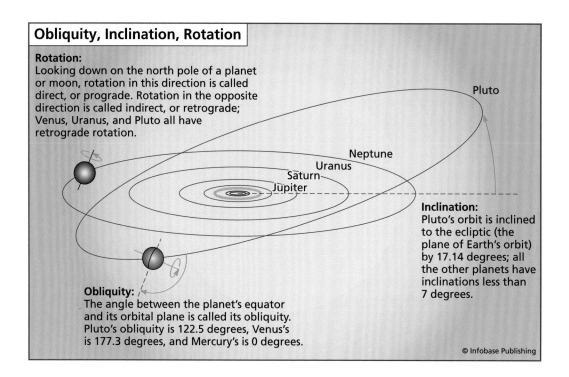

Obliquity, Inclination, Rotation

Rotation:
Looking down on the north pole of a planet or moon, rotation in this direction is called direct, or prograde. Rotation in the opposite direction is called indirect, or retrograde; Venus, Uranus, and Pluto all have retrograde rotation.

Pluto

Neptune
Uranus
Saturn
Jupiter

Inclination:
Pluto's orbit is inclined to the ecliptic (the plane of Earth's orbit) by 17.14 degrees; all the other planets have inclinations less than 7 degrees.

Obliquity:
The angle between the planet's equator and its orbital plane is called its obliquity. Pluto's obliquity is 122.5 degrees, Venus's is 177.3 degrees, and Mercury's is 0 degrees.

© Infobase Publishing

Obliquity, orbital inclination, and rotational direction are three physical measurements used to describe a rotating, orbiting body.

of the end of the strongly held belief that the Earth is the center of the solar system, as well as a beautiful example of a case where improved technology drove science forward.

The concept of the Earth-centered solar system is long gone, as is the notion that the heavenly spheres are unchanging and perfect. Looking down on the solar system from above the Sun's north pole, the planets orbiting the Sun can be seen to be orbiting counterclockwise, in the manner of the original *protoplanetary disk* of material from which they formed. (This is called *prograde* rotation.) This simple statement, though, is almost the end of generalities about the solar system. Some planets and dwarf planets spin backward compared to the Earth, other planets are tipped over, and others orbit outside the *ecliptic* plane by substantial angles, Pluto in particular (see figure above on *obliquity* and orbital *inclination*). Some planets and moons are still hot enough to be volcanic, and some produce *silicate* lava (for example, the Earth and Jupiter's moon Io), while others have exotic lavas made of molten ices (for example, Neptune's moon Triton).

Today, we look outside our solar system and find planets orbiting other stars, more than 400 to date. Now our search for signs of life goes beyond Mars and Enceladus and Titan and reaches to other star systems. Most of the science presented in this set comes from the startlingly rapid developments of the last 100 years, brought about by technological development.

The rapid advances of planetary and heliospheric science and the astonishing plethora of images sent back by missions motivate the revised editions of the Solar System set. The multivolume set explores the vast and enigmatic Sun at the center of the solar system and moves out through the planets, dwarf planets, and minor bodies of the solar system, examining each and comparing them from the point of view of a planetary scientist. Space missions that produced critical data for the understanding of solar system bodies are introduced in each volume, and their data and images shown and discussed. The revised editions of *The Sun, Mercury, and Venus, The Earth and the Moon,* and *Mars* place emphasis on the areas of unknowns and the results of new space missions. The important fact that the solar system consists of a continuum of sizes and types of bodies is stressed in the revised edition of *Asteroids, Meteorites, and Comets.* This book discusses the roles of these small bodies as recorders of the formation of the solar system, as well as their threat as *impactors* of planets. In the revised edition of *Jupiter and Saturn,* the two largest planets are described and compared. In the revised edition of *Uranus, Neptune, Pluto, and the Outer Solar System,* Pluto is presented in its rightful, though complex, place as the second-largest known of a extensive population of icy bodies that reach far out toward the closest stars, in effect linking the solar system to the Galaxy itself.

This set hopes to change the familiar and archaic litany *Mercury, Venus, Earth, Mars, Jupiter, Saturn, Uranus, Neptune, Pluto* into a thorough understanding of the many sizes and types of bodies that orbit the Sun. Even a cursory study of each planet shows its uniqueness along with the great areas of knowledge that are unknown. These titles seek to make the familiar strange again.

Acknowledgments

Foremost, profound thanks to the following organizations for the great science and adventure they provide for mankind and, on a more prosaic note, for allowing the use of their images for these books: the National Oceanic and Atmospheric Administration (NOAA) and the National Aeronautics and Space Administration (NASA), in conjunction with the Jet Propulsion Laboratory (JPL) and Malin Space Science Systems, the European Space Agency (ESA), the Russian Federation Space Agency, and the German Aerospace Agency.

A large number of missions and their teams have provided invaluable data and images, including the Mars Reconnaissance Orbiter, MESSENGER, Solar and Heliospheric Observer, Mars Global Surveyor, Mars Odyssey, the Mars Exploration Rovers, Galileo, Stardust, Near-Earth Asteroid Rendezvous, and Cassini. Special thanks to Steele Hill, SOHO Media Specialist at NASA, who prepared a number of images from the SOHO mission, to the astronauts who take the photos found at Astronaut Photography of the Earth, and to the providers of the National Space Science Data Center, Great Images in NASA, and the NASA/JPL Planetary Photojournal, all available on the Web (addresses given in the reference section).

Many thanks also to Frank K. Darmstadt, executive editor, Jodie Rhodes, literary agent, and Maria Zuber, Sam Bowring, Brad Hager, Tim Grove, and my other colleagues at MIT for their support, collaboration, and friendship.

Introduction

The MESSENGER mission to Mercury is opening a new window on the inner solar system. Starting in 2008, the mission began a number of years of flybys culminating in an orbital insertion around Mercury and is already producing unparalleled observations about this mysterious innermost planet. Mercury orbits so close to the Sun, from the point of view of Earth, that seeing it from the Earth against the Sun's glare is a great challenge. At the same time, the huge gravitational force of the Sun makes it a challenge to put a mission on Mercury without losing it into the Sun. Now, with dawning understanding of Mercury, we are also gaining understanding of the hot, close exoplanets in orbit around distant stars.

Studying these distant solar systems has also produced an unprecedented level of understanding of the formation of our own solar system. Looking back 4.5 billion years in this solar system is a challenge, since the violent and constant processes of planetary evolution have erased much of the early history. This history remains on the surface of Mercury, frozen, and it can be seen elsewhere in the galaxy in active motion. The current state of understanding of the formation of stars and planetary systems lies at the beginning of this six-book set that covers the state of scientific knowledge of the solar system's planets and smaller bodies, starting from the center, the Sun, and moving outward, as shown in this depiction of the solar system.

The Sun, Mercury, and Venus, Revised Edition discusses the Sun and the innermost planets in the context of new information about solar systems around other stars, revolutionizing our understanding of the nature of planet formation and planetary systems. In 2008 the MESSENGER mission flew

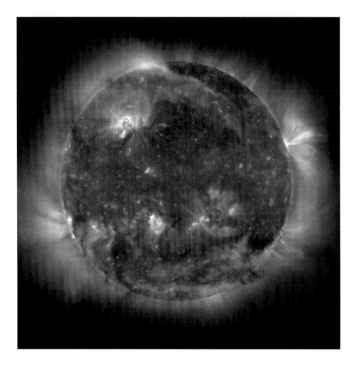

The Sun in infrared wavelengths shows activity in the chromosphere, a layer normally invisible to the human eye. (SOHO)

by Mercury for the first time and began sending its stream of new information, changing the fundamental understanding of that planet. The new information about Mercury and about planet-building processes in general is changing the understanding of our innermost solar system and drives the new edition of this volume.

In 350 B.C.E. Aristotle, the great Greek philosopher, published *De Caelo* (On the heavens), one of the most influential books in the history of science. Aristotle wrote that the Earth is the center of the solar system and that all the other bodies in the solar system orbit the Earth while set into a complex series of spheres. In his philosophy, the Earth was the only site of change, of birth, life, death, and decay, while the heavenly spheres were perfect and eternally changeless. Aristotle's system of spheres could not be reconciled with the apparent motions of the planets from the misleading perspective of a viewer on the planet Earth, which include speeding up, slowing down, and even moving backward (known as *retrograde* motion). About 500 years later Ptolemy, another Greek philosopher, published his masterwork *Hè Megalè Syntaxis* (*Almagest,* or The mathematical compilation). In *Almagest* Ptolemy develops a complex mathematical explanation for the apparent movement of the planets and thus supports the Aristotelian theory sufficiently for it to live on as the primary theory for the structure of the solar system for almost 2,000 years. The Aristotelian and Ptolemaic theories of an Earth-centered solar system thus may be one of the longest-lived theories in the history of science.

In 1514 C.E. Nicolas Copernicus, a Polish scientist and canon in the Catholic Church, published a tiny unsigned pamphlet

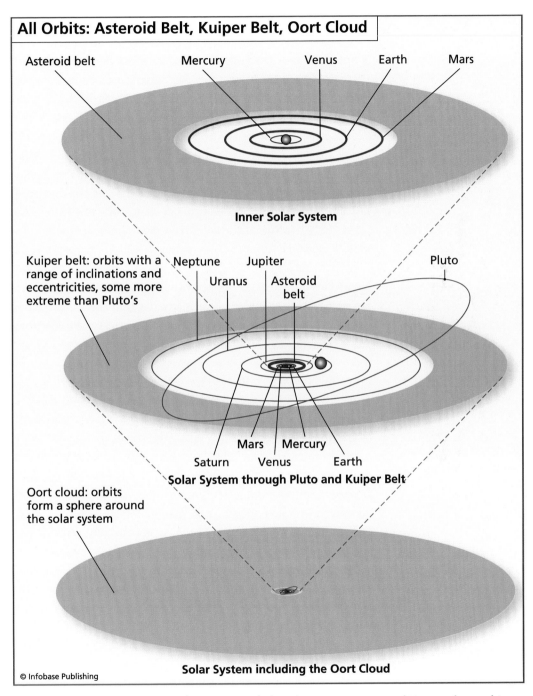

All Orbits: Asteroid Belt, Kuiper Belt, Oort Cloud

Asteroid belt — Mercury — Venus — Earth — Mars

Inner Solar System

Kuiper belt: orbits with a range of inclinations and eccentricities, some more extreme than Pluto's

Neptune — Uranus — Jupiter — Asteroid belt — Pluto

Saturn — Mars — Venus — Mercury — Earth

Solar System through Pluto and Kuiper Belt

Oort cloud: orbits form a sphere around the solar system

Solar System including the Oort Cloud

© Infobase Publishing

This book covers the innermost solar system, including the Sun, Mercury, and Venus, whose orbits are highlighted here. All the orbits are far closer to circular than shown in this oblique view, which was chosen to show the inclination of Pluto's orbit to the ecliptic.

called the *Commentariolus* (Little commentary). In this little handwritten book he posits that the center of the universe is not the Earth but near the Sun, that the distance from the Earth to the Sun is imperceptible compared to the distance to the stars, and that the apparent retrograde motion of the planets is due to observing them from the orbiting Earth. These axioms, now all known to be absolutely true, were earthshaking at the time. (Copernicus delayed a full publication of his theories until just before his death in 1543, when *De Revolutionibus Orbium* [On the revolutions of the celestial spheres] was published with the help of an assistant.) Galileo Galilei (1564–1642), the great Italian astronomer, was a great advocate of the Copernican system, for which he was condemned by an Inquisition at the Holy Office in Rome of heresy and lived the remainder of his life under house arrest. Galileo was fortunate not to have been executed for his belief that the universe did not orbit the Earth. Galileo's trial, held in 1633, further drove any Copernicans in Catholic countries into secrecy, and the theory was not held by a majority of natural philosophers until the late 17th century. The development of physics and in particular the theory of gravitation showed that only the Sun could be the center of the solar system, and slowly the world of science was won over to a Sun-centered system.

The new part one of this volume describes the state of understanding of how new planetary systems are formed. Observational astronomy has now demonstrated that almost all new young stars begin with planets forming around them, suggesting that many of the 200 to 400 billion stars in our galaxy may have planets orbiting them now. Observations also show that many planetary systems elsewhere in our solar system have gas giant planets closest to their stars, rather than small rocky planets like Mercury, Venus, Earth, and Mars, a pattern that challenges models for how planets are formed.

The Sun's huge mass (greater than 99 percent of the total mass of the solar system) controls the orbits of all the planets and smaller bodies of the solar system, and its radiation and magnetic field dominate the space environments of the inner planets and define the size of the solar system itself. The Sun, therefore, is the subject of part two of this volume.

Had Jupiter been just 15 times more massive, it also would have begun nuclear fusion reactions and become a small star itself. Instead, the Sun is the sole star of this solar system. The intense heat of fusion and its attendant complex and powerful magnetic fields are just beginning to be understood, though the importance of the Sun's energy has been recognized by mankind since prehistory.

Mercury, the topic of part three of this volume, is the subject of intense scientific attention because of the first flyby of the MESSENGER mission. *MESSENGER* is just the second spacecraft to visit the planet (*Mariner 10*, which flew by the planet three times in 1974 and 1975, was the first), and its advanced instruments are producing invaluable information about the planet.

Though Mercury is far closer to the Earth than are Jupiter or Saturn, more is known about those distant gas giant planets than about Mercury. Mercury is the least visited of terrestrial planets, as shown in the following figure. Mercury, Uranus, and Neptune have each been visited one time by space missions, and only Pluto has never been visited. Since space missions deliver the bulk of information about planets, Mercury is little known.

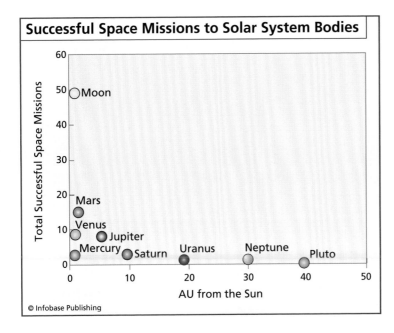

The approximate number of successful space missions from all nations shows that the Moon is by far the most visited body, only Pluto has had no mission visits, and Mercury is almost as neglected as Uranus and Neptune. The definition of a successful mission is arguable, so totals for Mars and the Moon in particular may be disputed.

Part four of this volume discusses Venus, the sister planet to Earth in size and distance to the Sun, though the two planets could not be more different in other ways. Lacking surface water and *plate tectonics,* Venus's surface is characterized by immense, roughly circular features sometimes hundreds of kilometers across volcanic and tectonic centers bounded by faults, some depressed and others raised in their centers. Venus's surface temperature is a blazing 855°F (457°C), hotter even than Mercury. The surface is dominated by dense clouds of acid creating a pressure about 90 times that of Earth's. Venus thus forms a perfect laboratory for studying the long-term effects of small differences in climate: Venus is the product of runaway greenhouse heating, where the Sun's energy is trapped within the atmosphere rather than reflected or radiated back into space. This same greenhouse effect is occurring on Earth with the alterations in the atmosphere caused by mankind. Though mankind may eventually drive the climate to dangerously high temperatures, it will not reach the extremes of Venus, where a human visitor would be simultaneously crushed by the atmospheric pressure, burned by its heat, and asphyxiated by its acids. The differences between Earth and Venus are exceptional, considering their similar positions in the solar system. Venus is also the subject of intense scientific interest and will receive more spacecraft visits in upcoming decades, adding to the 16 missions that have thus far taken images or even sent probes into the planet's atmosphere.

The conditions on Mercury and Venus today are the direct consequences of orbiting so close to the immensely powerful Sun, which baked Mercury, and which created the intense greenhouse heat on Venus. As the Sun's energy output changes over the coming hundreds of millions of years, the climates on the Earth and Mars will change as well. This volume describes the beginning of our solar system from its birth in a cloud of dust and gas and follows the evolution of the Sun and of the innermost planets, Mercury and Venus, to their present states.

PART 1

THE BIRTH OF STARS AND PLANETS

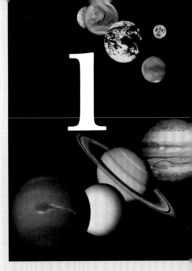

Searching
for Clues

Only since 2000 or so have observers with the most sophisticated telescopes begun to see what they think are young planet-forming regions elsewhere in the solar system. For the rest of human history, any understanding of the early development of the solar system had to rely on the evidence from meteorites and on basic theory, and the thought of other planetary systems around other stars remained the stuff of science fiction. Meteorites, the most critical clues of all, were misunderstood for millennia, though many were collected and studied for their interesting properties.

In 77 C.E. Pliny the Elder made a catalog of the meteorites already enshrined in Rome and described them as rocks that had fallen from the sky. However, he also listed as having fallen from the sky bricks, wool, and milk. The Greek philosopher Aristotle (384–322 B.C.E.) stated that it was impossible for stones to fall from the sky, as there was no matter up there to fall, apart from the planets themselves. Instead, he proposed a different solution: Meteorites are the tops of volcanoes that have been blown off at the site of some distant eruption and fall to Earth from a clear sky. This explanation was largely rejected at the time but came to be increasingly widely accepted, especially when Ptolemy (ca. 90–ca. 168

C.E.) hypothesized that the solar system consisted of a series of spheres nested inside each other, each bearing a planet and thus allowing their constant spinning motion. Since the spheres were solid, nothing could fall between one sphere and another, and so all meteorites had to originate on Earth.

Still, the fascination with meteorites never flagged. In 1492, a 280-pound (127-kg) meteorite fell in the town of Ensisheim, France. The emperor Maximilian happened to be traveling nearby and ordered that the meteorite be preserved in the church in Ensisheim as an omen of divine protection. Sir Isaac Newton, on the other hand, disbelieved that there could be small rocky bodies in space. He stated that "to make way for the regular and lasting motions of the planets and comets, it is necessary to empty the heavens of all matter." Though in the end proved incorrect, at least Newton had a scientific conjecture of why meteorites could not have fallen from space.

The general view of the 17th and 18th centuries was that God had put all things in the solar system in their rightful places and thus none should fall catastrophically into the others. Ernst Florens Friedrich Chladni, a German scientist whose primary field of study was not astronomy or geology but acoustics, disagreed with popular opinion and published in 1794 *On the Origin of the Pallas Iron and Other Similar to it, and on Some Associated Natural Phenomena*, what might be the seminal book on meteorites. In the book Chladni argued that meteorites fall from the sky and are extraterrestrial in origin. He stated that they are small bodies traveling through space that are attracted by Earth's gravity to fall through the atmosphere, and that fireballs are meteorites heated to incandescence (glowing from heat) by air friction. In these assertions scientists now find that he was completely right, but he was about a century ahead of his time in his thinking and received mainly ridicule when he published his carefully thought-out book.

As Ursula Marvin writes in her special paper "Ernst Florens Friedrich Chladni (1756–1827) and the origins of modern meteorite research," a 56-pound (25-kg) stone fell at Wold Cottage, England, at 3:30 P.M. on Sunday, December 13, 1775. Several people were startled by a whizzing sound and a series of explosions, and one laborer in particular was startled when the black stone broke through the clouds and struck the ground just 30 feet from where he stood. The impact showered him with earth, and when he ran up to investigate, he saw that the stone had penetrated 12 inches (30.5 cm) of soil and an additional half foot of the underlying limestone bedrock.

The landowner, a flamboyant writer, took full advantage of this unusual occurrence, displaying the stone in London and erecting a monument where it fell. The publicity meant that the stone came to the attention of researchers, and a sample finally came to the young chemist Edward C. Howard and his colleague Jacques-Louis, comte de Bournon (who had fled to England to escape the Reign of Terror in France). The two began the first chemical analysis of meteorites. They analyzed a number of fallen stones with the state-of-the-art techniques of the time, which were actually quite good at determining compositions.

Howard and de Bournon published a paper describing the four main components of the stones: "curious globules," martial pyrites, grains of malleable iron, and fine-grained earthy matrix. These were painstakingly separated and analyzed. The chemists correctly determined that the "martial pyrites" were unlike any known sulfide—in fact, they were troilite (FeS), a hallmark of meteorites, and rare on Earth. The abundance of nickel (~10 percent) in the malleable iron absolutely differentiated these rocks from anything yet found on Earth. This iron component is now thought to most closely resemble the Earth's core.

The paper went on to describe in great detail the compositions of the meteorites. These were the first meteorites to be taken apart, grain by grain, and compared to known terrestrial rocks, and a portion of scientists began to think carefully about whether meteorites might in fact come from space. Pierre-Simon Laplace, famous as a mathematician, suggested the rocks might actually be volcanic in origin, but from volcanoes on the Moon, rather than the Earth. Then, in 1803 the town of L'Aigle in France received an amazing meteorite shower that totaled about 3,000 stones following three loud explosive bangs. The whizzing sounds that accompanied the stones' falls and the thunderlike booming that continued for some minutes frightened the townspeople and created a large, irrefutable group of witnesses. People who immediately went to the stones found them warm to the touch and smelling of sulfur.

Within a decade most Europeans believed in an extraterrestrial origin for meteorites, but North American scientists lagged in this belief by about a century. In 1807 a meteorite fell in Weston, Connecticut, and two professors from Yale wrote in an essay that they had determined that the bolide had fallen from space. Throughout the literature there is a persistent story that Thomas Jefferson read their report and retorted: "I would find it easier to believe that two Yankee professors would lie, than that stones should fall from the sky." There appears to be no record of this comment, however, and Ursula Marvin of the Harvard-Smithsonian Center for Astrophysics reports that the closest remark recorded from Jefferson on the subject is as follows:

> We certainly are not to deny what we cannot account for. . . . it may be very difficult to explain how the stone you possess came into the position in which it was found. But is it easier to explain how it got into the clouds from whence it is supposed to have fallen? The actual fact, however, is the thing to be established.

Jefferson may not have believed the hypothesis wholeheartedly, but in the best scientific tradition what he wanted was for the truth to be proven in a clear way.

As populations rose and more falls were witnessed, and as scientific methods became better at demonstrating the differences between meteorites and terrestrial rocks, the extraterrestrial origin of meteorites has become absolutely clear. Understanding that these materials came from space immediately indicates that they carry clues to the origin and evolution of other solar system bodies. The different categories of meteorites carry different kinds of clues and mark different periods of early solar system development.

Meteorites are divided into four major classes: *chondrites,* achondrites, iron, and stony-iron meteorites. Chondrites are thought to contain the most primitive solar system material, while achondrites, iron, and stony-iron meteorites are thought to represent portions of larger asteroids that have undergone differentiation and other changes since solar system formation. Each of the major classes of meteorites contains many subclasses, often named after the fall location of the first example found, and in other cases differentiated according to mineral grain size, alteration by water, or other descriptive means.

The chondrite meteorites are named after tiny round bodies that they contain called *chondrules.* Chondrules are rounded, heterogeneous bodies that contain both crystals and glass. Because they are rounded, they are thought to have cooled before being incorporated into the meteorites (otherwise their round, smooth outlines would have been shaped by the crystals around them). They are further thought to be droplets that condensed from a liquid, and they reminded their first researchers of volcanic glass.

Most chondritic meteorites also contain small spheres called calcium-aluminum inclusions, or CAIs. At most there are ~5 percent by volume of CAIs in chondrites, and in some chondrites there are none. CAIs are made of many tiny minerals, which in turn consist mainly of the elements calcium, aluminum, titanium, and oxygen. These are the elements with the highest condensation temperatures, that is, when the initially hot mass of gas around the young Sun was cooling, these would have been the first materials to condense into solids.

The CAIs are thought to represent the most primitive, earliest solar system material. They are not like any other material yet found elsewhere in the solar system. Radioisotopic dating shows that the oldest CAIs formed at 4.568 billion years before the present, and that is the age of the solar system, the time when material first began to condense. The chondrules, by comparison, are mainly 1 to a few million years younger than the CAIs.

Precise radioisotope dating was not developed until after the 1950s, and these very precise dates for the age of the solar system were not made until around the year 2000. In the

One class of meteorites, the carbonaceous chondrites, have compositions almost exactly like the Sun, as shown in the plot, and so are thought to represent the bulk composition of the planetary disk that formed the planets. (modeled after Ringwood, 1979)

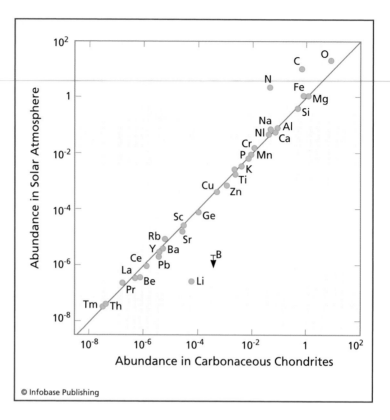

© Infobase Publishing

decades before the 1950s the solar system was thought to be on the order of 4 billion years old, but more precise ages were not attainable. The age of our solar system, therefore, is a very newly discovered fact.

The chondritic meteorites are thus thought to be the primitive earliest solids in the solar system and therefore to be the material that accreted into larger and larger bodies to eventually form the planets. Chondrites are divided further into four classes: ordinary, enstatite, carbonaceous, and other. The carbonaceous chondrites have the oldest CAIs. Of the carbonaceous chondrites, the most promising group is called the CI chondrites, after the first discovered in a fall in Tanzania in 1938. It was named Ivuna, hence the designation CI: carbonaceous Ivuna. Only five CI chondrites are known. The other four are Orgueil, Alais, Tonk, and Revelstoke.

To determine which meteorite composition represents the most primitive material, scientists have compared the concentrations of elements in the meteorites with the elements that make up the Sun (see the sidebar "Elements and Isotopes"). The Sun, since it contains more than 99 percent of the material in the solar system, is probably a good measure of an average solar system composition. If the material was processed by being smashed by other impactors, by being partly melting and having the solid and melted portions separated, perhaps repeatedly, or by being mixed and heated with water, its composition may no longer be similar to the Sun's.

The CI chondrites have compositions similar to the Sun's, except for the very volatile elements like helium and hydrogen. If the abundance of elements in the Sun is plotted against the abundance of elements in chondrite meteorites, the plot forms almost a perfect straight line, as shown in the figure on page 8. Other meteorites and especially planetary materials do not have comparable elemental abundances to the Sun.

Neither the Earth nor Mars, however, can be made from pure CI chondritic material: The bulk compositions do not match. No two known chondrites can be mixed to make the planet; nor any three, and in fact many meteorite compositions are required to match either planet. The building blocks of the planets must have been far richer in volatile elements, including hydrogen, helium, oxygen, carbon, and the noble gases than are the CI chondrites. Though the CI chondrites appear to be the oldest and most primitive material in the solar system, they are not the whole story for building the Earth, Moon, and Mars.

Nor are the chondrites the end of the meteorite story. While chondrites at first glance look similar to other Earth rocks (though they look entirely different when examined closely), the most distinctive meteorites are the iron meteorites. Iron meteorites consist of iron with 5 to 20 percent nickel and traces of gallium, germanium, carbon, sulfur, and iridium. These elements are arranged mainly into closely interlocked crystals of the minerals kamacite and tetrataenite. Kamacite generally consists of between 90 and 95 wt% iron, with the

(continues on page 12)

ELEMENTS AND ISOTOPES

All the materials in the solar system are made of *atoms,* or parts of atoms. A family of atoms that all have the same number of positively charged particles in their nuclei (the center of the atom) is called an *element:* Oxygen and iron are elements, as are aluminum, helium, carbon, silicon, platinum, gold, hydrogen, and well more than 200 others. Every single atom of oxygen has eight positively charged particles, called protons, in its *nucleus.* The number of protons in an atom's nucleus is called its *atomic number:* All oxygen atoms have an atomic number of eight, and that is what makes them all oxygen atoms.

Naturally occurring nonradioactive oxygen, however, can have eight, nine, or 10 uncharged particles, called neutrons, in its nucleus, as well. Different weights of the same element caused by addition of neutrons are called *isotopes.* The sum of the protons and neutrons in an atom's nucleus is called its *mass number.* Oxygen can have mass numbers of 16 (eight positively charged particles and eight uncharged particles), 17 (eight protons and nine neutrons), or 18 (eight protons and 10 neutrons). These isotopes are written as ^{16}O, ^{17}O, and ^{18}O. The first, ^{16}O, is by far the most common of the three isotopes of oxygen.

Atoms, regardless of their isotope, combine together to make molecules and compounds. For example, carbon (C) and hydrogen (H) molecules combine to make methane, a common gas constituent of the outer planets. Methane consists of one carbon atom and four hydrogen atoms and is shown symbolically this way: CH_4. Whenever a subscript is placed by the symbol of an element, it indicates how many of those atoms go into the makeup of that molecule or compound.

Quantities of elements in the various planets and moons and ratios of isotopes are important ways to determine whether the planets and moons formed from the same material, or different materials. Oxygen again is a good example. If quantities of each of the oxygen isotopes are measured in every rock on Earth and a graph is made of the ratios of $^{17}O/^{16}O$ versus $^{18}O/^{16}O$, the points on the graph will form a line with a certain slope (the slope is ½, in fact). The fact that the data forms a line means that the material that formed the Earth was homogeneous; beyond rocks, the oxygen isotopes in every living thing and in the atmosphere also lie on this slope. The materials on the Moon also show this same slope. By measuring oxygen isotopes in many different kinds of solar system materials, it has now been shown that the slope of the plot $^{17}O/^{16}O$ versus $^{18}O/^{16}O$ is one-half for every object, but each object's line is offset from the others by some amount. Each solar system object lies along a different parallel line.

At first it was thought that the distribution of oxygen isotopes in the solar system was determined by their mass: the more massive isotopes stayed closer to the huge gravitational force of the Sun, and the lighter isotopes strayed farther out into the solar system. Studies of very primitive meteorites called chondrites, thought to be the most primitive, early material in the solar system, showed to the contrary that they have heterogeneous oxygen isotope ratios, and therefore oxygen isotopes were not evenly spread in the early solar system. Scientists then recognized that temperature also affects oxygen isotopic ratios: At different temperatures, different ratios of oxygen isotopes condense. As material in the early solar system cooled, it is thought that first aluminum oxide condensed, at a temperature of about 2,440°F (1,340°C), and then calcium-titanium oxide ($CaTiO_3$), at a temperature of about 2,300°F (1,260°C), and then a calcium-aluminum-silicon-oxide ($Ca_2Al_2SiO_7$), at a temperature of about 2,200°F (1,210°C), and so on through other compounds down to iron-nickel alloy at 1,800°F (990°C), and water, at –165°F (–110°C) (this low temperature for the condensation of water is caused by the very low pressure of space). Since oxygen isotopic ratios vary with temperature, each of these oxides would have a slightly different isotopic ratio, even if they came from the same place in the solar system.

The key process that determines the oxygen isotopes available at different points in the early solar system seems to be that simple compounds created with ^{18}O are relatively stable at high temperatures, while those made with the other two isotopes break down more easily and at lower temperatures. Some scientists therefore think that ^{17}O and ^{18}O were concentrated in the middle of the protoplanetary disk, and ^{16}O was more common at the edge. Despite these details, though, the basic fact remains true: Each solar system body has its own line on the graph of oxygen isotope ratios.

Most atoms are stable. A carbon-12 atom, for example, remains a carbon-12 atom forever, and an oxygen-16 atom remains an oxygen-16 atom forever, but certain atoms eventually disintegrate into a totally new atom. These atoms are said to be unstable or radioactive. An unstable atom has excess internal energy, with the result that the nucleus can undergo a spontaneous change toward a more stable form. This is called radioactive decay.

Unstable isotopes (radioactive isotopes) are called radioisotopes. Some elements, such as uranium, have no stable isotopes. The rate at which unstable elements decay is measured as a *half-life*, the time it takes for half of the unstable atoms to have decayed. After one half-life, half the unstable atoms remain; after two half-lives, one-quarter remain, and so forth. Half-lives vary from parts of a second to millions of years, depending on the atom being considered. Whenever an isotope decays, it gives off energy, which can heat and also damage the material around it. Decay of radioisotopes is a major source of the internal heat of the Earth today: the heat generated by accreting the Earth out of smaller bodies and the heat generated by the giant impactor that formed the Moon have long since conducted away into space.

(continued from page 9)
remainder mainly nickel. In tetrataenite nickel makes up 20 to 65 wt% nickel, with the remainder iron.

Though iron meteorites make up only about 5 percent of observed meteorite falls, they make up the largest percent by mass of any meteorite group in collections. Their overrepresentation is simply explained by their durability and also their ease of recognition: Iron meteorites are highly distinctive and much easier to recognize. The largest iron meteorite yet found is a meteorite in Namibia, named Hoba, which weighs 123,000 pounds (55,000 kg). The reason no larger meteorites are found is that their fall would be at cosmic speeds, not significantly slowed by the atmosphere, and the meteorite itself would be destroyed when its shock wave strikes the surface of the Earth and the meteorite explodes.

Chondrites are thought to consist of the earliest solid materials in the solar system, but iron meteorites are believed to represent the cores of *planetesimals,* bodies tens to thousands of miles in diameter that were colliding and accreting on their way to becoming planets. As material in the early solar system collided and stuck together, it was also heated and began to melt. The iron and nickel metal in the chondritic accreting material was melted and sank through the rest of the silicate minerals to form an iron-nickel metal core in the planetesimal's interior. This process is called differentiation. (For more on this topic, see the sidebar "Accretion and Heating: Why Are Some Solar System Objects Round and Others Irregular?" in chapter 10.) Iron meteorites are thought to be parts of the cooled, solidified, metallic cores of failed planetesimals, planetesimals that were smashed apart by collision rather than bonding together to make a planet.

Further support for this theory comes from a group of meteorites called pallasites. In 1772 a German naturalist named Peter Pallas found a meteorite specimen near Krasnoyarsk in Siberia. This meteorite weighed 1,500 lbs (680 kg) and consisted of grains of the mineral olivine ($[Mg,Fe]_2SiO_4$) surrounded by two of the kinds of iron-nickel minerals found in iron meteorites, kamacite and taenite. This was the first meteorite found that combined iron-nickel metal with silicate minerals.

This pallasite, and the many that have since been found, are thought to be parts of the core-mantle boundary of these failed planetesimals. These are samples from the region at the bottom of the silicate mineral mantle of the planetesimal, just where it is merging into the sunken, growing iron-nickel metal core.

Another group of meteorites, the achondrites, represent yet another region from these differentiated planetesimals and even planets. Called achondrites because they lack chondrules, these meteorites are igneous rocks, that is, they have crystallized from a silicate melt. They are the remnants of larger bodies that formed early in the solar system and at least began the processes of differentiation. All early markers like chondrules and CAIs have been remixed into the bulk of the body, and the body had at least begun to melt internally and produce magmas that later crystallized. On these bodies the silicate mantles apparently also melted and erupted lava onto their surfaces: Pieces of the cooled, solidified lava from their surfaces were later broken off and sent to Earth and are now classified as achondrites. Achondrites therefore carry critical clues to the speed of accumulation and size of early bodies in the solar system.

Several classes of achondrite meteorites have been linked definitively to their parent bodies. Eucrites, howardites, and diogenites all come from the asteroid Vesta. Shergottites, nakhlites, and chassignites were blasted off Mars by a large impact. Another series of meteorites came from the Moon. A number of achondrite groups, however, have no parent body identified, including the aubrites, ureilites, acapulcoites, lodranites, brachinites, and angrites. Hypothesizing about the formation of these meteorites is a popular topic at meteoritical and space science conferences, and progress is constantly made toward better understanding of their origins.

Thus meteorites produce a time line and an image of early solar system development. The earliest solids, in the form of CAIs, formed at 4.568 billion years before the present. Within a few tens of millions of years material had accreted into planetesimals that differentiated internally into a metallic core, a silicate mantle, and a lava-covered surface, similar to the planets today.

Giant Molecular Clouds and Protoplanetary Disks

Though the birth of the solar system is distant in time and its evidence has been largely eliminated from the Earth by plate tectonics, internal mixing (called mantle convection), and surface erosion, high-powered telescopes can see young star- and planet-forming regions elsewhere in the galaxy. By watching them, it is possible to see the process that occurred 4.568 billion years ago.

The solar system is thought to have formed from an interstellar cloud of dust and gas that began to collapse upon itself through gravity and then to spin. Astronomers see many clouds of dust and gas at great distances from this solar system. Some of these clouds are large quiet masses of gas that slowly coalesce into stars here and there throughout their interiors. These giant molecular clouds, as they are called, slowly evolve without much interaction with surrounding bodies. (See the table on page 17 for definitions of the clouds, disks, and nebulae discussed here.) A second kind of cloud, called an H11 region, forms in an intense radiation environment near a massive star. When the nearby massive star dies in a supernova, the nearby cloud is sprayed with an isotope of iron that is only made in the center of massive stars. Evidence for this isotope of iron in primitive meteorites in this

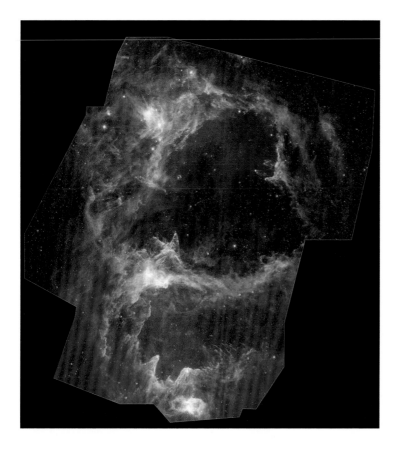

Generations of stars can be seen in this infrared portrait of the region W5 from NASA's Spitzer Space Telescope. The oldest stars can be seen as blue dots in the centers of the two hollow cavities. Younger stars line the rims of the cavities; others are pink dots at the tips of the elephant trunk–like pillars. The white knotty areas are where the youngest stars are forming. Red shows heated dust, while green highlights dense clouds. W5 is about 6,500 light-years away in the constellation Cassiopeia. (NASA/JPL-Caltech/ Harvard-Smithsonian CfA)

solar system indicates that it formed near such a massive star.

After the death of the massive nearby star, the dust cloud can begin to condense into a cluster of new stars through gravitational attraction to its center. The process that changes a molecular cloud to a cluster of new protostars (large dense clumps of matter that have not yet begun the nuclear processes of burning that make them stars), and then each protostar to a growing star with a planetary disk, is governed by a complex set of processes, including magnetic fields that support the cloud and prevent collapse, chemical and phase transitions in the heating and collapsing dust and gas, radiation from outside and, eventually, within the cloud, outflows and winds that vary from minutes to thousands of years, and thermal pressure from the protostar.

These cloud regions, the birthplaces of clusters of new protostars, are typically one-tenth to three-tenths of a parsec in diameter (a special unit of length used for huge distances in space, a parsec is equal to 1.9047×10^{13} miles, or 3.0857×10^{13} km, or 2.0626×10^{5} AU, or 3.26 light-years; one AU is the equiv-

This dramatic picture from the Hubble Space Telescope *show newborn stars emerging from dense, compact pockets of interstellar gas in the Eagle nebula, a nearby star-forming region 7,000 light-years from Earth in the constellation Serpens.* (NASA/ESA/STScI/J. Hester and P. Scowen [Arizona State University])

DEFINITIONS OF CLOUDS, DISKS, AND NEBULAE

giant molecular cloud	An interstellar cloud of dust and gas, typically 10^{12} miles (10^{13} km) in diameter; these are the birthplaces of clusters of new stars, formed as the cloud collapses under its own gravity.
protoplanetary disk	The flattened, spinning cloud of dust and gas surrounding a forming protostar; the material in this disk gradually accretes into larger and larger pieces, finally forming planets.
proplyd	A *protoplanetary disk*
primordial disk	Another name for protoplanetary disk
debris disk	Also a flattened, spinning cloud of dust and gas around a star, but formed by collisions among objects already formed in an aging solar system; does not lead to the formation of new solar systems
planetary nebula	A shell of gas ejected from stars at the end of their lifetimes. This name is credited to William Herschel, who in the 18th century looked at these objects through small, poor telescopes and mistook them for gas giant planets like Jupiter.
protostar	The central concentration of gas and dust in a protoplanetary disk that will eventually collapse sufficiently to begin nuclear processes and become a star.
solar nebula	The complete cloud of gas and dust orbiting and interacting with the protostar; this includes the protostar, the planetary disk, and the more spherical and diffuse cloud of gas and dust surrounding them both.

alent of about 93 million miles, or 150 million kilometers, the distance from the Sun to the Earth, and a light-year is the distance traveled in one year at the speed of light). Each of the new young protostars is far from its neighbors, and each one attracts its own slightly denser clump of molecular cloud.

As each protostar grows, it attracts matter from the edges of cloud more strongly through gravity. If spinning material is brought closer to the axis of its spin, it spins faster, like a spinning ice skater when he pulls in his arms (this is caused by conservation of angular momentum). The cloud contracts, spins faster, and flattens into a disk, called the protoplanetary disk, since it is the last structure prior to formation of the planets (see the sidebar "Forming Protoplanetary Disks").

FORMING PROTOPLANETARY DISKS

Why should the spinning cloud of dust around a protostar fall inward on itself and flatten into a disk? There is evidence that it does, because the planets in this solar system all move in the same direction around the Sun (thought of as the result of forming out of a uniformly spinning cloud), and their orbits are in or close to the plane of the Sun's equator (thought to be the result of forming out of a disk, rather than a sphere). This disk-forming is also seen around young stars elsewhere in the galaxy. There is a fairly simple explanation.

First, all the particles in the dust cloud are being attracted toward its center by gravity. Most of the particles are in orbits around a central spin axis for the cloud, and these orbits have a wide variety of radii: Some particles are close to the spin axis, and some are far away. The particles in orbits experience a centripetal force pulling them in and an opposing centrifugal force pushing them out. They also have a universal gravitational pull toward the center of the cloud. Their centrifugal and centripetal forces keep the particle in an orbit, not allowing it to go directly toward the cloud's center despite the gravitational force, and so the net result is that the gravitational force pulls the particles down to an equatorial plane without being able to pull them entirely into the center of gravity. There are also some particles that are on the spin axis, and since they have no centripetal or centrifugal forces, they simply move down or up the spin axis under the force of gravity, so the axis of spin flattens most easily and first.

In the equatorial plane, contraction is slowest because the orbits go out to the farthest distance from the gravitational center. When a particle is pulled in toward the gravitational center, its velocity increases (conservation of angular momentum again). Particles on the equatorial plane are pulled inward by gravity to the point that their velocity is high enough to keep them in orbit despite their gravitational attraction toward the center, and they are then at some stable orbit. This contributes to the assembly of dense elements in the inner solar system (their higher density makes their gravitational

Disks around stars can be divided into two major types, protoplanetary, or primordial disks, and debris disks. Protoplanetary disks, which are discussed in this chapter, are gas- and dust-rich and consist of material that is either falling in to a newly forming star, accreting into planetesimals, or being

pull stronger and requires a smaller and faster orbit to balance it) and lighter elements in the outer solar system: This is part of the story of why the inner planets are rocky and the outer planets gaseous.

This artist's concept shows a protoplanetary disk. (NASA/JPL-Caltech)

driven out of the star system by magnetic or radiation pressure. Debris disks, in contrast, can be of any age, and are made of dust produced in collisions among bodies orbiting the star.

Debris disks are colder than protoplanetary disks and do not lead to planetary system formation, but are worth describing briefly to contrast with protoplanetary disks. Between 10 and 20 percent of Milky Way stars (the Milky Way is our home galaxy, a collection of stars our Sun moves with) have debris disks. Some scientists characterize our Kuiper belt as a debris disk, because it is indeed a disk of rubble around a star (the Sun) that is past its planet-forming stage. Were the Kuiper belt around a distant star, though, it would be far too small to be seen by telescopes from Earth. The debris disks astronomers see are far larger and denser.

While debris disks are relatively uncommon, most, perhaps all, stars are born with protoplanetary disks. This understanding has been reached only in the last few years, as more and more young stars with disks have been imaged with improved telescopes. The great importance of this observation is this: Virtually every star ever born may have planets around it, and therefore the possibility of life.

Observations show that protoplanetary disks can be as wide as 400 AU. In our own solar system, *Voyager 1* passed the termination shock (the point at which the solar wind encounters the galactic wind, the virtual end of our solar system) at 94 AU from the Sun, and *Voyager 2* encountered it at 84 AU from the Sun. After the termination shock, a 50-AU wide region of mixing occurs, before pure galactic wind is encountered. Nonetheless, our entire solar system is far smaller than many observed disks.

Planets form from perhaps one-tenth to one-third of the original disk mass, based on models and observations. The remainder of the protoplanetary disk material falls into the protostar or is ejected from the developing solar system by radiation winds. For our own solar system, researchers have for years made calculations of the mass of the original protoplanetary disk. A common method is to sum the masses of the planets and estimate their bulk composition and then add sufficient hydrogen and helium to equal the solar composition.

This result is known as the minimum mass solar nebula, since it is the least massive nebula that is consistent with compositional constraints.

Our solar nebula was likely more massive than the calculated minimum mass solar nebula. The minimum mass solar nebula does not produce the temperatures and pressures in the inner nebula consistent with forming molten chondrules, the formation of Jupiter requires higher mass, and Uranus and Neptune would not form within the lifetime of the disk if it were as thin as a minimum mass model suggests.

Newer minimum mass solar nebula calculations, which take into consideration the recent suggestion that Jupiter and Neptune formed at different distances from the Sun and migrated, have a mass of 0.092 times the mass of the Sun, or 3.96×10^{29} lbs (1.8×10^{29} kg) (the mass of the Sun is 4.37×10^{29} lbs, or 1.9891×10^{30} kg), while some earlier nebula models totaled only one one-hundredth of a solar mass.

The total mass of the planets add up to 2.67×10^{27} kg, or only 1 percent of this new minimum mass solar nebula. This new model implies that only the smallest fraction of the solar nebula creates planets; the vast majority of the nebula either falls into the star or is expelled into space.

Collapse into a protostar and a disk from an initial molecular cloud can be very rapid. The process culminating in accreted planets can occur in less than 1 million years, according to observations. Most disks disperse in less than 3 Ma, meaning that a dense dust and gas disk is gone, possibly leaving only planets. Some disks disperse as early as 300,000 years after protostar formation, and others last as long as 20 million years. These are very brief periods of time in the context of the lifetime of a solar system. Because most planets cannot be imaged even by space-based telescopes, the apparently vacuous space around many stars may be inhabited by planets or in fact may be empty.

COMPOSITIONS AND TEMPERATURES OF PROTOPLANETARY DISKS

Initially, planetary disks have more gas than dust, sometimes to the extreme of 99 percent gas and just 1 percent dust. Space surveys suggest that primordial disks consist largely of molecular hydrogen, though some carbon monoxide has also been detected directly. Water is the next most common molecule measured in planetary disks around other stars. A few observations of disks have also shown the presence of carbon-rich dust, argon, sulfur, neon, and oxygen. The compositions of relatively cool objects so far away are very difficult to measure, and so much work remains to be done on the compositions of new star and planet regions.

In astrophysics all elements beyond hydrogen and helium are called metals, and so the proportion of heavier elements in disks and stars is referred to as their metallicity. There appears to be a correlation between higher metallicity and disk and planet formation. Judging from the solar systems that can be observed and using theory, the formation of giant planets like Jupiter appears to be encouraged by a star with iron levels higher than the Sun. Most giant exoplanets found orbit stars with higher iron. A simple assumption about the compositions of planetary disks is that they share the same bulk composition as their star, and so these higher-iron stars may have had higher-iron planetary disks.

The best-resolved imaging has been done for the disk around the star β Pictoris (often called β Pic), the second brightest star in the constellation Pictor. Small silicate grains have been detected in the β Pictoris disk within 20 AU of the star, with increasing crystalline silicate composition closer to the star. This observation is particularly exciting, since our terrestrial planets contain a large fraction of silicon (mainly bound into the crystals of silicate minerals in rocks).

When attempting to estimate the composition of the planetary disk that began our solar system, there are three measurements that can be used to inform the estimate. The first is the current composition of the Sun, as measured by the spectral properties of the photosphere. The second is the composition of CI chondrites, primitive material that condensed from the early planetary nebula, was never incorporated into a planet, and of all the primitive meteorites most resembles the current composition of the Sun. The last are the measurements made of nebular compositions elsewhere in the solar system.

Because the Sun holds more than 99 percent of the mass of the solar system, its composition is thought to be a good proxy for the bulk composition of the whole system. As a first estimate, the planetary nebula might be expected to have the same bulk composition as the Sun. Several questions might be asked about the accuracy of this assumption. First, does the photospheric composition of the Sun equal its bulk composition? Unfortunately it almost certainly does not. Young stars have higher metallicity than older stars do, and this is believed to be because heavier elements sink to the solar interior over time. So though the composition of the solar photosphere is the best measurement that can be made of the current bulk composition of the Sun, it is not the exact bulk composition of the Sun.

In summary, however, the composition of our Sun is dominated completely by hydrogen and helium, which are among the least important elements for building terrestrial planets. The solar photosphere has 74.91 wt% hydrogen, 23.77 wt% helium, and only 1.33 wt% of all the other elements together, including oxygen, nitrogen, carbon, silicon, aluminum, iron, magnesium, calcium, and all the other elements critical to building terrestrial planets.

Lastly, some information can be taken from spectroscopic analyses of other planetary nebulae and disks. Analyses as detailed as those for our Sun or for meteorites are not possible. Measurements do show that young stars and their disks appear to be somewhat more metal-rich than our current Sun, possibly because of the gravitational settling of metals. The photosphere of the Sun today is estimated to now have about 84 percent of the metallicity of the proto-Sun.

Because such a protoplanetary disk would have its highest temperatures in the center, from the heat caused by collapse of material inward and then later by the early heat of the Sun, gaseous elements and molecules nearer the Sun would be heated to temperatures high enough that they would remain as gases, rather than condensing into solids or ices. Models and observations indicate that midplane disk temperatures can approach 3,000°F (1,700°C) at 0.1 AU from the star, which is about twice as far from the Sun as is Mercury, near 1,300°F (700°C) at 1 AU, the distance of the Earth, dropping to 260 to −300°F (130 to −180°C) at 8 AU, which is a little closer to the Sun than is Saturn, and finally to less than −370°F (−220°C) at 100 AU.

The temperature gradient in the protoplanetary disk at the time of planetesimal and planet formation has a great influence on the compositions of the planets and therefore on their ability to support life. First, in the earliest, hottest disk, the temperature determines where the first solids will condense and what they will be. The oldest solar system solids, the calcium-aluminum inclusions (CAIs) in chondritic meteorites described above in the meteorite section, cannot condense until the disk cools below an estimated 2,000 to 3,000°F (to 1,100 to 1,600°C). The next oldest portions of primitive meteorites, the chondrules, require only 130 to 480°F (400 to 750°C). Thus the protoplanetary disk had cooled significantly before solids began to form.

At distances from the Sun less than two AU, only metals and silica-based molecules and compounds (called silicates) could condense and form planets. This is the reason that the inner, or terrestrial, planets are made primarily of silicates and metals. (The terrestrial planets include Mercury, Venus, Earth, and Mars, and their material is also similar to the asteroids in the asteroid belt between Mars and Jupiter.) The material that makes up the inner planets is denser than the gases and ices that make up much of the outer planets. The relationship between density and distance from the Sun is shown in the figure on page 25.

The elements that make up silicates and metals, primarily oxygen, silica, iron, magnesium, calcium, nickel, chromium, manganese, sodium, and potassium, are not the most common elements in the solar system. The most common elements in the solar system are hydrogen and helium, the major constituents of the Sun. Where, then, are hydrogen and helium in the planets? The simplest explanation follows the understanding that different elements have different weights and condense at different temperatures, as described in the sidebar "Elements and Isotopes" in chapter 1.

At distances farther from the early Sun, temperatures in the protoplanetary disk were cool enough that the most com-

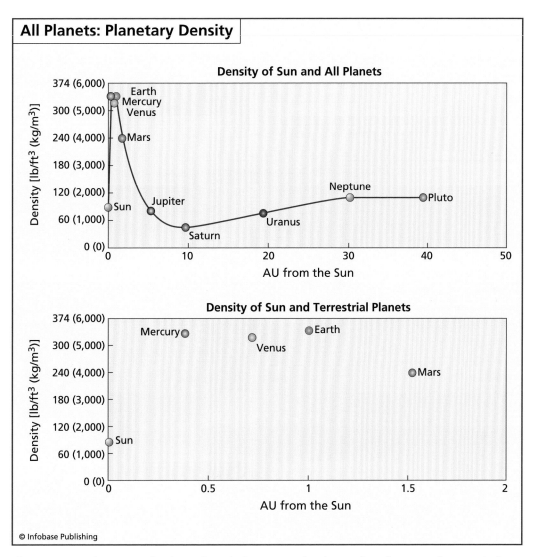

All Planets: Planetary Density

Density of Sun and All Planets

Density [lb/ft³ (kg/m³)]

AU from the Sun

Density of Sun and Terrestrial Planets

Density [lb/ft³ (kg/m³)]

AU from the Sun

© Infobase Publishing

The innermost planets, made of metals and silicates, are far denser than the outer planets, which consist mainly of ices and gases. The density gradient in the planets is a result of density gradients in the solar nebula.

mon molecules in the solar system could condense and form planets. (Condensation temperatures are shown in the table on page 35.) Molecules such as carbon dioxide (CO_2), water (H_2O), methane (CH_4), and ammonia (NH_3) condensed into ices and were abundant enough that, along with some silicate and metal components, they could form the *cores* of the giant planets

Jupiter, Saturn, Uranus, and Neptune. Once these giant condensed cores formed, they had enough gravitational attraction to pull in the clouds of hydrogen (H_2) and helium (He) gases that form by far the majority of all matter in the universe.

THE VIOLENT DYNAMICS OF THE DISK

Thus far gravity has been the main force controlling the evolution of the protoplanetary disk and its protostar. In general gas and dust are falling into the protostar from the disk from the force of gravity, but increasingly magnetic fields and eventually stellar winds are blowing material away from the star and eventually clearing the disk of gas and dust and leaving only larger bodies in orbit.

The flows out of the disk fall into two categories: constant inflows and outflows and violent, sporadic flows. Virtually all the material that is going to fall into the star and add to its mass does so before thermonuclear fusion begins in the star. (For more on thermonuclear fusion and the process of burning in a star, see "Solar Core" in chapter 5.) Once the star begins to burn, its own strong stellar radiation and material wind blow away the remaining dust and prevent any further disk accretion to the star, excepting the odd comet or asteroid sucked into the Sun by its huge gravity. Before the stellar wind turns on with the beginning of thermonuclear fusion, magnetic fields move material around almost as effectively as gravity does.

The protostar has a complex, active magnetic field, just as our Sun does today. Magnetic fields are created by electric currents. The gas and dust in the protostar are electrically charged, in the way

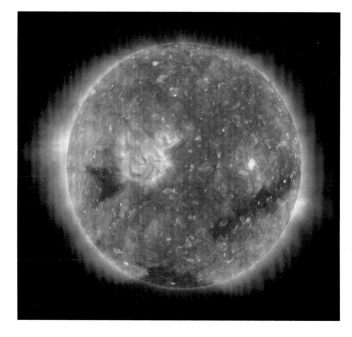

The violent patterns of convection (boiling movement) in the Sun's near-surface are caused by the heat from thermonuclear reactions in the star's interior. (NASA/JPL)

that dust can stick to plastic or cloth through static electricity. When the electrically charged gas and dust of the protostar flow turbulently, they act as an electric current and create a magnetic field. The magnetic field can grab and move material with it, so the interactions between the flowing material and the magnetic field become highly complex.

At the same time, the electrically charged dust and gas in the protoplanetary disk are orbiting the protostar, acting as separate electric currents and making its own magnetic field. In all protoplanetary disks found so far, there is an empty region of the disk next to the star, about 0.1 AU in radius. In this region dust and gas are either sucked into the protostar by the interactions between the magnetic fields and the gravity of the protostar (called funnel flow) or ejected away from the protostar and back into the outer disk.

The point at which these flows begin is the innermost edge of the protoplanetary disk, where it ends against the central empty region that surrounds the protostar. Some magnetic winds pull material into the pole of the protostar and other magnetic winds push material out away from the star; together these actions are called the x-wind, or sometimes disk wind.

There likely exists just a small amount of material in the empty region between the edge of the disk and the protostar. This material would be flash-melted by periodic X-ray flares from the protostar and by the high radiation in the region. Some scientists suggest that this is the origin of calcium-aluminum inclusions and that on timescales of tens of years the CAIs could be pressed back into the disk, to be incorporated into condensing solids that eventually become meteorites. CAIs formed in this region may even be carried back into the disk by the outward-flowing x-wind. These ideas, however, are entirely hypothetical—they have never been observed around any star, and some scientists say the chemistry of CAIs is inconsistent with this model for their formation.

Punctuating the constant violent motion of the magnetic fields, x-wind, disk rotation, and gravitational infall are massive, super-violent outflows from the protostar itself. Two major types of violent outflows occur in disks during planetary accretion. The first is the FU Orionis outflow, and the second, T-Tauri. These are named after the stars in which they were first observed, and indeed they have been seen through powerful telescopes in a number of distant young stars.

FU Orionis behavior, named after the star FU Ori, which underwent an observed outburst in 1937, occurs in protostars experiencing a sudden and high acceleration in the rate of gas and dust inflow to the protostar. FU Orionis behavior is the most violent bipolar outflow behavior exhibited by protostars. This occurs in stars before their disks are fully developed, while their molecular cloud envelopes are still partly in existence. These stars have not accreted the majority of their mass yet and, except for their violent FU Orionis jets, exist at temperatures less than 700°F (380°C), temperatures a home oven can almost reach.

When there is a great acceleration in infall to the protostar, perhaps caused by another protostar passing near, the protostar suddenly explodes jets out of its north and south poles. FU Orionis outburst jets can exceed 180 miles/sec (300 km/sec), can develop over just one to 20 years, and then subside back to quiet over five to 100 years. This process, of growing outburst and slow decay, has been observed using telescopes. FU Orionis jets can extend 1,000 to 10,000 AU from the star, 10 to 100 times the distance from the Sun to the edge of our solar system, and can reach temperatures of 8,500 to 10,000°F (5,000 to 6,000°C).

Computer models of star formation show that about 10 cycles of FU Orionis outbursts may occur before the disk becomes stable enough that planets might form. Because of the unpredictable mixing behavior of the magnetic fields and outbursts, the disk might not be well-mixed at the time of planet formation. Different regions may have different compositions, in contrast to the traditional view of protoplanetary disks, which says that at any given radius from the star the disk should have the same composition.

The second kind of violent outburst from a protostar is called the T-Tauri stage. T-Tauri refers to a class of protostars, generally less than about 2.5 times the mass of the Sun, before fusion begins; the stars shine only from heat of gravitational collapse. During this stage, which follows the FU Orionis stage (see figure on page 30), the protostar again emits giant jets from its north and south poles. These jets are large and hot, though not as large and hot as FU Orionis jets. About 30 percent of protostars of the appropriate size experience T-Tauri jets.

When the T-Tauri stage of stellar evolution was first discovered, scientists thought that the protostar emitted radiation and material jets in the plane of its protoplanetary disk, that is, straight toward and past its young accreting planets. The T-Tauri winds were called upon over and over by planetary scientists to strip the early atmospheres and surfaces off the young planets; that was the explanation for the chemically evolved atmosphere of the Earth and Mercury's lack of an atmosphere: It has been removed by the T-Tauri stage winds.

Soon after, astronomers discovered that the T-Tauri winds extend from the poles of the protostar and not in the plane of the planets. Planetary geology text, however, lagged behind this knowledge. To this day some texts call on T-Tauri winds to strip the early atmospheres from young planets and to remove the last dust and gas from the disk. Now it is known, however, that T-Tauri winds do not flow past the growing planets and planets are unlikely to have accreted by the time the T-Tauri stage occurs. Planet-building is just beginning, if at all, when the protostar undergoes this stage.

Throughout the cooling and condensing of the first materials and the violent magnetic storms and winds, gas and dust has continued to fall into the very center of the protoplanetary disk. At the center of this cooling, condensing disk is the protostar, which contains by far the greatest amount of mass. That central mass eventually condenses to the point that nuclear fusion begins in its center, and the star is born.

Nuclear processes begin in the young star during the T-Tauri stage, after the FU Orionis energetic outbursts. Radiation emissions from the young star are necessarily small at first, growing with time as the star increases its rate of fusion. The Sun, and all stars, begin glowing softly and their visible light increases over time as their internal nuclear processes expand.

Some stars have finished accreting and begun disk evolution in less than 1 million years, but others require as little as 100,000 years or as long as 10 million years. (modeled after Hartmann 1998, Fig. 1.7)

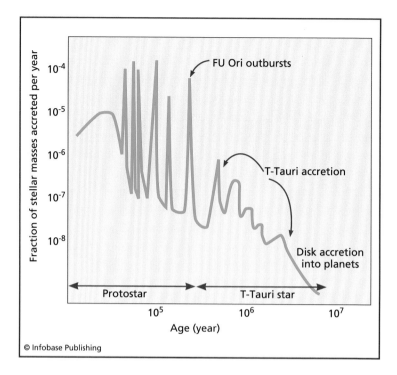

© Infobase Publishing

Carl Sagan, the famous astronomer from Cornell University, called this the "faint young Sun" hypothesis. Our Sun has likely increased its visible light output about 40 percent over its lifetime. If the Sun heats the Earth and produces the energy needed for life, how did the Earth become hot and wet enough for life so early, when the Sun was weak? The answer probably lies in the composition of the atmosphere: The early atmosphere was even more effective at trapping heat.

However, while the young Sun gave off far less visible light, it apparently gave off far more X-ray and ultraviolet emissions, the high-energy, destructive end of the radiation spectrum. These high-energy radiations were probably 10 to 60 times stronger when the Sun was young and would certainly have been a problem for early life.

The Sun is a category of star called a yellow dwarf, on the small side of stars in the universe. The majority of stars contain from 0.3 to three times the mass of the Sun, though giant stars as large as 27 solar masses are found occasionally.

The initial collapse under the influence of gravity of primordial material to form the Sun is thought to have taken about 100,000 years, based on computer modeling. This collapse is very fast in geological terms, only about 1/50,000 of the age of the solar system. Some stars observed from Earth appear to have formed in as little as 10,000 years. Thus the whole series of processes described to this point might have happened in just 10,000 years, a virtual eyeblink.

Building Planets
from Dust

To this point the planetary disk has been described as consisting of more gas than dust, just beginning to condense into solids. The processes that allow dust to accrete into planets have never been observed in action around any star. The processes happen on a scale too small to be seen by even the most powerful telescopes. (Astronomers are straining to detect planets as small as Earth around other stars, so seeing planetesimals or individual collisions is impossible in the present day.)

Even theory has trouble explaining this accretion process. There are few candidates for processes that would allow solid chunks from dust to house-size to stick together when they collide while orbiting the planetary disk. They are too small for gravity to be the dominant force, as it is with larger bodies. Nonetheless, it has to happen. Disks are known to start with gas and dust and to end with planets. On the way to making planets, the material has to accrete into bodies from tens to hundreds of miles in diameter, called planetesimals, and then into bodies thousands of miles in diameter, called planetary embryos, and finally into planets.

This composite image, combining data from NASA's Chandra X-ray Observatory and Spitzer Space Telescope, shows the star-forming cloud Cepheus B, located in our Milky Way galaxy about 2,400 light-years from Earth. Some of the young stars in the molecular cloud have detectable protoplanetary disks. (NASA/CXC/JPL-Caltech/PSU/CfA)

FROM GAS AND DUST TO PEBBLES AND MOUNTAINS

Though planetary nebulae start at temperatures near only a few tens of degrees above absolute zero (near $-429°F$, or $-250°C$), which is the temperature of molecular clouds observed elsewhere in our galaxy, the material heats rapidly due to conversions of kinetic and potential energies to heat as material collapses into a disk. Material in the protostar and in the inner disk is heated to $4,000°F$ ($2,200°C$) or higher, sufficient to break any molecules into atoms and to ionize most of them into a plasma. Before any accretion can begin, therefore, material must cool significantly and condense into solids.

Research by Denton Ebel at the University of Chicago and Katharina Lodders at Washington University in St. Louis, among others, has shown that as the plasma, gas, and dust cool, it condenses into small grains of crystalline minerals. It had been thought that the material might condense into droplets of glass, but that would require very fast cooling, too fast for the elements to organize themselves into a crystal lattice. (This very fast cooling is called quenching.) Apparently that did happen at times in the planetary disk, for example to make some of the chondrules, but that was the exception.

The minerals that condense at the highest temperatures contain the most calcium, aluminum, and titanium, as shown in the table on page 35. There are many more minerals expected to condense in the planetary disk than are shown in this table, but this table shows a number of the most important, including the first to condense at the highest temperatures.

The exact temperatures of solidification depend upon the bulk composition of the disk in that region. If there is more carbon than oxygen, for example, solidification occurs at lower temperatures. Lodders estimates that the planets, moons, asteroids, and comets, all the material left orbiting the Sun, condensed from only about 1.5 percent by weight of the original solar nebula that condensed into the planetary disk. Of that tiny 1.5 percent, only about one-third solidified into rocky material such as makes up the terrestrial planets; all the rest is ice and gas.

The composition of solid material therefore changes with time, as a part of the disk cools and allows more and more crystals to form. Composition also varies with radius from the star. The disk is hottest nearest the star and cooler at greater distances. Many scientists believe that water and other ices never condensed near the star, but only at greater distances where temperatures were always cooler. This model means that the material available to make planets near the star is dry,

CONDENSATION TEMPERATURES FOR SELECTED PLANET-FORMING MATERIALS

Material	Condensation temperature
corundum (Al_2O_3)	2,560°F (1,400°C)
hibonite ($CaAl_{12}O_{19}$)	2,520°F (1,380°C)
perovskite ($CaTiO_3$)	2,400°F (1,320°C)
anorthite feldspar ($CaAl_2Si_2O_8$)	2,040°F (1,110°C)
olivine (($Fe, Mg)_2SiO_4$), a common silicate *mineral* in the *mantles* of terrestrial planets)	1,980 to 930°F (1,100 to 500°C)
iron-nickel alloys (common core-forming material in terrestrial planets)	2,010 to 1,830°F (1,100 to 1,000°C)
water (H_2O)	32°F (0°C)
carbon dioxide (CO_2)	–112°F (–80°C)
methane (CH_4, exists as an ice on Pluto)	approximately –370°F (-225°C)
ammonia (NH_3, exists as a gas and an ice on Jupiter)	approximately –410°F (-245°C)

and water must be mixed in from greater distances to make a wet planet.

The chemistry of dust helps it accrete into larger bodies. Often the surface of crystals has a small electrical charge on it, which is caused by the crystal lattice being broken there, and the elements that make up the crystal not in the right quantities to cancel each other's charges. For example, the mineral quartz has a composition given as SiO_2. That is, two oxygens for each silicon. The silicon atom has an electric charge of +4, and each oxygen has a charge of –2. If, on the broken edge of a piece of quartz, oxygen atoms are exposed without their accompanying silicon, the surface of the grain will have a negative charge.

These electrical charges are exceptionally tiny—far too tiny to even be felt by a person—but when the crystal grains themselves are very small, the forces of the electrical charges can affect the grains. Very small crystals, 0.04 in (1 mm) or smaller in particular, can be pulled together and held together by opposing electrical charges on their surfaces. In this way, very small grains can be bonded together into larger clumps.

Small particles that are rich in iron may also carry magnetic fields. These magnetic fields could also help grains stick together. Between the electric and magnetic fields, then, accreting dust into clumps should happen.

These chemical interactions are only helpful with very small material. Very large bodies, like planetesimals and planetary embryos, can be attracted to each other by gravity. The transitional stage between pebble-sized objects and planetary embryos passes through an uneasy realm where chemistry is no longer helpful in accumulation, and yet gravity is not yet strong enough to force accretion. Here is the problem with the theory of planetary accretion: We know it happens, but the problem remains how pebble-sized material can accrete into planetesimal-sized material when chemistry does not help any more, and yet gravity is not yet effective.

A further problem arises with gas and dust in the planetary disk. Dust experiences two competing forces: radiation pressure forcing the dust outward and stellar gravity pulling the dust inward. Larger particles are quickly either pushed out of the system by radiation pressure or sucked into the star by gravity. Very tiny particles and molecules, those smaller than a micron, are all sucked inward. These particles and molecules are so small that radiation pressure from the protostar can actually slow down their orbital speed, much as a headwind slows down a bicyclist. When the speed of orbit goes down, the material drops into a smaller orbit closer to the star. This is referred to as orbital decay, in this case caused by Poynting-Robertson drag, and it is thought to be so effective that the planetary disk would quickly be cleared of gas and dust. Accretion, therefore, has to happen even more quickly.

All the gas and dust are orbiting the star. Accretion into larger bodies requires that two or more pieces of material collide. This collision could be just glancing, if the bodies are orbiting at similar speeds as neighbors, or the collision could be far more violent. The energy of the collision must have a large effect on whether the material sticks together (a constructive collision, sticking), just separates again (bouncing), or is further broken (a destructive collision, fragmentation). For solid spherical grains, there is a sharp change from sticking to bouncing at a relative velocity of 6.5 feet per second (2 m/sec). This means that two hard spherical grains can stick together if they collide when one is orbiting at 6,213 miles per second (10,000 km/sec) and the other at 6,216 miles per second (10,001 km/sec). Any larger difference in their velocities, and they will likely bounce apart again.

During constructive collisions microscopic particles grow into aggregates with high porosities, like sponges. Early solar system material is often described as fluffy, meaning it is largely space and little material. This porosity may have two important effects on accretion: First, it deadens the impact of two grains. The energy that would otherwise cause the grains to bounce can be taken up in smashing pore space and thus prevent a bounce. Second, porous grains melt much more easily from the heat of impact, and that can help them stick as well. For irregular and porous grains, sticking, rather than bouncing, can result even in collisions at relative velocities of 330 ft/sec (100 m/sec).

Dust particles thus move orbits in response to radiation pressure, Poynting-Robertson drag, stellar gravity, and also gas drag (friction with surrounding gas) and magnetic field forces. The ultimate fate of a particle of dust depends upon the cumulate effect of all these forces, plus the possibility of collision and accretion. By 5,000 years after disk formation the dust is expected to have accreted into centimeter-scale particles or to have been lost from the planetary disk, either into the protostar or out into space.

As clumps of material become larger, accretion is even more of a physical mystery. The energy of collisions becomes sufficient to create mostly destructive rather than constructive collisions beginning when the material is about four inches (10 cm) in diameter. After about three feet (one m) in diameter is attained, virtually all collisions should be destructive. These destructive collisions create collisional erosion, meaning that during collisions material is fragmented and larger pieces eroded into smaller pieces. Not until 33 feet (10 m) in diameter is reached do collisions become once again largely accretional rather than destructive.

Here is the problem in accretion: Collisions between clumps three to 33 feet (one to 10 m) in diameter should virtually always result in the clumps breaking into smaller pieces rather than joining together into larger pieces. Growth may stagnate for a million or more years at sizes less than a few meters, when these bodies hit the fragmentation limit. Growing from three to 33 feet may require the clumps to settle into the mid-plane of the disk and for the disk to develop turbulent flow. Recent research indicates that larger clumps may be formed in eddies in strong magnetic fields or in eddies between layers of gas and layers of dust in the planetary disk. This is hopeful work that may show the way for the physics of accretion to overcome the apparent destructive collision barrier, but far more work is needed.

Observations of our own and other solar systems, however, clearly show that accretion does proceed to make larger bod-

A schematic cross section of one-half of a planetary disk, with the protostar at the left and the disk stretching out to the right. (Modeled after the work of Hartmann, Kenyon, Boss, Ferriera, and Meyer)

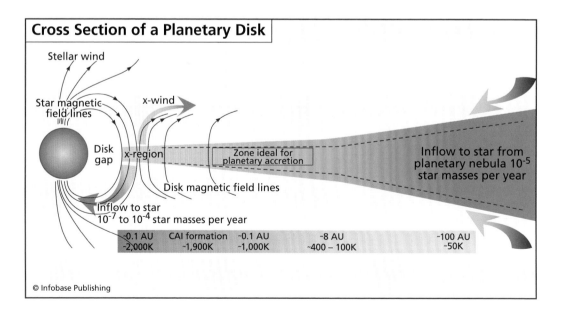

Cross Section of a Planetary Disk

Stellar wind

Star magnetic field lines

x-wind

Disk gap

x-region

Zone ideal for planetary accretion

Disk magnetic field lines

Inflow to star from planetary nebula 10^{-5} star masses per year

Inflow to star 10^{-7} to 10^{-4} star masses per year

| ~0.1 AU ~2,000K | CAI formation ~1,900K | ~0.1 AU ~1,000K | ~8 AU ~400 – 100K | ~100 AU ~50K |

© Infobase Publishing

ies, whether we understand the physics or not. Ian Sanders of Trinity College, Dublin, finds that planetesimals (bodies tens to hundreds of miles in diameter) are likely to accrete within a few million years of the first solids condensing in the disk. Within that rapid timeframe there are high concentrations of radioactive elements with short half-lives (radioactive elements that decay quickly, and indeed are all completely decayed by the present day).

These short-lived radioactive elements, notably an isotope of aluminum, create sufficient heat in the planetesimals that they are likely to melt from their centers outward. Thus they become the first spherical, rocky, differentiated bodies in the solar system, appearing much like small rocky moons. They would have had iron-nickel metal cores and silicate mineral mantles, just as the Earth has. They would orbit the star, waiting for further accretionary collisions to build them into larger bodies, and eventually, planets.

RUNAWAY ACCRETION: PLANETESIMALS TO PLANETARY EMBRYOS

Once planetesimals have formed, gravity plays a larger role in speeding accretion. This stage of accretion is called runaway growth, because the larger the bodies, the more gravitational attraction, and the faster the accretion. Therefore as bodies become larger, accretion moves faster, and, in effect, runs away.

Some accreting planetesimals are hard and differentiated, but others failed to melt and are still fluffy, porous, and poorly compacted. Computer models show that the regions over which mutual collisions create larger bodies, called the feeding zone of a given planet being formed, gets wider and wider as bodies grow and gravitational forces get larger. Because the inner disk is likely dry and most water and ices exist farther from the star, the inner, terrestrial planets begin to accrete from dry material, and then as their feeding zones widen, water is added. In some models of the solar system the Earth does not gain any water until about 10 million years after accretion begins.

This Spitzer Space Telescope image of the nebula NGC 1333 contains two dense regions of new star and planet formation. The northern group is shown as red light from warm dust. The southern region, in yellow and green, is in the densest part of the gas cloud. The knotty yellow-green features are glowing shock fronts where jets of material, shot from young embryonic stars, are plowing into the cold, dense gas nearby. The number of separate jets that appear in this region is unprecedented. (NASA/JPL-Caltech/Harvard-Smithsonian CfA)

Meanwhile, in the outer solar system, giant planets are accreting as well. They are thought to form from a rocky core, like a planetesimal or planetary embryo, which then attracts to it an envelope of gas through its gravitational field.

Computer models indicate that accretion continues among these bodies until the largest are about 100 times more massive than the smallest. Once this size range has been attained, the gravitational fields of the largest dominate completely further accretion; the smaller bodies move according to the gravitational fields of the large ones. Once this happens accretion moves on to the next stage, called the oligarchic stage.

OLIGARCHIC ACCRETION: EMBRYOS TO PLANETS

The oligarchic stage begins with planetary embryos, bodies thousands of miles in diameter. Between 10 and 100 planetary embryos are thought to have existed, depending upon the disk density and formation time. Mars, in fact, may be a leftover planetary embryo.

Oligarchic accretion is named after the political system called oligarchy, in which a small number of people rule over

This artist's concept shows a celestial body about the size of the Moon colliding with a body the size of Mercury. As the bodies slam into each other, a huge flash of light is emitted. The final result is a larger planet. The core of the smaller body and most of its surface have been absorbed by the larger one. This merging of rocky bodies is how planets like Earth are thought to have formed. (NASA/JPL-Caltech)

This artist's conception shows the binary star system HD 113766, where astronomers suspect a rocky Earthlike planet is forming around one of the stars. The system is located approximately 424 light-years away from Earth. The brown ring of material closest to the central star depicts a belt of dusty material, enough to build a Mars-sized planet or larger. The white outer ring shows a concentration of icy dust also detected in the system. A new planet has already cleared the disk between these dusty rings. (NASA/JPL-Caltech)

all but are largely equal within their group. In planetary formation, the largest growing planetary embryo in each region of the planetary disk comes to dominate its region by gravitationally interacting with smaller planetesimals, either scattering them into different orbits or accreting them into its growing mass.

Because gravitational interactions between smaller bodies and the dominant planetary embryo in a given orbital region can scatter the smaller bodies away like stones in a slingshot, the oligarchic stage creates a lot of mixing in the planetary nebula. These Moon- and Mars-sized bodies mix the compositions of the planetary nebula in a chaotic way and almost certainly lead to putting more water and other volatiles into the inner solar system, where compositions may have been dry previously.

Oligarchic accretion is considered to be self-regulating, as each oligarch accretes or scatters its supply of planetesimals; its own growth removes the source of mass for growth, and so growth is inevitably slowed. During oligarchic growth, therefore, the dominant bodies grow at about the same rate, in contrast to the runaway growth stage.

The time required to build planets from embryos appears to be from about 3 to 100 million years after the first solids formed. Therefore within a few tens to 100 million years, the solar system would have looked recognizably as it is today, 4.568 billion years later. The time of formation is dynamic and violent and brief.

PART TWO

THE SUN

4

fast facts
about the Sun

This set begins with the Sun, the center of the solar system, around which orbit all the planets, asteroids, and comets. The visible surface of the Sun is called the photosphere. Since the Sun is a ball of hot gases and plasma, it has no solid surface like those of the Earth, Mars, Venus, and Mercury. The Sun is large because of the pressure of the radiation from its center: There is so much radiation that it literally inflates the Sun, preventing it from collapsing under its own weight into a denser body.

The center of the Sun is a core where the nuclear reactions occur that provide the energy for the entire solar system. The energy created in the core is transported through the bulk of the Sun (through layers called the radiative and convective zones) to reach the photosphere. In the photosphere, the energy from the center of the Sun has lessened to the point that it can interact with atoms, and the atoms give off visible light. Though the photosphere is the layer of the Sun visible to the eye, above the photosphere are several additional layers of hotter material that are not visible to the human eye because that material does not emit light in the visible spectrum. The Sun emits wavelengths of 171, 195, and 284 angstroms, all within the ultraviolet spectrum (not visible to the human

47

eye). This energy range highlights the loops and spots in the chromosphere, the layer of the Sun just outside the photosphere, normally invisible to the eye. The Sun's gigantic magnetic field powers the outermost layer of the Sun, the corona, which forms huge loops and ejects great bubbles of matter and is the source of the solar wind.

The final product from the Sun, the solar wind, consists of particles emitted at supersonic speeds, along with radiation. The Sun also creates an immense magnetic field that flows through the entire solar system and well beyond Pluto. Thus though the Sun is often thought of as simply another object in the solar system, it could be thought of as the solar system itself, with the planets and other bodies simply afterthoughts swimming through the Sun's huge flowing volume of flowing particles and magnetic field. The size of the Sun and other basic statistics are listed in the sidebar "Fundamental Information about the Sun," on page 49.

Each large object in the solar system has its own symbol, a sort of astronomer's shorthand. The symbol for the Sun is shown in the figure below.

The solar wind and the magnetic field of the Sun affect everything in the solar system. Planets with their own magnetic fields are protected from the Sun's solar wind and magnetic field to a large degree, but planets with weak or nonexistent fields are bombarded by the particles of the solar wind and have their atmospheres removed by the Sun's magnetic field. The energy of the Sun in the form of light and heat reaches all the objects in the solar system, even the most distant. Though the large planets still emit heat from their interiors from *radioactive* decay, most of the energy for everything that happens in the solar system comes from the Sun. On the Earth, the Sun's energy and water combine to make life possible: Plants use water and the heat and light of the Sun to grow, and animals eat those plants, forming the basis for the food chain.

Following his publication of the theory of relativity, Albert Einstein published a series of papers addressing relativistic effects on gravity. He predicted that masses actually warp space itself in their near environs. Mercury, the planet that

FUNDAMENTAL INFORMATION ABOUT THE SUN

The Sun contains 99.6 percent of the mass in the solar system, as shown in the table below. Its huge mass generates the nuclear reactor in its interior that produces almost all the energy for the planets—running their weather systems, shaping their magnetic fields, and making life possible on Earth. Though there is the remote possibility of life on Europa and on Mars in the past, Earth remains the only place in the universe that life is known to exist.

FUNDAMENTAL FACTS ABOUT THE SUN	
equatorial radius where atmospheric	432,000 miles (695,000 km), or 10 times
pressure is one bar	Jupiter's radius and 104 times Earth's radius
ellipticity	0.00005 (almost a perfect sphere)
volume	3.38×10^{17} cubic miles (1.41×10^{18} km³), or 1,306,000 times the volume of the Earth
mass	4.385×10^{30} pounds (1.989×10^{30} kg), or 333,000 times the mass of Earth
average density	87.9 pounds per cubic feet (1,410 kg/m³)
acceleration of gravity where	900 feet per second squared (274.4 m/sec²),
atmospheric pressure is one bar	or 28 times the gravitational acceleration on Earth's surface
magnetic field strength near sunspots	0.1 to 0.4 T, as much as 20,000 times stronger than Earth's magnetic field
magnetic field strength in polar regions	~0.001 T
rotational period	at its equator the surface rotates once every 25.38 Earth days; near the poles, rotation takes as long as 36 Earth days (this is called *differential rotation*)

Many solar system objects have simple symbols; this is the symbol for the Sun.

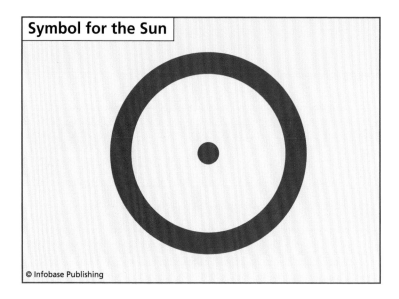

Symbol for the Sun

© Infobase Publishing

orbits closest to the Sun, has irregularities in its precession (gradual change of the orientation of the orbit in space) of its elliptical orbit that could not previously be explained. (For a long time, people looked for a planet orbiting closer to the Sun than Mercury, with a gravity field that could alter Mercury's orbit as the closer planet lapped Mercury.) Einstein asked Erwin Finlay Freundlich, an astronomer at the Royal Observatory in Berlin, to look into Mercury's orbital discrepancy by carefully measuring Mercury's orbit. Freundlich published his results in 1913 and thus was among the first scientists brave enough to contradict Newton's theories and support Einstein's. His paper and subsequent papers by Einstein showed that Mercury's orbital irregularities are perfectly explained by the predicted relativistic effects of the Sun's giant gravity field. This announcement pleased Einstein greatly and settled a centuries-old debate about Mercury.

Composition and Internal Structure of the Sun

The Sun consists of 92.1 percent hydrogen, 7.8 percent helium, and 0.1 percent other elements, on an atom basis (in other words, by count, not by weight). The abundances of minor elements in the Sun is not known because of the difficulty of measuring them remotely, and none of the ratios of isotopes in the Sun are known (the Genesis space mission is hoping to fill in some of those gaps). Because the Sun makes up the vast majority of the mass of the solar system it is reasonably assumed that its composition is the same as the original dust nebula from which the solar system was made.

Because of the extreme temperatures in the Sun's deep interior and in its outermost structures, the corona and solar wind, most of the atoms have been broken apart into a plasma. Plasma is material made of freely moving atomic nuclei, or even separate protons, neutrons, and electrons, which have been stripped from their nuclei by heat (see the following sidebar "Elementary Particles," on page 53). The higher the temperature of an atom, the more the electrons vibrate, until they have too much energy to continue orbiting the atomic nucleus, and they fly off separately. Though the plasma consists of positively, negatively, and neutrally charged particles, it is electrically neutral as a whole, since each atom was electrically neutral (positive charges equaling negative charges) before it was disassociated by heat.

The core of the Sun takes up about a quarter of its depth and is the site of all the nuclear reactions that create the Sun's energy. Above the core is the radiative zone, reaching to 71 percent of the radius of the Sun. In the radiative zone, the radiation from the core is still too energetic for plasma particles to absorb their heat, and the waves simply radiate through this zone. Above the radiative zone is the convective zone, where the radiation works to heat the Sun's matter, and it boils like water in a pot. Finally, above the convective zone is the thin layer called the photosphere, from which visible light is radiated and which viewers think of as the surface of the Sun as seen from Earth. The layers of the Sun are shown in the figure on page 56.

Though the Sun appears as a discrete disc in the sky, a spherical, separate object like a planet, it is actually a continuous body through the entire solar system. The Sun is not as dense as Earth's air until depths 10 percent below the photosphere (the surface that is seen in visible light). Outside the photosphere, which appears to be the edge of the Sun because it is the only solar structure that is seen in visible light, are the transition zone, the corona, and the solar wind. The solar wind is a continual, pulsating wave of particles and radiation sent out from the Sun that permeates all the space between the planets and continues past the orbits of the most distant solar system objects until it collides with the radiation of interstellar space. The Sun sends a billion kilograms of electrons and protons into space each second, and these form the solar wind. Though the solar wind is very sparse, it is a major force in solar system space, and the Sun might be thought of more accurately as filling the entire solar system, with the orbiting planets embedded within it. (The space in the solar system is actually filled with three things: the matter of the solar wind, the radiation from the Sun, and interstellar cosmic rays, which constantly shoot through all the space and matter in the solar system, on paths from the distant star systems that created them.)

ELEMENTARY PARTICLES

Molecules, like carbon dioxide (CO_2), are built from atoms, which are the basic units of any chemical element. The atom in turn is made from the subatomic particles called the proton, the electron, and the neutron. Protons and neutrons in turn are made of varieties of still smaller particles called quarks, which are members of the most basic group known, the fundamental particles. This progression is shown in the table below.

Known fundamental particles include the lepton, the quark, the photon, the gluon (which holds together material in atomic nuclei), and the boson (not discussed here). At this time it appears that the two basic constituents of matter are the lepton and the quark, and there are believed to be six types of each. Each type of lepton and quark also has a corresponding antiparticle—a particle that has the same mass but opposite electrical charge and *magnetic moment* (direction in which it is moved by a magnetic field).

An isolated quark has never been found: Quarks appear to almost always be found in twos or threes with other quarks and antiquarks. A theoretically predicted five-quark particle, called a pentaquark, has been produced in the laboratory. Four- and six-quark particles are also predicted but have not been found. The six quarks have been named up, down, charm, strange, top (or truth), and bottom (or beauty).

(continues)

BUILDING BLOCKS OF MATTER		
Type of matter	**Built from**	**Example**
molecule	atoms	CH_4, a methane molecule, is built from four hydrogen atoms and one carbon atom
atom	subatomic particles	H, a hydrogen atom, is built from one electron and one proton (the variety called deuterium also contains a neutron)
subatomic particle	fundamental particles	a proton is built from two "up" quarks and one "down" quark

(continued)

The mass of the truth quark is greater than an entire atom of gold and about 35 times heavier than the next biggest quark. The truth quark may be the heaviest particle in nature. The quarks found in ordinary matter are the up and down quarks, from which protons and neutrons are made. A proton, for instance, consists of two up quarks and a down quark, and a neutron consists of two down quarks and an up quark (quarks have fractional charges of one-third or two-thirds of the basic charge of the electron or proton).

The electrons that orbit atomic nuclei are a type of lepton. Like quarks, there are six types of leptons. The most familiar lepton is the electron. The other five are the muon, the tau particle, and the three types of neutrino associated with each: the electron neutrino, the muon neutrino, and the tau neutrino. Neutrinos are made in the Sun and flow outward from the Sun continuously and in great numbers. They are almost massless and actually pass through matter without interacting with it. Exiting at great speeds from the Sun, they pass through the planets and everything on them, including people, all the time.

The following is a brief list of glossary terms on this topic:

electron   A lepton; the least massive electrically charged particle, hence is absolutely stable

fundamental particle   A particle with no internal substructure; quarks, leptons, photons, gluons, and bosons are fundamental; all other objects are made from these, including protons and neutrons

SOLAR CORE

The core is thought to be as hot as 28,080,000°F (15,600,000°C) and to sustain pressures as high as 2,961,000 atm (300 GPa). The pressure at the center of the Earth is thought to be between 3,553,000 atm (360 GPa) and 3,750,000 atm (380 GPa) but temperatures are far lower. The Sun's temperatures and pressures allow the nuclear reactions that provide the energy for the Sun to proceed.

In the core, the Sun creates its energy by a process called *hydrogen burning*. In this process, four hydrogen nuclei are fused to create one helium nucleus. Since the hydrogen nuclei each consist of one proton, while the helium nucleus consists

lepton A category of fundamental particles; the electrically charged leptons are the electron, the muon, the tau, and their antiparticles; electrically neutral leptons are called neutrinos

neutrino A lepton with no electric charge; neutrinos participate only in weak and gravitational interactions and are therefore very difficult to detect; there are three known types of neutrinos, all of which are very light and could possibly have zero mass

neutron A subatomic particle with no electric charge, made of two down quarks and one up quark (held together by gluons); the neutral component of an atomic nucleus is made from neutrons; different isotopes of the same element are distinguished by having different numbers of neutrons in their nucleus

photon The fundamental particle that is the carrier particle of electromagnetic radiation

proton The most common subatomic particle, with electric charge of +1; protons are made of two up quarks and one down quark, bound together by gluons; the nucleus of a hydrogen atom is a proton. A nucleus with atomic number Z contains Z protons; therefore the number of protons is what distinguishes the different chemical elements

positron The antiparticle of the electron

quark A category of fundamental particles; quarks combine in groups to make subatomic particles such as protons and neutrons; the six quarks are named truth, beauty, charm, strange, up, and down

subatomic particle A particle used to make atoms; is itself made of fundamental particles

of two protons and two neutrons, several hydrogen nuclei are required to make one helium nucleus. The process takes several steps because the positive electrical charges of the protons repel each other, and it would be virtually impossible to cause four to collide at the same instant.

The process of creating the helium nucleus is called the proton-proton chain because it uses the protons one at a time. Hans A. Bethe, professor of physics at Cornell University, and Charles Critchfield, then a graduate student of George Gamow at George Washington University, first demonstrated in the late 1930s how a series of nuclear reactions could make the Sun shine. Bethe won the Nobel Prize in physics in 1967 for their work (Critchfield had since died).

Internal Structure of the Sun

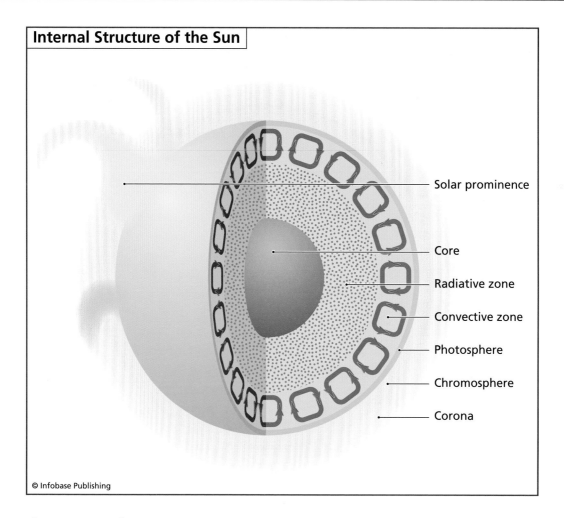

Solar prominence

Core

Radiative zone

Convective zone

Photosphere

Chromosphere

Corona

The Sun consists of a number of distinct layers, with differing temperatures and convection patterns.

In the first step of the proton-proton chain, two protons (the stripped nuclei of hydrogen atoms, denoted ^{1}H) come together to form a deuteron (D), which is a nucleus with one proton and one neutron. In the process, they emit two subatomic particles: a positron and an electron neutrino (these particles are defined in the sidebar "Elementary Particles," on page 53). Another proton (^{1}H) then collides with the deuteron (D) to form the nucleus of a rare isotope of helium, consisting of two protons and one neutron (denoted ^{3}He), and in the process, they emit a gamma ray. Finally, two of these ^{3}He nuclei fuse to create a ^{4}He nucleus, and in the process return two ^{1}H to the plasma in the core. The steps in the proton-proton chain are shown in the figure on page 57.

The basic law of physics that allows radiation energy to be produced from matter is the famous equation that Albert Einstein first stated:

$$E = mc^2$$

This equation states that energy, E, is equal to mass, m, times the speed of light squared, c^2. What this means is that mass and energy are interchangeable, a critical and revolutionary concept. Because the speed of light is such a huge number (9.8×10^8 feet per second, or 2.9979×10^8 meters per second), only a small amount of mass is needed to create a large amount of energy. One gram of hydrogen can be converted to energy equivalent to 20 kilotons of explosive!

But where in the proton-proton chain is the lost mass that makes all the energy that the Sun emits? After careful measurements, scientists were able to determine that a ^{4}He nucleus is just seven-tenths of 1 percent (0.7 percent) less massive than four protons. This tiny amount of lost mass is converted into energy each time one proton-proton chain is completed, and through Einstein's equation, creates all the energy that the Sun radiates. Every second, the Sun creates 10^{38} helium nuclei from about 700 million tons of hydrogen. In this process, every second, 5 million tons (0.7 percent) of this matter disappears as pure energy, creating the radiation that shines from the Sun.

There was a further mystery about hydrogen burning that needed to be solved: Protons are positively charged and therefore repel each other. Electrical forces work strongly over a wide range of distances between the protons, from long distances down to an atomic-scale separation. If the protons move closer than a certain extremely small distance, a stronger force, called the nuclear force (the force that bonds protons and neutrons together in an atomic nucleus), takes over and pulls the protons together with great strength. The hotter the protons are, the more energy they have to collide with each other and push close together despite the electrical repulsive force. Unfortunately, the temperature required to allow protons to come close enough for the strong nuclear force to take over is 11 billion degrees, about 10 times as hot as the center of the Sun. So how do protons ever combine to make deuterons?

The answer was also provided by Einstein, along with Louis de Broglie, at the time a professor of theoretical physics at the Henri Poincaré Institute, and Satyendranath Bose, a professor of physics at the University of Dacca. They explained in the 1920s that protons could act as waves or particles or have

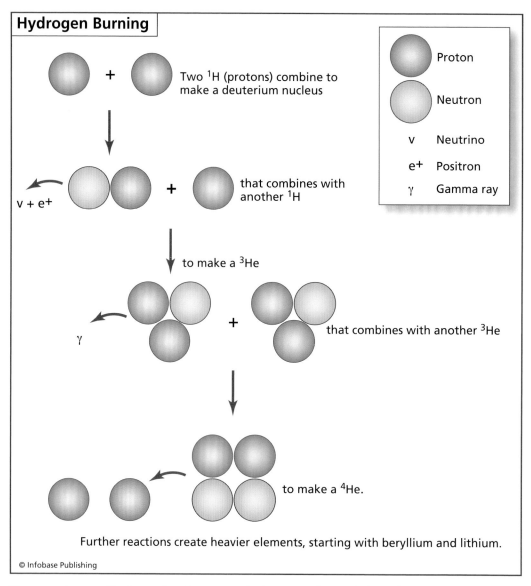

Hydrogen Burning

Two ^{1}H (protons) combine to make a deuterium nucleus

Proton

Neutron

v   Neutrino

e+   Positron

γ   Gamma ray

v + e+

that combines with another ^{1}H

to make a ^{3}He

γ

that combines with another ^{3}He

to make a ^{4}He.

Further reactions create heavier elements, starting with beryllium and lithium.

© Infobase Publishing

The several steps of hydrogen burning convert hydrogen nuclei into helium, thus creating new atoms and releasing the heat that drives the Sun and provides energy for the planets.

characteristics of both at the same time (this is also a result of the equivalency of matter and energy, stated in $E = mc^2$). If the wave positions of two protons can extend past their particle size enough to overlap, then the protons can overcome the electrical force and be pulled together by the nuclear force. This is called tunneling. The average proton in the Sun has a velocity of 2.03×10^6 feet per second (6.2×10^5 m/s), which along with the density of protons in the Sun's core caused each proton to collide with other protons 20 million times per second. Tunneling is such a delicate process, however, that it takes the average proton 10^{25} collisions before tunneling occurs!

In total, the process of hydrogen burning produces, along with a helium atom (^{4}He), a positron, an electron neutrino, two protons, and one gamma ray. The gamma rays move outward from the core of the Sun, colliding with and being absorbed by atoms, and then being reemitted. If they moved out of the Sun unimpeded at their original energies, they would pass out of the Sun in less than two seconds. Because of their constant collisions, the passage of a single gamma ray from the core of the Sun into space takes about 1 million years, and all the collisions and reemissions take away so much of the gamma ray's energy that by the time it passes out of the surface of the Sun it has been reduced from a gamma ray to the wavelength of visible light.

Though it is a small star, the Sun gives off 9.20×10^{23} calories per second (3.85×10^{26} J/s; a joule/second is a watt; for more information, see Appendix 1, "Units and Measurements"). The Sun seems to be the great constant in the life of Earth, but its luminosity has changed over time, and it will continue to change as the Sun ages.

The neutrinos created by hydrogen burning pass relatively unobstructed through the layers of the Sun and stream out into space at the unimaginable rate of 10^{38} every second. Because neutrinos interact very little with matter, they pass through the Sun—as well as through atmospheres, planets, and even our own bodies—unobstructed. Every second, 150 million neutrinos pass through every cubic centimeter of your body!

If neutrinos refuse to interact with mass and seem to have none themselves, how does anyone know they exist? When instruments had been developed that could accurately measure radioactivity, people found that radioactive rocks gave off energy that varied by unpredictable amounts. In a kind of *radio-decay* called β-decay (beta decay), a neutron turns into a proton and emits an electron. When measured in the lab, electrons emerged from the reaction with values of energy that varied over a wide range, rather than with one fixed and predictable energy value. More distressingly, no electron that emerged had enough energy to balance the reaction (remember that the fundamental law of physics is that energy is always conserved, whether as electromagnetic radiation or as mass). In 1930, physicist Wolfgang Pauli proposed a "desperate way out" of the β-decay problem: A low-mass, unseen, unknown particle was emitted at the same time as the electron. However, there was absolutely no evidence for such a thing to occur. This kind of complex and unsupported theory is often called "desperate pleading" in science. Of course Pauli was right: In 1956, neutrinos were first detected as flashes of light in a 2,640-gallon (10,000-l) tank of water placed next to a nuclear reactor.

Scientists have spent entire careers trying to detect and count neutrinos, and the best efforts to date have only been able to detect between one-third and two-thirds of the number predicted by theory. Whether the error is in the detection or in the theory has yet to be determined. One experiment to detect neutrinos was built in a 1.24-mile- (2-km-) deep mine in Sudbury, Ontario. There, a tank 13 yards (12 m) in diameter was filled with heavy water, so called because each molecule of this water is created with a deuterium atom rather than a hydrogen atom. Deuterium is an atom with a proton and a neutron in its nucleus, where hydrogen has only a proton (regular water is shown chemically as H_2O, meaning two hydrogens and one oxygen bonded together, and heavy water is sometimes shown as D_2O, for two deuteriums and one oxygen). Heavy water is used because neutrinos have a weak interaction with it: When a neutrino collides with a molecule of heavy water, a tiny flash of light is emitted. The flashes can be then counted.

RADIATIVE ZONE

From the top of the core to about 71 percent of the radius of the Sun is the area called the radiative zone. When the gamma rays produced by hydrogen burning in the core pass through the radiative zone, they are so energetic that rather than heating the plasma of the Sun in this region they simply collide and are reemitted over and over. The repeated collisions slowly remove energy from the gamma rays, lengthening their wavelengths and lowering their frequencies. Energy transfer in the radiative zone, therefore, is by continuous absorption and reemission of electromagnetic waves, which bounce ever closer to the surface of the Sun. Despite the intense electromagnetic radiation bouncing around in the radiative zone, the matter is relatively calm and stationary, especially when compared to the convective zone above it. From the temperature of the core, 28,080,000°F (15,600,000°C), it takes 170,000 years for the colliding and rebounding gamma rays to pass upward and gradually drop to a temperature of 2,700,000°F (1,500,000°C). At this temperature, atoms and particles in the Sun can absorb the radiation and become hotter themselves; this transition marks the bottom of the convective zone.

CONVECTIVE ZONE

By the time it reaches the top of the radiative zone, the electromagnetic radiation from the Sun's core has lost enough energy that matter in the convective zone can absorb the waves and become hotter itself. This hot matter circulates upward in a process called *convection,* and in this way energy is passed through the convective zone by hot matter. Convection is mixing due to temperature or density differences in a liquid or gas. One example of convection is boiling oatmeal in a pot: Heat put in at the bottom of the pot causes the water and oatmeal at the bottom to expand. Almost every material expands when it is heated, and since it retains its original mass, it becomes less dense. Lowering the density of the material at the bottom makes it buoyant, and it rises to the top. Cooler material from the top sinks to the bottom to take its place, and the cycle continues. Convection can create "cells," regular patterns of circulation with material moving up and down.

Temperatures in the Sun become cooler with distance from the core. Though the temperature at the top of the radiative zone is still in the millions of degrees, by the time material reaches the edge of the convective zone, the temperature has fallen to about 11,000°F (6,000°C), even though the convective zone takes up less than the final third of the Sun's radius. The Sun's material forms giant convection cells as it transfers heat from the top of the radiative zone to the surface. A complex pattern called granulation is visible in white light: These "granules" are the shapes of the tops of convective cells inside the Sun. The normal pattern of convective cells creates about a million granules over the surface of the convective zone, of which each granule is 870 miles (1,400 km) across.

In addition to the normal granules, giant convective cells up to 21,700 miles (35,000 km) in diameter are seen, called "supergranules." Material flowing to create the supergranules has a velocity between 160 and 1,300 feet per second (50 and 400 m/s). Supergranules therefore seem like a contradiction: The supergranules themselves rotate a few percent faster than the gas from which they are made. The supergranules seem to be waves moving through the surface of the convective zone, much like waves on the oceans of Earth.

The rotation of the Sun can be measured by observing the motion of sunspots—dark, cooler markings on the photosphere of the Sun, just above the convective zone. The Sun rotates west to east (in a prograde, or *direct,* sense), just like the Earth. Unlike the Earth, different latitudes on the Sun rotate at different rates. This is called differential rotation. The differential rotation persists into the Sun about one-third of the way to the core. Beneath this point, the Sun behaves as a solid body and rotates at the same rate at all latitudes, as the Earth does. The point where the Sun stops rotating differentially is the bottom of the convective zone. This means that velocities in the Sun change sharply at this boundary, creating a shear zone about 12,400 miles (20,000 km) thick, known as the *tacholine.* The relative speeds of material on each side of the tacholine oscillate on a 16-month period. When the

Sun's material at 0.72 of the Sun's radius is moving quickly, the material at 0.63 solar radii is moving slowly, and then the relative velocities change such that the deep material is moving fast and the shallow material slowly.

MAGNETIC FIELD

The Sun's magnetic field is immense and influential to all aspects of solar structure, and it extends far out into the solar system. The magnetic field is included here in the structure of the Sun, not because it is a discrete layer, but because it is believed to originate at the base of the convective zone. The hot gases and plasma inside the Sun are good conductors of electricity. The area of the tacholine, where on one side the gases are convecting and on the other side they are stationary, is a similar structure to the core of the Earth and is thus thought to be where the Sun's magnetic field is generated.

Most of the time the Sun, like Earth, has a north and a south magnetic pole, with magnetic field lines flowing out of the south magnetic pole and into the north magnetic pole. This arrangement is called a dipolar field, since it has two poles. At solar maximum (the maximum of the sunspot cycle and of all solar activity, occurring every 11 years or so), the most recent space missions have shown that the Sun's magnetic field becomes chaotic. This is to be expected, since the magnetic field controls the Sun's activity, from sunspots to prominences to loops and coronal mass ejections, but now the Sun's magnetic field can be accurately tracked. For nearly a month beginning in March 2000, the Sun's south magnetic pole faded, and a north pole emerged to take its place. The Sun had two north poles. As outrageous as this may sound, it is apparently a common occurrence at solar maximum. The south magnetic pole migrated north and formed a band roughly around the Sun's equator. By May 2000, the south pole had returned to its usual place, but in 2001, the Sun's magnetic field reversed itself and through 2003 remained with the south magnetic pole at the north rotational pole and vice versa. Though the Sun's magnetic field most generally resembles a *dipole,* there are other, more complex configurations possible for magnetic

On July 24, 1999, this large, looping prominence reached 35 Earth radii in length (image of the Earth included for scale). (SOHO/MDI, NASA/ESA)

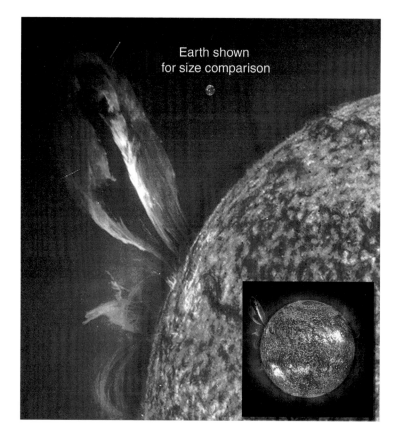

Earth shown for size comparison

fields. The next most complex after the dipole is the quadrupole, in which the field has four poles equally spaced around the sphere of the planet. After the quadrupole comes the octupole, which has eight poles. The Earth's magnetic field is thought to degenerate into quadrupole and octupole fields as it reverses, and then reforms into the reversed dipole field. The Sun's magnetic field also showed complex combinations of quadrupole and octupole fields when it went through its solar maximum contortions.

PHOTOSPHERE

The photosphere is only 310 miles (500 km) thick. This is the outermost layer of the Sun that emits energy in the visible light spectrum, and so it is the layer that seems to define the surface of the Sun. The photosphere maintains a steady average temperature of 9,900°F (5,500°C). The photosphere oscillates by 30 miles (50 km) in height, five or six times per half hour. These are giant acoustic compressions and are detected by the Doppler effect in wavelengths of solar spectral lines (see the sidebar "Doppler Effect" on page 66). Scientists from the SOHO (Solar and Heliospheric Observatory) mission have taken images showing "sunquakes" creating waves similar to those formed by a pebble falling into water, though these waves were formed by the eruption of a solar flare. The waves accelerated from 22,000 miles per hour (14,000 k/h) to more than 10 times that speed and carried the energy equivalent to 40,000 times the devastating San Francisco earthquake of 1906.

Because the convection that creates the magnetic field is so active, and because the surface of the Sun rotates faster at its equator than it does nearer the poles, the magnetic field itself is twisted as it is formed. When particularly concentrated twisted areas of the magnetic field emerge into the photosphere, they create both sunspots and especially active regions and can even trigger solar flares. Sunspots are usually

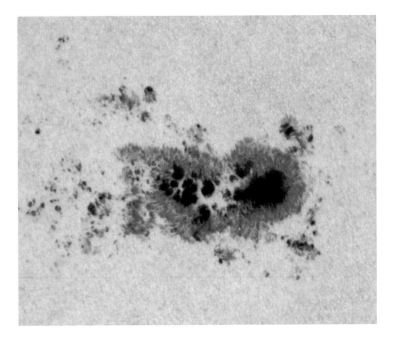

An unusually large sunspot cluster, seen during a period of high solar activity in September 2000 (SOHO/MDI, NASA/ESA)

DOPPLER EFFECT

Sound is produced by waves passing through a substance. The sound of a voice is produced by vibrations of the vocal chords making waves in air. These waves strike the eardrum and allow the person to hear them. Sounds can pass through water as well, but no sound passes through space because space is a near vacuum with no substance to carry the sound waves. For more on waves, wavelength, and frequency, see appendix 2, "Light, Wavelength, and Radiation."

The term *Doppler effect* is most often used to describe the ways sounds appear to change when an observer is standing still and the object making the sounds is moving past. A good example is the sound of a car horn while the car is speeding past: As the car approaches, the car horn sounds shriller, until after it passes, when the sounds becomes deeper and deeper. The car horn produces a uniform sound, and to the driver, the sound does not seem to change: It only seems to change for the observer, standing still as the car rushes past.

In 1842, Christian Doppler, director of the Institute of Physics at Vienna University, explained this effect in a presentation regarding the colors of starlight to the Royal Bohemian Society of Sciences. Though he applied the science to stars moving toward or away from the Earth, the same physics apply to the sounds of objects moving toward or away from an observer. As the speeding, noisy object is coming toward an observer, the wavefronts of the sound it is producing are pressed closer together by the object's movement, and the sound the observer hears seems to have a higher and higher frequency. Frequency is the number of wavefronts that strike the ear per second, and the higher the frequency, the higher the pitch of the sound. When the noisy object passes the observer, the frequency of the wavefronts seem to be less and less, spreading out behind the speeding object, and so the noise the observer hears seems lower in pitch.

The Doppler effect for sound can be expressed as an equation for f, the frequency perceived by the observer:

about 8,670°F (4,800°C), about 1,830°F (1,000°C) cooler than their surroundings. The largest sunspots have diameters on the order of five times the diameter of the Earth and can actually be seen with the naked eye, though of course, to restate, no one should ever look directly at the Sun because its intense radiation will permanently damage the eyes. Because they are

$$f = \frac{f_o}{\left(1 - \frac{v_s}{v}\right)},$$

where f_o is the actual frequency of the sound, v_s is the speed of the source, and v is the speed of the sound through the air. If the source is approaching the listener, its velocity v_s is positive, and the frequency the listener hears is higher than f_o. If the source is moving away from the listener, its velocity v_s is negative, and the frequency the listener hears is lower than f_o.

Now imagine the source is moving at or above the speed of sound in the medium. The speed of sound in air at sea level is about 1,115 feet per second (340 m/s). If the source's speed is equal to the speed of sound ($v_s = v$), the source's speed is called Mach 1; if the source's speed is twice the speed of sound ($v_s = 2v$), it is called Mach 2, and so forth. The wavefronts in front of the source are now cascading behind the sound source in a cone. As a result, an observer in front of the source will detect nothing until the source arrives, for Mach 1, or until it has passed, for higher Mach numbers. The pressure front will be quite intense (a shock wave), due to all the wavefronts adding together, and will not be perceived as a pitch but as a bang or crack of sound and a physical feeling of pressure as the pressure wall passes. Pressure fronts from jets flying above Mach 1 can shake objects off shelves and even break glass.

A similar effect happens to light. The equations and relationships are more complex and involve some special relativity, one of the contributions of Albert Einstein. The principal, though, is the same: Light seen on Earth emitted from objects moving away is shifted toward lower frequencies ("red shift"), and light emitted from objects moving toward the Earth is shifted toward higher frequencies ("blue shift"). The Doppler effect, then, allows scientists to determine the movement of celestial objects relative to Earth.

visible without telescopes or special instruments, sunspots were first reported by the Chinese some 2,000 years ago. The sunspots shown in the photo on page 65 appeared on September 20, 2000, during an especially active period for the Sun. This cluster is more than 10 times the area of the Earth's surface and was the largest sunspot group seen in nine years.

Several large sunspot clusters were visible on the Sun on October 28, 2003. (SOHO, NASA/ESA)

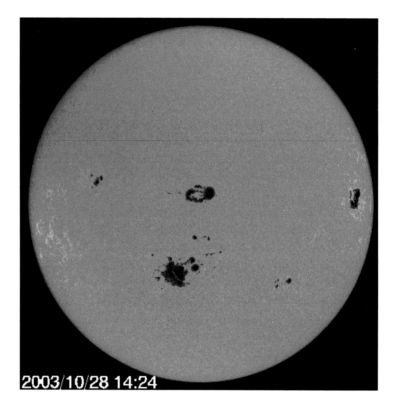

2003/10/28 14:24

Sunspots can last months or only a few hours. This image of the whole Sun shown above was taken on October 28, 2003, as a part of NASA's catalog that contains one sunspot image of the Sun for every day (http://sohowww.nascom.nasa.gov). Sunspots can coalesce or move past or even through each other. Each cluster is assigned a number and tracked as it moves across the Sun's surface. In this image, the lower cluster is numbered 0486, and the central cluster is 0484.

Simple sunspots have a dark center, called the umbra, almost invariably making up 17 percent of the area of the sunspot, for unknown reasons. The umbra is surrounded by a lighter penumbra, consisting of radial light and dark filaments, along which matter is flowing at a few kilometers per second. Sunspots usually form at about 40° latitude on the Sun and move toward the equator progressively during a regular cycle. About every 11 years, there is a maximum number of sunspots, and then fewer and fewer, until the next cycle begins again. The solar cycle is commonly described as exactly 11 years, but it actually varies from about nine to 14 years. David Hathaway and Bob Wilson, scientists at NASA's Marshall Space Flight Center, have analyzed records of sunspots and found that the solar minimum occurs about 34 months after the first day with no sunspots. In the most recent cycle, the first day with no sunspots occurred January 18, 2004. According to their hypothesis, the solar minimum should have occurred in 2006. After the solar minimum, solar activity rises sharply and should have reached its next maximum in only four years, in 2010. The solar cycle is not forever unchanging though: In 2010, we were still in a solar minimum, and from the years 1645 to 1715, there were very few sunspots visible on the Sun at all, and no one knows why.

CHROMOSPHERE

The chromosphere is a 15,500-mile- (25,000-km-) thick layer over the photosphere. The chromosphere is dimmer and more diffuse than the photosphere, so it cannot be seen without devices called spectrohelioscopes or during solar eclipses, when it appears as a bright red crescent a few seconds before and after totality of the eclipse. Both the chromosphere and corona just beyond it are so diffuse that they would count as vacuums on Earth.

Though dim and diffuse, the chromosphere is an astonishingly active region, with many different dynamic structures. Narrow, pointed plasma jets called spicules rise 9,300 miles (15,000 km) from the Sun for durations of five to 10 minutes. These jets are moving at 12–20 miles per second (20–30 km/s) and are only a couple of miles wide. There may be a half-million spicules on the chromosphere at any time, and they tend to cluster into "hedgerows" or "tufts." Sunspots also extend into the chromosphere as dark areas and are associated with various structures called surges, sprays, and loops. Much more massive loops of cool gas called filaments stretch up to halfway across the face of the Sun, appearing as dark threads. When they are seen from the side (so that they appear to extend into space), they are called prominences. As shown in the photo on page 70, prominences and

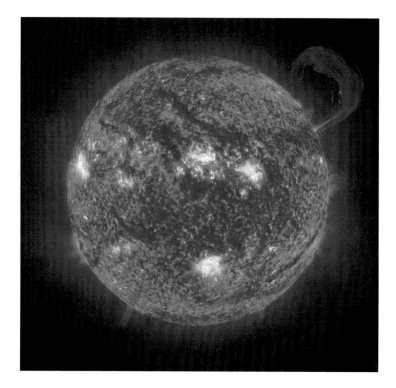

This large erupting prominence, seen in the ultraviolet, shows some of the activity and scale of the Sun's magnetic field. (SOHO/EIT, NASA/ESA)

filaments are the same phenomenon—thin arches of chromospheric material drawn out by the magnetic field and seen from different angles.

Prominences can be 60,000 miles (100,000 km) long, and their temperatures vary from 9,000°F–27,000°F (5,000°C–15,000°C), hundreds of times cooler and denser than the rest of the chromosphere. The prominences (or filaments) shown in the photo on page 71 in ultraviolet light were precursors to a coronal mass ejection, an immense solar event described later in this chapter.

The strangest thing about the chromosphere, and one of the main mysteries about the Sun, is its temperature structure. From a low of about 9,900°F (5,500°C) in the photosphere, temperatures actually rise through the chromosphere. In the top 300 miles (500 km) of the chromosphere, the temperature rises to 36,000°F (20,000°C). This makes little obvious sense: Since the source of the heat is in the Sun's core, one would assume it would be the hottest. In fact the corona, further out from the surface of the Sun, is hotter still.

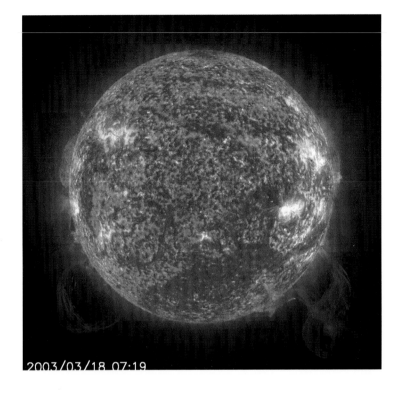

This extreme ultraviolet image captured twin erupting prominences. The prominences were about 20 Earth diameters in length and lasted less than a day. (SOHO, NASA/ESA)

TRANSITION ZONE

The transition zone is a thin layer separating the chromosphere from the corona, but it has distinctive properties. The transition zone is tens of kilometers thick. Its temperature rises from 36,000°F (20,000°C) on its inside edge to 3,600,000°F (2,000,000°C) at its outside edge. The abruptness of the temperature change is thought to be linked to the Sun's magnetic field, but it makes little sense when compared to temperature transition on Earth. On Earth, abrupt temperature changes rapidly smooth out through heat conduction or convection. The transition zone on the Sun is maintained by physics that are not yet fully understood.

CORONA

The corona is dimmer and more diffuse than the chromosphere, so like the chromosphere, it cannot be seen except during eclipses, when it shines pearly white, mainly from reflected sunlight. The corona reaches out from the Sun millions of kilometers, emitting energy in the ultraviolet spectrum, and structures called arches, loops, plumes, and streamers rise from it. The corona is highly variable in density, and less dense areas called coronal holes allow the Sun's magnetic field to stream outward. The corona is the major source of the solar wind, consisting largely of protons and electrons. The image of the shining corona shown in the photo below was taken by the *SOHO* craft, an international cooperative effort between the European Space Agency (ESA) and the National Aeronautics and Space Administration (NASA). The *SOHO* craft has an instrument called the Large Angle and Spectrometric Coronagraph (LASCO), which blocks the Sun itself with a disk so that the instrument can take images of the wispy corona. The strong streaks seen in the corona are called polar plumes and extend past the edges of this 5.25-million-mile-wide (8.4-million-km-wide) view. The curving streak of

The Sun's corona and sungrazing comet SOHO-6: The size of the Sun's disk out to its photosphere is outlined in white on the blocking disk that allows the less bright corona to be seen. (SOHO, NASA/ESA)

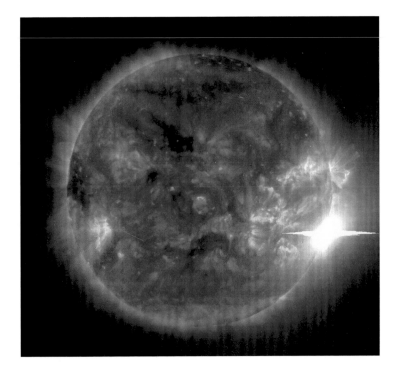

On November 4, 2003, NOAA's GOES satellite detected the largest X-ray flare of the last solar maximum. The radiation was so intense that it saturated the detectors on the satellite, causing the bright horizontal line. (SOHO/EIT/ESA/NASA)

comet SOHO-6 is also captured in this same image; the comet later fell into the Sun.

There are also strongly energetic emissions from the corona, including solar flares. A flare is defined as a rapid and intense increase in brightness, but it can be broken into several categories. Some are very rapid, small X-ray flares that suddenly release enough energy to heat the corona hundreds of thousands of degrees; others are ultraviolet flares; and still others are flares consisting primarily of plasma. Solar flares consisting of plasma can for short periods of time be the hottest material on the Sun, at tens of millions of degrees, containing electrons and protons accelerated almost to the speed of light. These flares are always located near sunspots and can last for minutes to hours. They are often accompanied by X-ray and gamma-ray bursts. The superheated, supersonic material and high radiation in the flare can be thrown out into space, where it can damage satellites and even strike the Earth's magnetic field with enough disruptive energy to damage electrical grids.

Skylab, the American space station that functioned in the 1970s, took the first high-resolution images of the corona. Because the corona is normally invisible in the visible light spectrum, the images were taken using ultraviolet and X-ray telescopes. Skylab and several later missions (involving SOHO craft, TRACE [Transition Region and Coronal Explorer], and RHESSI [Reuven Ramaty High Energy Solar Spectroscopic Imager]; see the mission list on page 101) have made detailed images of the corona over time, recording huge domes and bubbles of plasma that erupt from the corona at up to 620 miles per second (1,000 km/s) and burst, flying out into space. These eruptions, called coronal mass ejections, occasionally reach out far enough to collide with Earth and other planets. A large coronal mass ejection, covering 45° of the disk of the Sun, can send literally billions of tons of material at a million degrees flying out into space, fast enough to reach the Earth in four days. The image at right, taken with the LASCO instrument on the SOHO craft, shows the bright comet NEAT passing the Sun as a large coronal mass ejection fades. The

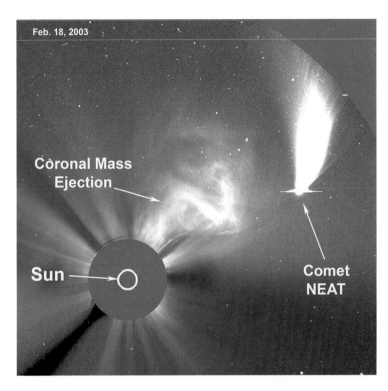

Feb. 18, 2003

Coronal Mass Ejection

Sun

Comet NEAT

The LASCO instrument took this image of the Sun's corona. The image also captured the comet NEAT (its exceptionally bright nucleus saturated the instrument's sensors, creating false horizontal lines), as well as a fading coronal mass ejection. (SOHO, NASA/ESA)

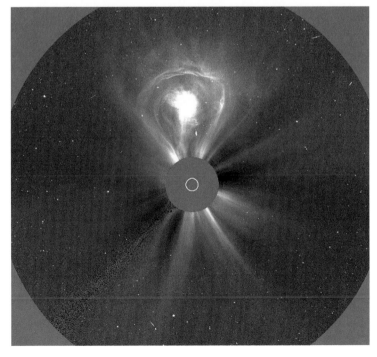

A perfect example of the normal lightbulb shape of a coronal mass ejection (SOHO, NASA/ESA)

An unusual helical coronal mass ejection may have been twisted by magnetic field lines. (SOHO, NASA/ESA)

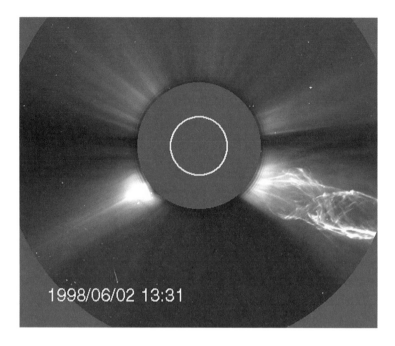

1998/06/02 13:31

visible-light Sun is blocked by a disc in the instrument that allows the far dimmer coronal events to be imaged.

Violent and gigantic as they are, coronal mass ejections occur three to five times a day at peak and seldom less often than once every five days. Like all other solar activity, coronal mass ejection events vary with the 11-year sunspot cycle. The first example of an immense coronal mass ejection is shown in the photo on page 75. It has the classic exploding lightbulb shape. The second example, shown on this page, has a highly unusual and beautiful twisted shape. In these figures, the bright disk of the Sun is blocked by the imaging instrument, and the blocking plate contains the white ring, which shows the size and position of the Sun itself.

Thinner streamers of coronal material also streak out and back into the corona. The *TRACE* satellite has shown that arches in active regions are extremely thin, only a few hundred kilometers wide. The high-resolution images also show that the arches and streamers flicker constantly, an indication of the strength and variability of the magnetic field. In fact, strongly magnetic flares have been observed to create oscillations in nearby thin loops, and the rate at which these oscillations die can be used to test the theory of magnetic interactions; the arches, plumes, streamers, and holes in the corona are all the product of the Sun's magnetic field. The corona is the first part of the Sun that is diffuse enough that it is molded by the Sun's magnetic field, rather than the magnetic field being molded by the Sun's movements (recall that in the convective and photosphere regions, the magnetic field is molded by the convective movements of the Sun, being twisted and folded until it erupts in sunspots and solar flares). The Sun's magnetic field is 20–200 times stronger than the Earth's, but that does not explain the profound effect it has on the solar corona. The corona conforms tightly to the magnetic field lines: Coronal holes and streamers have very sharp edges. This is because the corona is so hot that its material is a plasma. Most of the atoms have been ionized, that is, they have lost electrons and are no longer electrically neutral but instead are charged particles, and other atoms have been completely disassembled into electrons and bare nuclei. These charged particles stream in helices up and down the magnetic field lines, bound by the fundamental physical relations between electrical currents (streams of charged particles) and magnetic fields. Thus, the shapes of the corona are entirely controlled by the magnetic field. At the edges of the corona, the magnetic field molds its gases into long, pointed petal shapes called helmet structures. The points of helmet structures can reach tens of millions of kilometers into space and temperatures of up to 3,600,000°F (2,000,000°C).

Just as the temperature in the Sun rises through the chromosphere and transition zone, in the corona the temperature continues to rise, from 3,600,000°F to 5,400,000°F (2,000,000°C to 3,000,000°C). The parts of the corona associated with sunspots are even hotter. The first observations that indicated something about the outrageous temperatures in the chromosphere and corona came in the 1800s, when scientists were measuring spectral lines during an eclipse. They were using a technique called spectrometry. *Spectrometers* are instruments that spread light out into spectra, in which the strength of the energy being emitted at each wavelength is measured separately. The spectrum ends up looking like a bar

This image shows two coronal mass ejections heading in symmetrically opposite directions from the Sun. An image of the Sun from a different day was enlarged and superimposed on the occulting disk for effect. (SOHO, NASA/ESA)

graph, in which the height of each bar shows how strongly that wavelength is present in the light. These bars are called spectral lines. Each type of atom can only absorb or emit light at certain wavelengths, so the location and spacing of the spectral lines indicate which atoms are present in the object emitting the light. In this way, scientists can determine the composition of something simply from the light shining from it (see the following sidebar "Remote Sensing," on page 79). Some of the spectral lines for the Sun could not be matched with any known elements and were not identified until the 1940s, when physicists discovered that iron atoms that had been stripped of up to half of their usual 26 electrons created these spectral lines. Very hot temperatures can cause atoms to lose most or all of their electrons. Later, instruments sent into space on rockets and satellites detected X-ray and ultraviolet radiation being emitted from the Sun, which also required hot temperatures, near or above 1,800,000°F (1,000,000°C).

The high temperatures in the chromosphere and corona are still not completely understood, though finally there are at least some theories. The extreme heat likely has something

(continues on page 86)

REMOTE SENSING

Remote sensing is the name given to a wide variety of techniques that allow observers to make measurements of a place they are physically far from. The most familiar type of remote sensing is the photograph taken by spacecraft or by giant telescopes on Earth. These photos can tell scientists a lot about a planet; by looking at surface topography and coloration photo geologists can locate faults, craters, lava flows, chasms, and other features that indicate the weather, volcanism, and tectonics of the body being studied. There are, however, critical questions about planets and moons that cannot be answered with visible-light photographs, such as the composition and temperature of the surface or atmosphere. Some planets, such as Venus, have clouds covering their faces, and so even photography of the surface is impossible.

For remote sensing of solar system objects, each wavelength of radiation can yield different information. Scientists frequently find it necessary to send detectors into space rather than making measurements from Earth, first because not all types of electromagnetic radiation can pass through the Earth's atmosphere (see figure on page 80), and second, because some electromagnetic emissions must be measured close to their sources, because they are weak, or in order to make detailed maps of the surface being measured.

Spectrometers are instruments that spread light out into spectra, in which the energy being emitted at each wavelength is measured separately. The spectrum often ends up looking like a bar graph, in which the height of each bar shows how strongly that wavelength is present in the light. These bars are called spectral lines. Each type of atom can only absorb or emit light at certain wavelengths, so the location and spacing of the spectral lines indicate which atoms are present in the object absorbing and emitting the light. In this way, scientists can determine the composition of something simply from the light shining from it.

Below are examples of the uses of a number of types of electromagnetic radiation in remote sensing.

GAMMA RAYS

Gamma rays are a form of electromagnetic radiation; they have the shortest wavelength and highest energy. High-energy radiation such as X-rays and gamma rays are

(continues)

(continued)

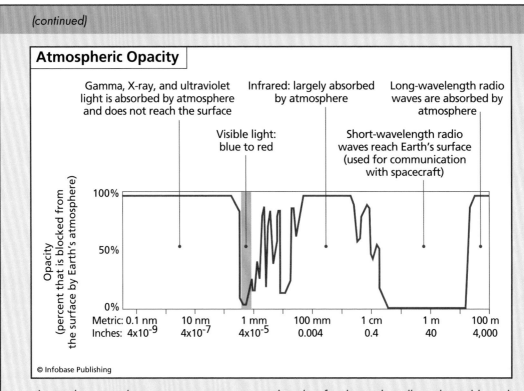

Atmospheric Opacity

Gamma, X-ray, and ultraviolet light is absorbed by atmosphere and does not reach the surface

Infrared: largely absorbed by atmosphere

Long-wavelength radio waves are absorbed by atmosphere

Visible light: blue to red

Short-wavelength radio waves reach Earth's surface (used for communication with spacecraft)

© Infobase Publishing

The Earth's atmosphere is opaque to many wavelengths of radiation but allows the visible and short radio wavelengths through to the surface.

absorbed to a great degree by the Earth's atmosphere, so it is not possible to measure their production by solar system bodies without sending measuring devices into space. These high-energy radiations are created only by high-energy events, such as matter heated to millions of degrees, high-speed collisions, or cosmic explosions. These wavelengths, then, are used to investigate the hottest regions of the Sun. The effects of gamma rays on other solar systems bodies, those without protective atmospheres, can be measured and used to infer compositions. This technique searches for radioactivity induced by the gamma rays.

Though in the solar system gamma rays are produced mainly by the hottest regions of the Sun, they can also be produced by colder bodies through a chain reaction of events, starting with high-energy cosmic rays. Space objects are continuously bombarded with cosmic rays, mostly high-energy protons. These high-energy protons strike the surface materials, such as dust and rocks, causing nuclear reactions in the atoms of the surface material. The reactions produce neutrons, which collide with surrounding nuclei. The nuclei become excited by the added energy of neutron impacts, and reemit gamma rays as they return to their original, lower-energy state. The energy of the resultant gamma rays is characteristic of specific nuclear interactions in the surface, so measuring their intensity and wavelength allow a measurement of the abundance of several elements. One of these is hydrogen, which has a prominent gamma-ray emission at 2.223 million electron volts (a measure of the energy of the gamma ray). This can be measured from orbit, as it has been in the Mars Odyssey mission using a Gamma-Ray Spectrometer. The neutrons produced by the cosmic ray interactions discussed earlier start out with high energies, so they are called fast neutrons. As they interact with the nuclei of other atoms, the neutrons begin to slow down, reaching an intermediate range called epithermal neutrons. The slowing-down process is not too efficient because the neutrons bounce off large nuclei without losing much energy (hence speed). However, when neutrons interact with hydrogen nuclei, which are about the same mass as neutrons, they lose considerable energy, becoming thermal, or slow, neutrons. (The thermal neutrons can be captured by other atomic nuclei, which then can emit additional gamma rays.) The more hydrogen there is in the surface, the more thermal neutrons relative to epithermal neutrons. Many neutrons escape from the surface, flying up into space where they can be detected by the neutron detector on Mars Odyssey. The same technique was used to identify hydrogen enrichments, interpreted as water ice, in the polar regions of the Moon.

X-RAYS

When an X-ray strikes an atom, its energy can be transferred to the electrons orbiting the atom. This addition of energy to the electrons makes one or more electrons leap from their normal orbital shells around the nucleus of the atom to higher orbital shells, leaving vacant shells at lower energy values. Having vacant, lower-energy orbital shells is an unstable state for an atom, and so in a short period of time the electrons fall back into their original orbital shells, and in the process emit another X-ray. This X-ray has energy equivalent to the difference in energies between the higher and lower orbital shells that the electron moved between. Because each element has a unique set of energy levels between electron orbitals, each element produces X-rays with energies that are characteristic of itself and no other element. This method can

(continues)

(continued)

be used remotely from a satellite, and it can also be used directly on tiny samples of material placed in a laboratory instrument called an electron microprobe, which measures the composition of the material based on the X-rays the atoms emit when struck with electrons.

VISIBLE AND NEAR-INFRARED

The most commonly seen type of remote sensing is, of course, visible light photography. Even visible light, when measured and analyzed according to wavelength and intensity, can be used to learn more about the body reflecting it.

Visible and near-infrared reflectance spectroscopy can help identify minerals that are crystals made of many elements, while other types of spectrometry identify individual types of atoms. When light shines on a mineral, some wavelengths are absorbed by the mineral, while other wavelengths are reflected back or transmitted through the mineral. This is why things have color to the eye: Eyes see and brains decode the wavelengths, or colors, that are not absorbed. The wavelengths of light that are absorbed are effectively a fingerprint of each mineral, so an analysis of absorbed versus reflected light can be used to identify minerals. This is not commonly used in laboratories to identify minerals, but it is used in remote sensing observations of planets.

The primary association of infrared radiation is heat, also called thermal radiation. Any material made of atoms and molecules at a temperature above absolute zero produces infrared radiation, which is produced by the motion of its atoms and molecules. At absolute zero, −459.67°F (~273.15°C), all atomic and molecular motion ceases. The higher the temperature, the more they move, and the more infrared radiation they produce. Therefore, even extremely cold objects, like the surface of Pluto, emit infrared radiation. Hot objects, like metal heated by a welder's torch, emit radiation in the visible spectrum as well as in the infrared.

In 1879 Josef Stefan, an Austrian scientist, deduced the relation between temperature and infrared emissions from empirical measurements. In 1884 his student, Ludwig Boltzmann derived the same law from thermodynamic theory. The relation gives the total energy emitted by an object (E) in terms of its absolute temperature in Kelvin (T), and a constant called the Stefan-Boltzmann constant (equal to 5.670400×10^{-8} W m^{-2} K^{-4}, and denoted with the Greek letter sigma, σ):

$$E = \sigma T^4.$$

This total energy *E* is spread out at various wavelengths of radiation, but the energy peaks at a wavelength characteristic of the temperature of the body emitting the energy. The relation between wavelength and total energy, Planck's Law, allows scientists to determine the temperature of a body by measuring the energy it emits.

The hotter the body, the more energy it emits at shorter wavelengths. The surface temperature of the Sun is 9,900°F (5,500°C), and its Planck curve peaks in the visible wavelength range. For bodies cooler than the Sun, the peak of the Planck curve shifts to longer wavelengths, until a temperature is reached such that very little radiant energy is emitted in the visible range.

Humans radiate most strongly at an infrared wavelength of 10 microns (*micron* is another word for micrometer, one millionth of a meter). This infrared radiation is what makes night vision goggles possible: Humans are usually at a different temperature than their surroundings, and so their shapes can be seen in the infrared.

Only a few narrow bands of infrared light make it through the Earth's atmosphere without being absorbed, and can be measured by devices on Earth. To measure infrared emissions, the detectors themselves must be cooled to very low temperatures, or their own infrared emissions will swamp those they are trying to measure from elsewhere.

In thermal emission spectroscopy, a technique for remote sensing, the detector takes photos using infrared wavelengths and records how much of the light at each wavelength the material reflects from its surface. This technique can identify minerals and also estimate some physical properties, such as grain size. Minerals at temperatures above absolute zero emit radiation in the infrared, with characteristic peaks and valleys on plots of emission intensity versus wavelength. Though overall emission intensity is determined by temperature, the relationships between wavelength and emission intensity are determined by composition. The imager for *Mars Pathfinder*, a camera of this type, went to Mars in July 1997 to take measurements of light reflecting off the surfaces of Martian rocks (called reflectance spectra), and this data was used to infer what minerals the rocks contain.

When imaging in the optical or near-infrared wavelengths, the image gains information about only the upper microns of the surface. The thermal infrared gives information about the upper few centimeters, but to get information about deeper materials, even longer wavelengths must be used.

(continues)

RADIO WAVES

Radio waves from outside the Earth do reach through the atmosphere and can be detected both day and night, cloudy or clear, from Earth-based observatories using huge metal dishes. In this way, astronomers observe the universe as it appears in radio waves. Images like photographs can be made from any wavelength of radiation coming from a body: Bright regions on the image can correspond to more intense radiation, and dark parts, to less intense regions. It is as if observers are looking at the object

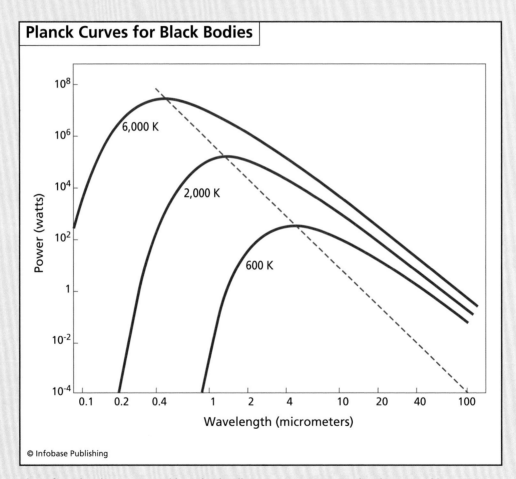

Planck Curves for Black Bodies

The infrared radiation emitted by a body allows its temperature to be determined by remote sensing. The curves showing the relationship between infrared and temperature are known as Planck curves.

through eyes that "see" in the radio, or ultraviolet, or any other wavelength, rather than just visible. Because of a lingering feeling that humankind still observes the universe exclusively through our own eyes and ears, scientists still often refer to "seeing" a body in visible wavelengths and to "listening" to it in radio wavelengths.

Radio waves can also be used to examine planets' surfaces, using the technique called radar (radio detection and ranging). Radar measures the strength and round-trip time of microwave or radio waves that are emitted by a radar antenna and bounced off a distant surface or object, thereby gaining information about the material of the target. The radar antenna alternately transmits and receives pulses at particular wavelengths (in the range 1 cm to 1 m) and polarizations (waves polarized in a single vertical or horizontal plane). For an imaging radar system, about 1,500 high-power pulses per second are transmitted toward the target or imaging area. At the Earth's surface, the energy in the radar pulse is scattered in all directions, with some reflected back toward the antenna. This backscatter returns to the radar as a weaker radar echo and is received by the antenna in a specific polarization (horizontal or vertical, not necessarily the same as the transmitted pulse). Given that the radar pulse travels at the speed of light, the measured time for the round trip of a particular pulse can be used to calculate the distance to the target.

Radar can be used to examine the composition, size, shape, and surface roughness of the target. The antenna measures the ratio of horizontally polarized radio waves sent to the surface to the horizontally polarized waves reflected back, and the same for vertically polarized waves. The difference between these ratios helps to measure the roughness of the surface. The composition of the target helps determine the amount of energy that is returned to the antenna: Ice is "low loss" to radar, in other words, the radio waves pass straight through it the way light passes through window glass. Water, on the other hand, is reflective. Therefore, by measuring the intensity of the returned signal and its polarization, information about the composition and roughness of the surface can be obtained. Radar can even penetrate surfaces and give information about material deeper in the target: By using wavelengths of 3, 12.6, and 70 centimeters, scientists can examine the Moon's surface to a depth of 32 feet (10 m), at a resolution of 330 to 985 feet (100 to 300 m), from the Earth-based U.S. National Astronomy and Ionosphere Center's Arecibo Observatory!

Venus is imaged almost exclusively in radar because of its dense, complete, permanent cloud cover. Radar images of Venus have been taken by several spacecraft

(continues)

(continued)

The far greater resolution obtained by the Magellan *craft (right) shows the relative disadvantage of taking images of Venus from the Earth (left) using the Arecibo Observatory. (NASA/Magellan/JPL)*

and can also be taken from Arecibo Observatory on Earth. The image above makes a comparison between the resolution possible from Earth using Arecibo (left), and the resolution from the *Magellan* spacecraft (right). Arecibo's image is 560 miles (900 km) across and has a resolution of 1.9 miles (3 km). The *Magellan* image corresponds to the small white rectangle in the Arecibo image, 12 × 94 miles (20 × 120 km) in area. *Magellan*'s resolution is a mere 400 feet (120 m) per pixel.

(continued from page 79)

to do with the Sun's magnetic field, since where the magnetic field is strongest, the corona is hottest. The bright loops of active regions can be as hot as 7,200,000°F (4,000,000°C), while huge, slow arches of quiet regions with weak fields are often only about 1,800,000°F (1,000,000°C). The temperature of the Sun with distance from its center is shown in the figure on page 88. The magnetic field can transfer energy without transferring material, which may allow heat to be moved to the very diffuse corona without requiring dense material transfer. The exact mechanism for changing magnetic field energy back into heat is unknown, though there are several complex hypotheses.

The extreme length of the points of the corona means that it can sometimes extend past the orbit of the Earth, and at that distance from the Sun, coronal electrons still have temperatures on the order of 250,000°F (140,000°C). Why do these burning hot particles not incinerate the outer atmosphere of the Earth and also any satellites and spacecraft? The corona has such a low density at this distance from the Sun that although each particle has a very high kinetic energy (corresponding to a high temperature), as a material, it is too sparse to heat anything.

SOLAR WIND

The Sun emits a vast cloud of particles that stream past and through all the planets and out of the solar system. This continuous emission is called the solar wind, or as it is sometimes called, corpuscular radiation. The solar wind varies both in the density of particles that issue from different regions of the surface of the Sun, and it varies in time. On average, the solar wind consists of 5 million electrons and 5 million protons per cubic meter. There are two components of the solar wind: a fast, hot, and uniform wind, moving at about 460 miles per second (750 km/s), and a slower, highly variable wind, moving at about 250 miles per second (400 km/s). The slow wind is formed by coronal loops and streamers, while the magnetic network radiating through coronal holes is thought to create

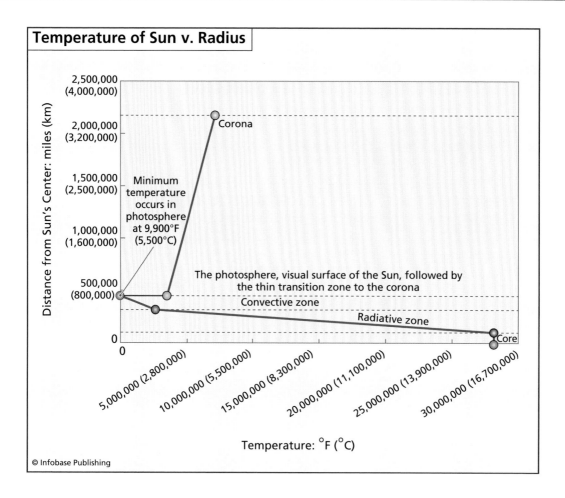

Temperature of Sun v. Radius

Distance from Sun's Center: miles (km)

2,500,000
(4,000,000)

2,000,000
(3,200,000)
Corona

1,500,000
(2,500,000)
Minimum
temperature
occurs in
photosphere
1,000,000
(1,600,000)
at 9,900°F
(5,500°C)

500,000
(800,000)
The photosphere, visual surface of the Sun, followed by
the thin transition zone to the corona
Convective zone
Radiative zone
Core

0
0

5,000,000 (2,800,000)
10,000,000 (5,500,000)
15,000,000 (8,300,000)
20,000,000 (11,100,000)
25,000,000 (13,900,000)
30,000,000 (16,700,000)

Temperature: °F (°C)

© Infobase Publishing

This graph of temperature in the Sun versus radius shows the peaks of temperature in the corona.

the fast wind. Coronal loops are lines of streaming plasma trapped within tubes of magnetic flux. Close images of coronal loops are shown in the infrared image from the *SOHO* orbiter on page 89.

In addition to the solar wind, the Sun projects its magnetic field into space, and this effects the solar wind. The solar wind is divided roughly along the ecliptic by a wave interface where the Sun's magnetic field changes from north to south. This interface is called the current sheet because it carries electric currents that are created by the opposing magnetic fields. The current sheet acts as a barrier to cosmic rays, since when they strike the sheet they flow along it rather than through it. Because the shape of the sheet is irregular and changes with time, the Earth passes through it, moving from above it to below it and back, at irregular times during its orbit. When the Earth is on the south magnetic side of the sheet, the Sun's magnetic field tends to cancel the effects of the Earth's magnetic field, making us more susceptible to geomagnetic storms from solar emissions.

While hydrogen is ejected from the Sun preferentially over other larger, heavier atoms and particles, the solar wind also contains helium and neon. The composition of the solar wind is impossible to measure from Earth because the charged particles of the solar wind interact with the Earth's magnetic field and do not reach the Earth's surface. The Moon, however, has no atmosphere and a negligible magnetic field, and so its surface is bombarded with the solar wind continuously. All the materials on the surface of the Moon have elements of the solar wind embedded into their surfaces. The mineral ilmenite (titanium iron oxide), for example, does not naturally contain hydrogen, helium, or neon, so samples of ilmenite returned to Earth by the Apollo or Luna missions can be analyzed to determine the composition of the solar wind: The solar wind constituents are literally embedded in the crystal.

The extreme ultraviolet image enables us to see tight, looplike magnetic fields that extend above the Sun's surface: These magnetic fields carry spinning charged particles near 1 million degrees Kelvin. (SOHO, NASA/ESA)

The solar wind components are extracted from the crystal by gradually heating the crystal under a vacuum. As the heat adds energy to the solar wind gases, they escape the crystal into the surrounding vacuum because they are not bound into the framework of the crystal with atomic bonds. The gases released are then fed into a mass spectrometer, an instrument that separates the elements and even isotopes according to their weights using a series of large magnets. The different elements or isotopes are accelerated through a series of tubes

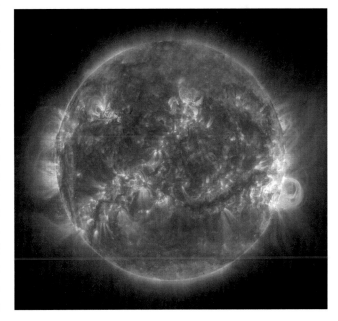

by the magnets, and strike detectors that count them one by one. In this way the exact abundances of the constituents of the solar wind can be measured. In fact, using these techniques, any change in composition of the solar wind over time can also be measured.

While the hydrogen to helium ratio on the surface of the Sun can be measured using spectroscopy and is found to be about 10 to one, the hydrogen to helium ratio found on the lunar surface is 20 to one. This confirms the idea that hydrogen is ejected preferentially from the Sun. Any change in the isotopic composition of the solar wind over time can also be measured; members of the Ulysses mission team have determined that the neon and helium isotopic compositions have remained constant over the lifetime of the Sun.

The solar wind radiates between and among the planets, expanding and becoming cooler as it travels. The solar wind fills all the space in the solar system except those volumes that are protected by planetary magnetic fields. Though solar wind flows outward constantly from the Sun, it does have an outside edge, where it meets the interstellar wind. This edge is known as the heliopause.

HELIOPAUSE

Even outside the solar system, space is not truly empty but is filled with waves of electromagnetic radiation and with the interstellar wind. Scientists have theorized for years that the solar wind will reach a point, far past Pluto, where it is so cool and weak that it can no longer expand against the pressure of the interstellar wind. The surface that bounds the solar wind is called the heliopause.

The heliopause was thought to be located at 110–160 AU from the Sun, based on models that used guesses for the pressure of the interstellar wind (that pressure is unknown). Now it has been found that the shock where the solar wind strikes the interstellar wind creates a hiss in radio frequencies.

The intrepid *Voyager 1,* as it moved farther and farther from Earth, heard this hiss. Based on the radio sounds, it is now estimated that the heliopause is 90 to 120 AU from the

Sun. After traveling through space for more than 26 years, *Voyager 1* reached 90 AU from the Sun on November 5, 2003. (An AU, or astronomical unit, is the average distance from the Sun to the Earth, or approximately 93 million miles, or 150 million km.) *Voyager 1* is the only spacecraft to have made measurements in the solar wind at such a great distance, and it is the most distant man-made object in the universe. *Voyager 2* is close behind, also on its way out of the solar system.

Voyager 1 is moving away from the Sun at about 3.6 AU per year, 35 degrees out of the ecliptic plane (the plane of Earth's orbit) to the north, in the general direction of the solar apex (the direction of the Sun's motion relative to nearby stars). *Voyager 2* is also escaping the solar system, at a speed of about 3.3 AU per year, 48 degrees out of the ecliptic plane to the south. Each spacecraft is expected to be able to communicate with Earth until about 2020. On NASA's excellent Voyager mission Web site (URL: http://voyager.jpl.nasa.gov/), weekly reports on each spacecraft are posted. On the first week of 2004, each spacecraft had about 66 pounds (30 kg) of propellant left, *Voyager 1* was 90.1 AU from the Sun, and *Voyager 2* was 71.8 AU from the Sun. A year later, *Voyager 1* had attained a distance of 94.3 AU, and *Voyager 2* 75.4. By the beginning of 2009, *Voyager 1* was at 108.8 AU from the Sun, and *Voyager 2* was at 88.1 AU. *Voyager 2* is not scheduled to reach 90 AU from the Sun until December 2009.

Communications with the spacecraft are accomplished using the worldwide Deep Space Network, an international coalition of giant radar dishes. The spacecraft are now so far away that the dishes 110 feet (34 m) in diameter cannot reach them, and only the three largest, 230-foot (70-m) dishes can make the transmissions. These huge dishes are located 120 degrees apart around the world, in Canberra, Australia; near Madrid, Spain; and near Barstow, California, to make continuous radio communication possible as the Earth rotates. Transmissions take about 10 hours to reach the spacecraft, even though the transmissions are traveling at the speed of light, and success requires that the dish be pointed exactly at the spacecraft, billions of kilometers away in space. The success of the Voyager missions is truly one of mankind's most astonishing and exciting accomplishments.

The *Voyagers* have reached (and, in the case of *Voyager 1,* possibly passed) the termination shock, which is the point inside the solar system where the solar wind is radically slowed by the external pressure of the heliopause (see figure below). At the termination shock, the solar wind slows from supersonic to subsonic speeds (from about 276 to 70 miles per second [440 km/s to 110 km/s]), the direction of the solar wind changes and may become chaotic, and the magnetic field also changes directions.

The spacecraft are expected to encounter powerful, short wavelength magnetic field disruptions, of increasing ampli-

Different parts of the interaction between the Sun's magnetic field and the interstellar wind are shown schematically: the solar wind termination shock, heliopause, and the bow shock.

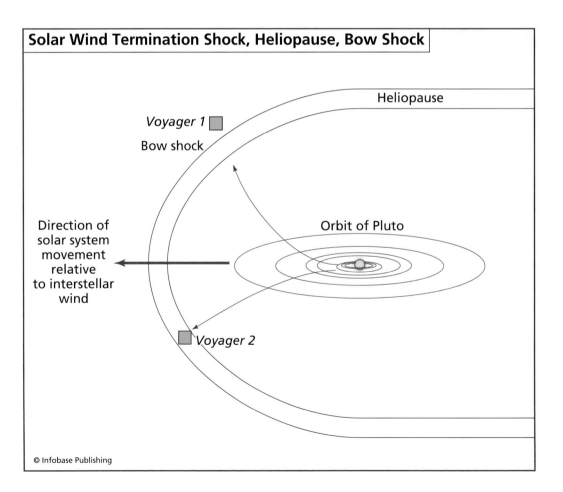

Solar Wind Termination Shock, Heliopause, Bow Shock

Heliopause

Voyager 1

Bow shock

Direction of solar system movement relative to interstellar wind

Orbit of Pluto

Voyager 2

© Infobase Publishing

tude toward the termination shock. Ions should be accelerated violently in this compressed, oscillating magnetic field. *Voyager 1* has already reported these conditions; it passed into the termination shock at 94 AU in December 2004. Scientists argued about that passage for several years. The first indications that the solar wind was slow and chaotic came in 2002, and some researchers reported that the craft had encountered the termination shock. When the solar wind around *Voyager 1* returned to supersonic speeds and smoothness others hypothesized that the momentary storminess have been some sort of pre-termination shock, or a local termination storm. As data continued to come in from the spacecraft the true termination revealed itself at 94 AU.

Now *Voyager 2* has also passed into the termination shock, on August 30, 2007, at only 83 AU, about a billion miles closer to the Sun than *Voyager 1* encountered the edge of the solar system. This confirms that the heliopause is not a sphere, but that it is squashed closer to the Sun by interstellar magnetic fields and the relative movement of the solar system.

Between the exits of *Voyagers 1* and *2* and the close inspection of the SOHO mission and other solar orbiters, mankind now has instruments inspecting the Sun over its entire range of influence. Because scientists are now watching solar activity continuously, coronal mass ejections and other events that affect the Earth are seen long before they strike the Earth's *magnetosphere*. Local news stations are even connecting to this information source and adding space weather to their forecasts; some stations in Massachusetts and elsewhere now warn about impending electrical disturbances and possible lively auroral displays. The careful analysis of the increasing quantities of high-quality solar data is rapidly driving knowledge about the Sun forward.

6

The Sun's Effects on the Planets

HEAT AND LIGHT

Energy from the Sun allows plants to grow and hence is the source of the energy for all life on Earth. On the Earth and on other planets with atmospheres, solar heat creates clouds and wind and is therefore the major source of energy for all weather, except on planets with very high levels of heat flow from their interiors (Jupiter, Saturn, and Neptune, though not Uranus). For the last several hundred years, people have known that the energetic output of the Sun varies. This variance can be seen in sunspot and aurora change, as well as the amount of solar wind that makes it past the Earth's magnetic field to reach the Earth's surface. This can be measured in both beryllium-10 in ice layers in polar ice cores, and in carbon-14 in the rings of long-lived trees. These markers have been correlated recently with Earth's climate by Kevin Pang, from the Jet Propulsion Laboratory, and Kevin Yau, from the University of Durham, England.

These researchers documented that over the past 1,800 years there have been nine cycles of solar energy output. Some of the periods of lowest solar output have names, such as the Oort, Wolf, Sporer, Maunder, and Dalton Minima. The

Maunder Minimum is perhaps the most famous because of its strong effects on civilization in Europe during recorded time. This minimum occurred between 1645 and 1715, and even dedicated scientists with observatories were hard pressed to see more than one or two sunspots per decade. At the same time, the Earth experienced what is called the Little Ice Age, from about 1600 to 1800 (scientists disagree about the proper beginning of the Little Ice Age, some putting the start as early as 1400). Throughout the world, glaciers in mountainous areas advanced. In many parts of the world, average temperatures fell and harsh weather was more common. The Little Ice Age was a time of repeated famine and cultural dislocation, as many people fled regions that had become hostile even to subsistence agriculture.

In addition to short-term fluctuations, the Sun changes luminosity over time as it ages. The Sun is already 30 percent more luminous than it was 4.6 billion years ago. This poses an interesting problem: If the Sun were much less luminous than it is now, the Earth would be expected to freeze over and become a dry and lifeless place, much like Mars. In fact, that is thought to be in part why Mars is freeze-dried: not enough heat from the Sun (see the table on page 96). In the very young solar system, the Sun certainly gave too little heat to sustain liquid water and life on Earth. The atmosphere at that time may have been significantly different: If it had 1,000 times more carbon dioxide (CO_2) in the past than it has now, life would have been preserved by the increased retention of solar heat that the carbon dioxide allows. Perhaps as life took off and created more oxygen in the atmosphere, the decrease in carbon dioxide was offset by the natural increase in solar luminosity, and in this delicate way life was preserved.

In part because of the great variety of orbital radii in the solar system, the Sun has different effects on the different planets. Sunlight takes 40 times longer to reach Pluto than it does to reach the Earth, and by the time solar radiation reaches Pluto, it is much weaker than it was at the Earth's orbit, for two reasons: A shell of radiation becomes less dense as it expands in three dimensions, and at the same time, wavelengths lengthen due to energy loss. A planet's ability to use

SUNLIGHT TRAVEL TIMES

Planet	Average distance from the Sun (miles [km])	Average distance from the Sun (AU)	Average time it takes light to travel from the Sun to this planet
Mercury	37,230,000 (59,910,000)	0.4	3 minutes, 20 seconds
Venus	67,240,000 (108,210,000)	0.72	6 minutes, 1 second
Earth	92,960,000 (149,600,000)	1	8 minutes, 19 seconds
Mars	141,640,000 (227,940,000)	1.52	12 minutes, 40 seconds
Jupiter	483,650,000 (778,340,000)	5.2	43 minutes, 16 seconds
Saturn	886,727,000 (1,427,010,000)	9.54	1 hours, 19 minutes, 20 seconds
Uranus	1,783,136,000 (2,869,600,000)	19.18	2 hours, 39 minutes, 31 seconds
Neptune	2,794,200,000 (4,496,700,000)	30.06	4 hours, 9 minutes, 59 seconds
Pluto	3,666,200,000 (5,900,000,000)	39.44	5 hours, 27 minutes, 59 seconds

solar radiation for warmth is also a function of the strength of its magnetic field and its atmosphere. A dense atmosphere of carbon dioxide like that of Venus will retain much of the heat from the Sun, keeping the planet warm, while a weak atmosphere like that of Mars allows most of the solar heat to escape.

SOLAR WIND

The ubiquitous solar wind has both positive and negative effects on the Earth and other planets. The solar wind causes auroras, gorgeous to watch on Earth and also remotely on other planets. The solar wind and other solar ejections also cause magnetic disturbances in the Earth's field, sometimes

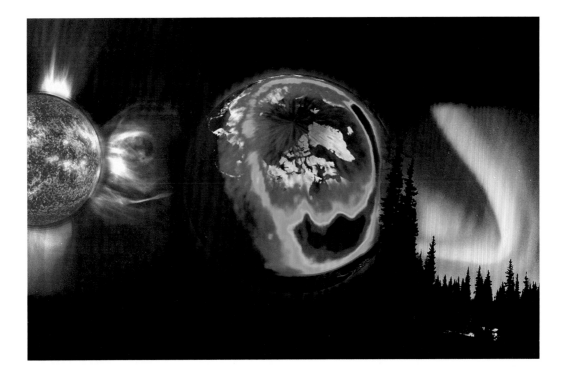

strong enough to actually damage electrical grids on Earth badly enough that they fail and cause blackouts and also strong enough to interrupt satellite transmissions.

The Sun's magnetic field can either enhance the Earth's, or weaken it, depending on whether the Earth is in the north or south half of the Sun's dipole field. If the Earth's magnetic field is weakened, then more high-energy radiation can enter the atmosphere and cause damage to living tissue on an atomic level.

This composite image shows the relationship between solar flares (left), charged particles from the wind released by flares interacting with the Earth's magnetic field (center), and the resulting display of aurora borealis in the northern night sky (right). (SOHO/LASCO/EIT/POLAR/VIS)

CONNECTION BETWEEN VISION AND LIGHT FROM THE SUN

The most intense radiation from the Sun is in the visible range, and that is one of the ranges of wavelengths that travels largely unimpeded through the atmosphere to the surface of the Earth, as shown in the figure on page 80 in the sidebar "Remote Sensing" in chapter 5. The development of vision based on this portion of the light spectrum is entirely a result of life developing on Earth and learning to use the wavelengths of radiation that enter the atmosphere most easily and interact with Earth-temperature objects most effectively.

DEATH OF THE SUN

Stars the size of the Sun are expected to shine constantly for 10 to 20 billion years. The Sun has been shining for almost 5 billion years, so at some point between about 5 and 15 billion years from now (some say as soon as 2 billion years), the Sun will run low of hydrogen to burn. At this point it will expand to many times its present size, becoming a red giant, a huge smoldering dark star with a much cooler surface temperature. When it becomes a red giant, theorists say that its burning, expanding surface will travel through the solar system at thousands of kilometers per second, incinerating the entire inner solar system at least. After this flare, the Sun will continue to burn until all its hydrogen fuel is gone, and then the red giant will collapse and cool into a small, cool, dense star known as a white dwarf. The death of the Sun, then, means the death of the solar system as it is now, though billions of years lie between now and that time.

Stars larger than the Sun explode into supernovae rather than expand into red giants. A supernova is such a strong explosion that when one happens in this galaxy, it will burn for a few weeks, with more than the combined brightness of all the other stars in the galaxy. There is one supernova in the Milky Way galaxy about every 100 years. Stars smaller than the Sun burn more slowly and have longer lifetimes. Because the universe is only about 10 billion years old, this means that all the smaller stars that have ever existed are still burning today.

One of the most lovely things to think about in the whole science of astronomy and planetary science is the origin of the elements. Hydrogen and helium were created in the big bang, the initial formation of the universe. By nuclear fusion in the cores of stars, hydrogen and helium can be converted into heavier elements in the largest, hottest stars. Nuclear fusion in the normal burning lifetimes of even the hottest, largest stars can only create elements up through iron (^{56}Fe) and as far as nickel (^{62}Ni), though, and no heavier (see the sidebar "Elements and Isotopes" on page 10). In the final years of a red giant's life, a special process that involves emitting gamma rays can produce elements up to atomic number 209. Every naturally occurring element beyond atomic number 209 was created in supernova explosions, including bismuth, radon, thorium, and uranium. This solar system is thought to have originated from a dust and gas cloud, and it must have had the remnants of one or more supernova explosions in it, since the solar system contains elements up to atomic weight 254 or so. Most of the elements in the periodic table are present in our bodies in trace amounts. This means that our bodies, and the other things in the solar system, are made of a mixture of material from the primordial universe, the cores of stars, and the products of immensely huge stellar explosions. We are literally made of stardust from before and beyond our solar system.

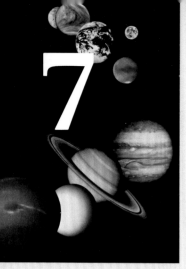

Missions
to the Sun

The most basic structures of the surface of the Sun, including sunspots and prominences, have been known since the 1700s. Only visible and radio wavelengths emitted by the Sun efficiently enter the Earth's atmosphere, and so all early observation was made in visible light. Once radio telescopes were developed, the Sun could be observed from the ground in radio frequencies, even on cloudy days. To see the Sun in detail images need to be made in the short ultraviolet and X-ray wavelengths, and to use them, scientists had to wait for the space age, when observing satellites and spacecraft could be sent above the atmosphere.

In the 1940s and 1950s, some rocket-based observations were made from the upper atmosphere. True space observations began in 1957 when the Soviets launched *Sputnik 1,* the first artificial Earth satellite. The herald of the space race between the United States and the Soviet Union, *Sputnik 1* was simply a metal sphere about the size of a basketball sent into Earth orbit. *Sputnik 1*'s instruments measured the density of the upper atmosphere and solar wind flux and radioed the results back to Earth. The mission lasted only three weeks. Other early spacecraft, such as *Luna 2* in 1960 and *Mariner 2* in 1962 also measured solar wind. More recent missions have measured solar

MISSIONS TO THE SUN

Launch date	Mission	Country	Comments
March 11, 1959	*Pioneer 5*	United States	Successful orbiter
December 16, 1965	*Pioneer 6*	United States	Probe is still transmitting from solar orbit
August 17, 1966	*Pioneer 7*	United States	Probe transmitted until recently
December 13, 1967	*Pioneer 8*	United States	Probe is still transmitting from solar orbit
November 8, 1968	*Pioneer 9*	United States	Probe transmitted until March 3, 1987
May 26, 1973	*Skylab*	United States	First U.S. manned space station
June 10, 1973	*Explorer 49*	United States	Solar physics probe placed in lunar orbit
December 10, 1974	*Helios A*	United States and Germany	Probe in solar orbit
January 16, 1976	*Helios B*	United States and Germany	Probe in solar orbit
February 14, 1980	*Solar Maximum Mission*	United States	The mission failed in orbit, but was fixed by a shuttle mission team in 1984; probe returned data until 1989
October 6, 1990	*Ulysses*	United States and European Space Agency	Probe to study solar poles
August 31, 1991	*Yokoh*	Japan, United States, England	Probe to study solar flares
December 12, 1995	*Solar and Heliospheric Observatory (SOHO)*	United States and European Space Agency	Solar orbiter; still operating in 2010

(continues)

MISSIONS TO THE SUN *(continued)*			
Launch date	**Mission**	**Country**	**Comments**
August 25, 1997	Advanced Composition Explorer (ACE)	United States	Orbiting at the L1 point in the Earth-Sun system; still operating in 2010
April 2, 1998	Transition Region and Coronal Explorer (TRACE)	United States	Still operating in 2010
December 20, 1999	ACRIMsat	United States	Measures total solar energy output; still operating in 2010
August 8, 2001	Genesis	United States	Solar wind sample return mission
February 5, 2002	Reuven Ramaty High Energy Solar Spectro-scopic Imager (RHESSI)	United States and Switzerland	Still operating in 2010
September 18, 2006	STEREO	United States	This pair of spacecraft orbit the Sun, one leading and one trailing the Earth; still operating in 2010
September 22, 2006	Hinode	Japan leads, with NASA, the European Space Agency, and Britain's Particle Physics Astronomy Research Council	Still active in 2010
October 19, 2008	Interstellar Boundary Explorer (IBEX)	United States	Earth orbiter, still operating in 2010

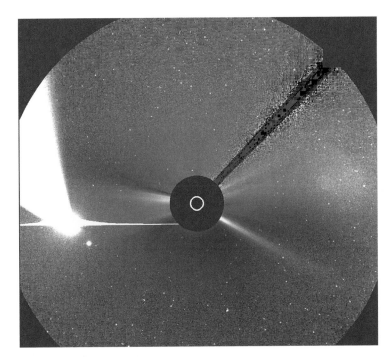

In 2006 the SOHO mission captured this image of comet McNaught, the brightest comet observed in over 40 years. McNaught was so bright it could be seen from Earth during the day with the naked eye. The disk in the center of the image is a shade to block out the light of the Sun. (SOHO)

wind on their way to other goals and objects. All the recent missions have gorgeous Web sites containing images, data on ongoing missions, and press releases of the most important scientific results. Solar missions are summarized in this table, and some are discussed in more detail below.

Orbiting Solar Observatories 1 through 8
1962–1975
American

These early orbiting satellites were designed to look at the Sun through an entire sunspot cycle. The first of the eight *OSO* satellites was launched March 7, 1962. *OSO 1* orbited Earth at about 575 km altitude. Its primary mission objectives were to measure the solar electromagnetic radiation in the ultraviolet, X-ray, and gamma-ray regions and to investigate dust particles in space. Data transmission ended on August 6, 1963, and the satellite reentered the Earth's atmosphere and burned on October 8, 1981. The final satellite, *OSO 8,* was launched June 21, 1975, and ended its mission on October 1, 1978.

Skylab 1973–1979
American

Skylab was launched May 14, 1973, and had three crews of astronauts who kept it in use continuously until February 1974. *Skylab* was the premier solar observatory of its time and used its X-ray and ultraviolet light telescopes to take the first good images of the Sun's corona, showing that coronal loops happen constantly. *Skylab* was going to remain in space for another 10 years, perhaps being visited by astronauts from the space shuttle. Unfortunately, on July 11, 1979, *Skylab*'s orbit was disturbed by extreme solar activity and it reentered Earth's atmosphere and disintegrated into pieces across western Australia and the southeastern Indian Ocean.

Helios A and Helios B 1974–1976
German and American

Helios A launched December 10, 1974, and *Helios B* launched January 15, 1976, both joint missions of the Federal Republic of Germany and NASA. The instruments were launched from American Titan rockets at Cape Canaveral and went into orbit around the Sun about one-third the distance from the Sun to the Earth. *Helios A* and *B* survived the high temperatures and sent back data for over 10 years. They both measured the content of the solar wind, the strength and direction of the Sun's magnetic and electric fields, and high-energy gamma and X-rays emitted from the Sun. Though the instruments can no longer transit data, they remain in their orbits around the Sun. (Oddly, they are also called *Helios 1* and *Helios 2*, names similar to the top-secret French satellites *Helios 1A* and *1B* of the late 1990s, advanced surveillance imaging satellites that are widely believed to have one meter resolution capability.)

Voyager 1 and 2 1977
American

Voyager 2 actually launched August 20, 1977, several days before *Voyager 1*, which launched September 5, 1977. They were both launched from Cape Canaveral, Florida, aboard Titan-Centaur rockets. Although these spacecraft were designed to visit planets, which they did between 1977 and 1989, they have continued to transmit data back to Earth as they travel out of the solar system. In 2003 or early 2004, the *Voyager* spacecraft would be the first spacecraft to leave the region of space dominated by the Sun, when they passed through the termination shock and entered the region where the heliosphere merges into the interstellar medium. In 2007 scientists detected the *bow shock,* where the supersonic solar wind strikes the interstellar gas. For more on these missions, see the section on the heliopause in chapter 5.

Solar Maximum Mission 1980
American

Launched February 14, 1980, by NASA, this satellite examined ultraviolet, X-ray, and gamma ray emissions from solar flares. The launch was set to coincide with a period of high solar activity. In 1984 the instrument was rescued and repaired by the space shuttle *Challenger,* and as a result the Solar Maximum Mission (SMM) was able to continue taking data. This mission was the first to demonstrate that the Sun is actually brighter during periods of high sunspot activity. Though the spots themselves are dark, the regions around the spots are far brighter and make up more than the deficit of the spots themselves. SMM observations showed that energetic X-rays are emitted from the bases of solar flare magnetic loops and that large coronal loops with temperatures up to 10 million degrees Fahrenheit are probably always present in the corona. The mission relayed its last data in 1989.

Ulysses 1990
European and American

A joint project between NASA and the European Space Agency, the *Ulysses* spacecraft was launched October 6, 1990, and is now orbiting the Sun to study its north and south poles. The spacecraft went over the solar south pole for the first time in 1994 and the north pole for the first time in 1995. *Ulysses* had an unexpected encounter with the tail of comet Hyakutake, indicating that the comet's tail might be much longer than previously estimated. Its main mission is to measure and map the heliosphere in three dimensions. *Ulysses* made a second polar orbit around the Sun in 2001. In 2004 *Ulysses* was at the *aphelion* of its huge orbit, near Jupiter.

Yohkoh 1991
Japanese

Yohkoh, meaning "sunbeam" in Japanese, was a mission from the Institute of Space and Astronautical Science launched August 30, 1991. *Yohkoh* had the ability to image the entire Sun at once, with the highest-resolution X-ray instrument available at the time. In 1997 the solar minimum was reached, and the mission continued to gather X-ray data through the rise to the solar maximum in 2000. At times the missions Yohkoh, SOHO, and TRACE (see below) were all able to take images of the same solar structures at the same time, thus gathering invaluable data in several wavelengths simultaneously. The Yohkoh mission ended in December 2001 after 10 years of excellent data gathering. The Yohkoh team has produced an excellent Web site for public outreach, filled with accessible information, at http://solar.physics.montana.edu/YPOP/.

Solar and Heliospheric Observatory (SOHO) 1995
European and American

The *SOHO* satellite is a joint European-American effort, launched December 2, 1995, which orbits 930,000 miles (1.5 million km) from the Earth. Among its many instruments is one called the Large Angle and Spectroscopic Coronagraph (LASCO), which, by blocking the Sun with an opaque disk, can take images of the corona in visible light. *SOHO* has successfully taken images of coronal mass ejections, dangerous and little understood phenomena. *SOHO*'s primary scientific goals are to measure the structure and dynamics of the Sun's interior, to gain an understanding of the heating mechanisms of the corona, and to study the source and acceleration of the solar wind. *SOHO* has viewed amazing and unique events, including, on June 2, 1998, two Sun-grazing comets following

The SOHO spacecraft being prepared for launch (SOHO, NASA/ESA)

similar orbits entering the tenuous outer atmosphere of the Sun and failing to reappear on the other side of the Sun, having been melted and engulfed. Visit its excellent Web site at http://sohowww.nascom.nasa.gov/.

Transition Region and Coronal Explorer (TRACE) 1998
American

Stanford-Lockheed Institute for Space Research launched this satellite, called *TRACE,* into a polar orbit around the Earth on

The SOHO craft being launched by the Atlas II-AS launch vehicle at the Cape Canaveral Air Force Station, December 2, 1995 (SOHO, NASA/ESA)

April 1, 1998. The mission's objectives are to follow the evolution of magnetic field structures from the solar interior to the corona, to investigate the mechanisms of the heating of the outer solar atmosphere, and to investigate the triggers and onset of solar flares and mass ejections. Its ultrahigh resolution ultraviolet telescope has revealed many new aspects of thin coronal loops. As of 2010, *TRACE* is still successfully orbiting, and movies of solar dynamics can be seen on its Web site: http://trace.lmsal.com/.

Genesis 2001
American

The *Genesis* spacecraft was launched August 8, 2001, and placed into orbit around the Lagrangian point L1, a point between Earth and the Sun where the gravity of both bodies is balanced, to collect particles of the solar wind. In September 2004 the return capsule crashed in the desert and broke open the sample container in the dust and a shallow puddle. Despite this heartbreaking failure, excellent data has been extracted from the damaged capsule.

Reuven Ramaty High Energy Solar Spectroscopic Imager (RHESSI) 2002
American launch and management, with team participants from Switzerland, Scotland, Japan, and France

After several launch delays, this spacecraft, *RHESSI* for short, was launched February 5, 2002, and is taking images of the Sun in the short-wavelength X-ray and gamma ray spectra. Its results have already led to new understanding about the temperatures and processes in solar flares and coronal mass ejections. Recently *RHESSI, SOHO,* and *TRACE* together took data on an emerging coronal mass ejection and were able to show that as the mass ejection begins to rise off the Sun at 1 million to 5 million miles per hour (1.6 million to 8 million km/hr), the solar magnetic field acts like a lid, holding down the ejection that is trying to rise. Suddenly and in ways that are not understood, the magnetic lid opens, associated with a solar flare, and the mass ejection rises from the Sun. The magnetic field lines are dragged out with the ejection, and magnetic reconnection into a normal configuration continues to energize the associated solar flare for over 12 hours. *RHESSI* is considered the most successful solar mission to date, and it has been recommended for additional funding to lengthen its mission.

The burst of fascinating data on the Sun has slowed, not because the instruments have reached their lifetimes or stopped working (solar missions are continuing to function at high levels), but because the Sun is now in an extended period of quiescence, a solar minimum. There are fewer dramatic images of mass ejections and sunquakes from the *SOHO* mission, fewer solar flares for *RHESSI* to record.

Simultaneously, though, other space missions will be spared some of the intensity of the solar wind and radiation as solar activity dies down. The flush of data taken during this solar maximum will help predict the onset and progress of the next solar maximum, to the benefit of space missions and the activities of mankind on Earth.

PART THREE

MERCURY

Mercury:
Fast Facts about
a Planet in Orbit

Mercury is the innermost planet in the solar system. Though Mercury is much closer to the Earth than Jupiter and Saturn, less is known about it. Its tiny orbit keeps it close to the Sun, as seen from the Earth, and so viewing the planet from the Earth is especially difficult. The *Hubble Space Telescope,* along with many Earth-based telescopes, is forbidden to view Mercury because of the damage strong solar radiation would do to its optics. Only a few Earth-based optical telescopes attempt to look at Mercury: the Abastumany Astrophysical Observatory in the Republic of Georgia recently obtained images of Mercury that allowed science teams to identify features as small as 75 miles (120 km). This is still a coarse resolution, and much better images are required for good research and understanding of the planet.

Earth-based radar telescopes like Arecibo in Puerto Rico can make images of Mercury, and this has led to some important new discoveries about the planet. *Mariner 10* is the only spacecraft to have visited Mercury; it flew by the planet three times in 1974 and 1975, taking photos of the surface. Mercury's neglect by space missions is detailed in the table on page 114; it is by far the least explored of the inner planets. The United States has visited Venus far more times than it has Mercury, but the Soviet Union investigated Venus intensively compared to the United States (see chapter 16, on Venus missions).

Space scientists have high hopes for the MESSENGER mission, launched by NASA in August 2004, and the BepiColombo mission, planned for launch after 2011 by the European Space Agency and the Institute of Space and Astronautical Science in Japan. These missions should bring back critical information that will allow scientists to begin to solve some of Mercury's strange mysteries, including the source of Mercury's continuing magnetic field and why the planet contains far more metal than any other terrestrial planet. For basic statistics on Mercury, see the following sidebar "Fundamental Information about Mercury," on page 115.

Mercury is also of interest for another reason: In the last few years, scientists have been discovering increasing numbers of planets that are orbiting around stars in distant solar systems. The majority of these planets are very large, like Jupiter, but orbit very close to their stars. Sixteen percent of the *extrasolar* planets discovered (more than 100 so far) orbit closer than one AU to their stars. These extrasolar planets

U.S. SPACE MISSIONS TO THE INNER PLANETS

Launch date	Mission craft	Comments
July 22, 1962	*Mariner 1*	destroyed just after launch
August 27, 1962	*Mariner 2*	Venus flyby
June 14, 1967	*Mariner 5*	Venus flyby with descent vehicle
November 3, 1973	*Mariner 10*	Mercury flyby and Venus flyby and soft *lander*
May 20, 1978	*Pioneer Venus Orbiter*	Venus satellite and soft lander
August 8, 1978	*Pioneer Venus bus and probes*	Venus orbiter and four probes
May 4, 1989	*Magellan*	Venus orbiter
August 3, 2004	*MESSENGER*	Mercury orbiter

FUNDAMENTAL INFORMATION ABOUT MERCURY

Mercury stands out from the rest of the terrestrial planets in several ways. It is the smallest of the four (the others are Venus, Earth, and Mars; see the table below), but it has the largest core. Mercury's core takes up three-quarters of the planet's radius and contains twice the metal than do Earth's, Venus's, or Mars's cores. Mercury's huge core makes the bulk planet exceptionally dense and therefore also gives it a strong gravity field for its size. The cause of its large core is unknown, as is the cause of its magnetic field. These and other mysteries about Mercury may be partially solved from data sent back by two new missions to the planet, the first to visit since 1975.

FUNDAMENTAL FACTS ABOUT MERCURY	
equatorial radius	1,515 miles (2,440 km), or 0.38 of the Earth's radius
ellipticity ([equatorial radius–polar radius]/polar radius)	0, meaning the planet is almost a perfect sphere, within the accuracy of the current radius measurements
volume	1.30×10^{10} cubic miles (5.4×10^{10} km³), 0.05 times Earth's volume
mass	7.3×10^{23} pounds (3.3×10^{23} kg), or 0.055 times the Earth's mass
average density	341 pounds per cubic feet (5,430 kg/m³), the second densest after Earth, and if gravitational compression is not considered, Mercury is the densest planet
acceleration of gravity on the surface at the equator	12.1 feet per second squared (3.70 m/s²), 0.37 times the Earth's gravity
magnetic field strength at the surface	2×10^{-7}
rings	0
moons	0

all appear to have been giant icy planets formed far enough from their stars that ices could condense, and then thought to have migrated inward. Mercury, on the other hand, is a rocky planet that probably formed close to where it is now in the solar system. Despite these differences, Mercury may be an important analog to these strange extrasolar bodies. Mercury is the only planet in this solar system significantly closer to the Sun than one AU, and although it is not a giant planet, its conditions may help us understand the conditions under which these exotic extrasolar planets exist.

The astronomical symbol for Mercury has upstanding lines that resemble the wings on the helmet of the god Mercury, as shown in the illustration below. Each planet, the Sun, and a number of asteroids have their own symbols, which are often used in scientific figures and notes and other places where shorthand is helpful or space is at a premium.

Because of their spin, most planets are not perfect spheres. Spinning around an axis creates forces that cause the planet to swell at the equator and flatten slightly at the poles. Planets are thus usually shapes called oblate spheroids, meaning that they have different equatorial radii and polar radii. Mercury's radii, to the extent that they have been measured, are almost equal. Mercury is probably not truly spherical (Venus is the

Many solar system objects have simple symbols; this is the symbol for Mercury.

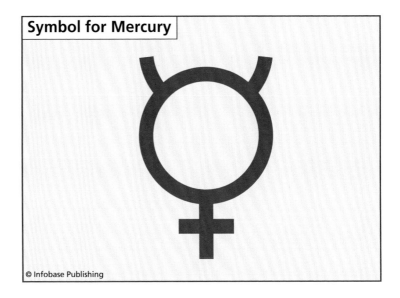

Symbol for Mercury

© Infobase Publishing

WHAT MAKES GRAVITY?

Gravity is among the least understood forces in nature. It is a fundamental attraction between all matter, but it is also a very weak force: The gravitational attraction of objects smaller than planets and moons is so weak that electrical or magnetic forces can easily oppose it. At the moment about the best that can be done with gravity is to describe its action: How much mass creates how much gravity? The question of what makes gravity itself is unanswered. This is part of the aim of a branch of mathematics and physics called string theory: to explain the relationships among the natural forces and to explain what they are in a fundamental way.

Sir Isaac Newton, the English physicist and mathematician who founded many of today's theories back in the mid-17th century, was the first to develop and record universal rules of gravitation. There is a legend that he was hit on the head by a falling apple while sitting under a tree thinking, and the fall of the apple under the force of Earth's gravity inspired him to think of matter attracting matter.

The most fundamental description of gravity is written in this way:

$$F = \frac{Gm_1 m_2}{r^2},$$

where F is the force of gravity, G is the universal gravitational constant (equal to 6.67 $\times$ 10^{-11} Nm^2/kg^2), m_1 and m_2 are the masses of the two objects that are attracting each other with gravity, and r is the distance between the two objects. (N is the abbreviation for newtons, a metric unit of force.)

Immediately, it is apparent that the larger the masses, the larger the force of gravity. In addition, the closer together they are, the stronger the force of gravity, and because r is squared in the denominator, gravity diminishes very quickly as the distance between the objects increases. By substituting numbers for the mass of the Earth (5.9742×10^{24} kg), the mass of the Sun (1.989×10^{30} kg), and the distance between them, the force of gravity between the Earth and Sun is shown to be 8×10^{21} pounds per foot (3.56×10^{22} N). This is the force that keeps the Earth in orbit around the Sun. By comparison, the force of gravity between a piano player and her piano when she sits playing is about 6×10^{-7} pounds per foot (2.67×10^{-6} N). The force of a pencil pressing down in the palm of a hand under the influence of Earth's gravity is about 20,000 times stronger than the gravitational attraction between the player and the piano! So, although the player and the piano are attracted to each other by gravity, their masses are so small that the force is completely unimportant.

planet closest to a sphere, probably because it rotates exceptionally slowly), and better measurements will clarify Mercury's shape.

Because most planets' equatorial radii are longer than their polar radii, the surface of the planet at its equator is farther from the planet's center than the surface of the planet at the poles. To a lesser extent, the distance from the surface to the center of the planet changes according to topography, such as mountains or valleys. Being at a different distance from the center of the planet means there is a different amount of mass between the surface and the center of the planet. Mass pulls with its gravity (for more information on gravity, see the sidebar "What Makes Gravity?" on page 117). Gravity is not a perfect constant on any planet: Variations in radius, topography, and the density of the material underneath make the gravity vary slightly over the surface. This is why planetary gravitational accelerations are generally given as an average value on the planet's equator. On Mercury, gravity changes according to the density of the material beneath the place being measured, and according to the topography. Small changes in gravity can be used to calculate models of the planet's interior.

The MESSENGER and BepiColombo missions will return new scientific data. The complexity of its magnetic fields, along with its topography, will be completely revealed in new detail.

Mercury's Orbital Physics and the Theory of Relativity

Mercury does not return to exactly the same point in space at the end of each orbit. Instead, on a given day of its year, Mercury is some small distance ahead in its orbit from its location of the year previous. Mercury's precession, as this orbital change is called, amounts to about 570 arc seconds per century (an orbit or circle can be divided into 360°; each degree contains 60 arc minutes, and each arc minute contains 60 arc seconds, so an arc second is 1/3600 of a degree, or 1/1,296,000 of a circle). Almost all of the precession is due to gravitational interactions with the other planets, but 43 arc seconds cannot be explained by this mechanism. Forty-three arc seconds per century is a tiny distance: It translates to less than 1/10 of an arc second per year. If Mercury's orbit was a circle with a radius of one meter (about three feet), then that 1/10 of an arc second change would be the equivalent of 1/100 the width of a human hair. Tiny though they may be, the extra 43 arc seconds contradict Kepler's laws of orbital motion and demand an explanation.

In 1845, Urbain-Jean-Joseph Le Verrier, then director of the Paris Observatory, was the first to notice the discrepancy between Mercury's orbit and what was predicted according to classical Newtonian and Keplerian mechanics. He suggested the existence of a smaller planet orbiting between the Sun and Mercury and perturbing Mercury's orbit with its small gravitational field. Le Verrier spent years searching for this body, which he named Vulcan, but with no success. Other hypotheses were proposed to explain the orbital anomaly: Was there an unseen moon orbiting Mercury and pulling it off a straight path? Was it sharing its orbit with a swarm of asteroids? Was there another planet orbiting inside Mercury? Months and years were spent searching for the fabled inner planet, mainly between 1826 and 1850.

Centuries after this anomaly was noticed, Einstein finally explained it. His theory of relativity predicts that huge masses, like the Sun, actually bend the space around them. Relativity perfectly predicts the tiny anomaly in Mercury's orbit, caused by the bending of space by its huge neighbor the Sun. Reportedly the discovery of this perfect prediction by his theory (and therefore part of his theory's validation) pleased Einstein immensely. Data on Mercury's orbit are given in the table on page 121.

Mercury's rotation is tied to the Sun by a phenomenon called *tidal locking*. Gravitational attraction between the planet and the Sun produces a tidal force on each of them, stretching each slightly along the axis oriented toward its partner. This causes them to become slightly egg-shaped; the extra stretch is called a tidal bulge (the bulge is significant on pairs such as the Earth and Moon, but the Sun's mass is so large compared to Mercury that the Sun does not bulge). If either of the two bodies is rotating relative to the other, this tidal bulge is not stable. The rotation of the body will cause the long axis to move out of alignment with the other object, and the gravitational force will work to reshape the rotating body. Because of the relative rotation between the bodies, the tidal bulges move around the rotating body to stay in alignment with the gravitational force between the bodies. This is why ocean tides on Earth rise and fall with the rising and setting of its Moon, and the same effect occurs to some extent on all rotating orbiting bodies.

The rotation of the tidal bulge out of alignment with the body that caused it results in a small but significant force acting to slow the relative rotation of the bodies. Since the bulge

MERCURY'S ORBIT	
rotation on its axis ("day")	58.65 Earth days (the Aricebo observatory used Doppler effects to measure rotation)
rotational speed at equator	6.8 miles per hour (10.9 km/hr)
rotational direction	prograde (counterclockwise when viewed from above the North Pole)
sidereal period ("year")	87.97 Earth days, or two-thirds of an orbit
orbital velocity (average)	29.9 miles per second (47.9 km/s)
sunlight travel time (average)	3 minutes, 20 seconds to reach Mercury
average distance from the Sun	35,984,076 miles (57,909,175 km), or 0.387 AU
perihelion	28.58 million miles (46.0 million km), or 0.31 AU
aphelion	43.38 million miles (69.82 million km), or 0.47 AU
orbital eccentricity	0.2056; this is the second-highest eccentricity in the solar system, after Pluto; the next most eccentric is Mars, at only 0.093
orbital inclination to the ecliptic	7.01°
obliquity (inclination of equator to orbit)	0° (though some say it is 180°)

requires a small amount of time to shift position, the tidal bulge of the moon is always located slightly away from the nearest point to its planet in the direction of the moon's rotation. This bulge is pulled on by the planet's gravity, resulting in a slight force pulling the surface of the moon in the opposite direction of its rotation. The rotation of the satellite slowly decreases (and its orbital momentum simultaneously increases). This is in the case where the moon's rotational period is faster than its *orbital period* (the time required to make a complete orbit) around its planet. If the opposite is true, tidal forces increase its rate of rotation and decrease its orbital momentum.

Almost all moons in the solar system are tidally locked with their primaries, since they orbit closely and tidal force strengthens rapidly with decreasing distance. Mercury is tidally locked with the Sun in a 3:2 *resonance* (when two orbital periods make an integer ratio). Mercury is the only solar system body in a 3:2 resonance with the Sun. For every two times Mercury revolves around the Sun, it rotates on its own axis three times. More subtly, the planet Venus is tidally locked with the planet Earth, so that whenever the two are at their closest approach to each other in their orbits Venus always has the same face toward Earth (the tidal forces involved in this lock are extremely small). In general, any object that orbits another massive object closely for long periods is likely to be tidally locked to it.

Just as planets are not truly spheres, the orbits of solar system objects are not circular. Johannes Kepler, the prominent 17th-century German mathematician and astronomer, first realized that the orbits of planets are ellipses after analyzing a series of precise observations of the location of Mars that had been taken by his colleague, the distinguished Danish astronomer Tycho Brahe. Kepler drew rays from the Sun's center to the orbit of Mars and noted the date and time that Mars arrived on each of these rays. He noted that Mars swept out equal areas between itself and the Sun in equal times and that Mars moved much faster when it was near the Sun than when it was farther from the Sun. Together these observa-

KEPLER'S LAWS

Kepler's first law:	A planet orbits the Sun following the path of an ellipse with the Sun at one focus.
Kepler's second law:	A line joining a planet to the Sun sweeps out equal areas in equal times (see figure below).
Kepler's third law:	The closer a planet is to the Sun, the greater its speed. This is stated as: The square of the period of a planet T is proportional to the cube of its semimajor axis R, or $T \propto R^{\frac{3}{2}}$ as long as T is in years and R in AU.

tions convinced Kepler that the orbit was shaped as an ellipse and not as a circle, as had been previously assumed. Kepler defined three laws of orbital motion (listed in the table on page 122), which he published in 1609 and 1619 in his books *New Astronomy* and *The Harmony of the World*. These three laws are still used as the basis for understanding orbits.

As Kepler observed, all orbits are ellipses, not circles. An ellipse can be thought of simply as a squashed circle, resembling an oval. The proper definition of an ellipse is the set of all points that have the same sum of distances to two given fixed points, called foci. To demonstrate this definition, take two pins, push them into a piece of stiff cardboard, and loop a string around the pins (see figure on page 124). The two pins are the foci of the ellipse. Pull the string away from the pins

Kepler's second law shows that the varying speed of a planet in its orbit requires that a line between the planet and the Sun sweep out equal areas in equal times.

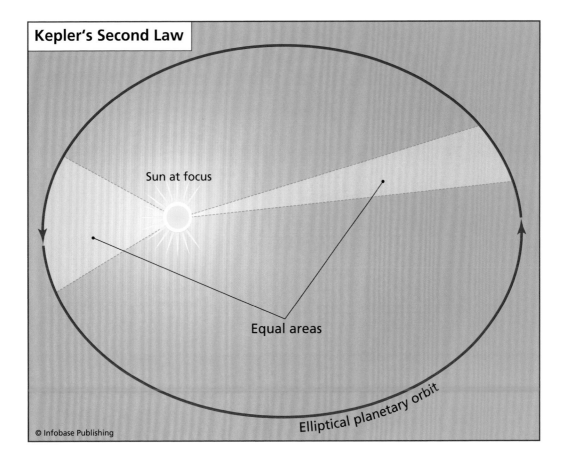

Kepler's Second Law

Sun at focus

Equal areas

Elliptical planetary orbit

© Infobase Publishing

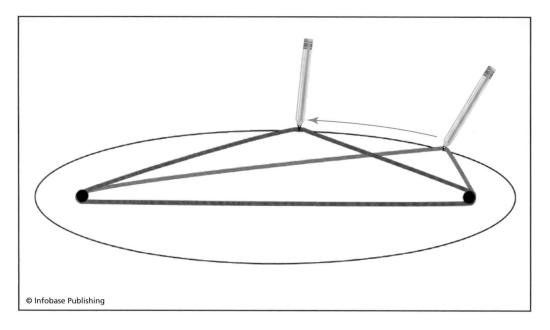

Making an ellipse with string and two pins: Adding the distance along the two string segments from the pencil to each of the pins will give the same sum at every point around the ellipse. This method creates an ellipse with the pins at its foci.

with a pencil and draw the ellipse, keeping the string taut around the pins and the pencil all the way around. Adding the distance along the two string segments from the pencil to each of the pins will give the same answer each time: The ellipse is the set of all points that have the same sum of distances from the two foci.

The mathematical equation for an ellipse is

$$\frac{x^2}{a^2} + \frac{y^2}{b^2} = 1,$$

where x and y are the coordinates of all the points on the ellipse, and a and b are the *semimajor* and *semiminor axes,* respectively. The semimajor axis and semiminor axis would both be the radius if the shape was a circle, but two radii are needed for an ellipse. If a and b are equal, then the equation for the ellipse becomes the equation for a circle:

$$x^2 + y^2 = n,$$

where n is any constant.

When drawing an ellipse with string and pins, it is obvious where the foci are (they are the pins). In the abstract, the foci can be calculated according to the following equations:

Coordinates of the first focus

$$= (+\sqrt{a^2 - b^2}, 0)$$

Coordinates of the second focus

$$= (-\sqrt{a^2 - b^2}, 0)$$

In the case of an orbit the object being orbited (for example, the Sun) is located at one of the foci.

An important characteristic of an ellipse—perhaps the most important for orbital physics—is its eccentricity: a measure of how different the semimajor and semiminor axes of the ellipse are. Eccentricity is dimensionless and ranges from 0 to 1, where an eccentricity of zero means that the figure is a circle, and an eccentricity of 1 means that the ellipse has gone to its other extreme, a parabola (the reason an extreme ellipse becomes a parabola results from its definition as a conic section). One equation for eccentricity is

$$e = \sqrt{1 - \frac{b^2}{a^2}},$$

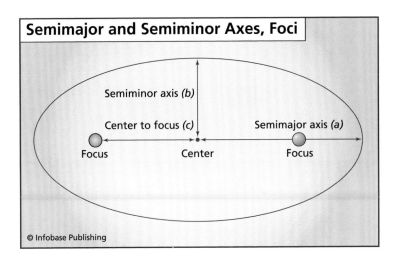

Semimajor and Semiminor Axes, Foci

Semiminor axis (b)

Center to focus (c)

Semimajor axis (a)

Focus   Center   Focus

© Infobase Publishing

The semimajor and semiminor axes of an ellipse (or an orbit) are the elements used to calculate its eccentricity, and the body being orbited always lies at one of the foci.

where *a* and *b* are the semimajor and semiminor axes, respectively (see figure on page 125). Another equation for eccentricity is

$$e = \frac{c}{a}$$

where *c* is the distance between the center of the ellipse and one focus. The eccentricities of the orbits of the planets vary widely, though most are very close to circles, as shown in the figure below. Pluto has the most eccentric orbit at 0.244, and Mercury's orbit is also very eccentric, but the rest have eccentricities below 0.09.

While the characteristics of an ellipse drawn on a sheet of paper can be measured, orbits in space are more difficult to characterize. The ellipse itself has to be described, and then the ellipse's position in space, and then the motion of the body as it travels around the ellipse. Six parameters are needed to specify the motion of a body in its orbit and the position of the orbit. These are called the orbital elements (see the figure below). The first three elements are used to determine where a body is in its orbit.

Though the orbits of planets are measurably eccentric, they deviate from circularity very little. This figure shows the eccentricity of Pluto's orbit in comparison with a circle.

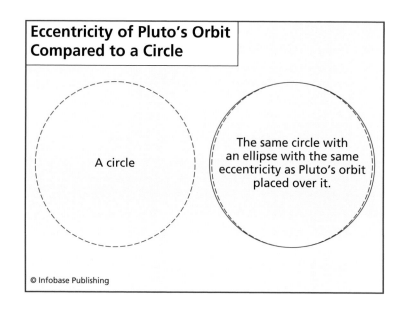

Eccentricity of Pluto's Orbit Compared to a Circle

A circle

The same circle with an ellipse with the same eccentricity as Pluto's orbit placed over it.

© Infobase Publishing

Orbital Elements

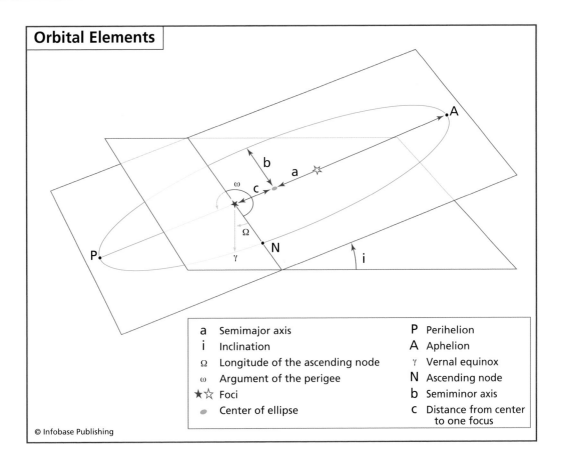

a	Semimajor axis		P	Perihelion
i	Inclination		A	Aphelion
Ω	Longitude of the ascending node		γ	Vernal equinox
ω	Argument of the perigee		N	Ascending node
★☆	Foci		b	Semiminor axis
●	Center of ellipse		c	Distance from center to one focus

© Infobase Publishing

a **semimajor axis** The semimajor axis is half the width of the widest part of the orbit ellipse. For solar system bodies, the value of the semimajor axis is typically expressed in units of AU. Mercury's semimajor axis is 0.387 AU.

e **eccentricity** Eccentricity measures the amount by which an ellipse differs from a circle, as described above. An orbit with *e* of 0 is circular, and an orbit with *e* of one stretches into infinity and becomes a parabola. In between, the orbits are ellipses. The orbits of all large planets are almost circles: The Earth, for instance, has an eccentricity of 0.0068, and Mercury's eccentricity is 0.2056.

M **mean anomaly** Mean anomaly is an angle that moves in time from 0° to 360° during one revolution,

A series of parameters called orbital elements are used to describe exactly the orbit of a body.

as if the planet were at the end of a hand of a clock and the Sun were at its center. This angle determines where in its orbit a planet is at a given time, and is defined to be 0° at *perigee* (when the planet is closest to the Sun) and 180° at *apogee* (when the planet is farthest from the Sun). The equation for mean motion M is given as

$$M = M_0 + 360\left(\frac{t}{T}\right),$$

where M_o is the value of M at time zero, T is the orbital period, and t is the time in question.

The next three Keplerian elements determine where the orbit is in space.

i   **inclination** For the case of a body orbiting the Sun, the inclination is the angle between the plane of the orbit of the body and the plane of the ecliptic (the plane in which the Earth's orbit lies). For the case of a body orbiting the Earth, the inclination is the angle between the plane of the body's orbit and the plane of the Earth's equator, such that an inclination of zero indicates that the body orbits directly over the equator, and an inclination of 90 indicates that the body orbits over the poles. If there is an orbital inclination greater than zero, then there is a line of intersection between the ecliptic plane and the orbital plane. This line is called the line of nodes (see figure on page 127). Mercury's orbital inclination is 7.01°. The inclinations of all the planets are listed in the table on page 129.

Ω **longitude of the ascending node** After inclination is specified, there are still an infinite number of orbital planes possible: The line of nodes could cut through the Sun at any longitude around the Sun. Notice that the line of nodes emerges from the Sun in two places. One is called the ascending node (where the orbiting planet crosses the Sun's equator from south to north). The other is called the descending node (where the orbiting planet crosses the Sun's equator from north to south). Only one node needs to be specified, and by convention the ascending node is used. A second point in a planet's orbit is the vernal *equinox,* the spring day in which day and night

OBLIQUITY, ORBITAL INCLINATION, AND ROTATIONAL DIRECTION FOR ALL THE PLANETS

Planet	Obliquity (inclination of the planet's equator to its orbit; tilt); remarkable values are in italic	Orbital inclination to the ecliptic (angle between the planet's orbital plane and the Earth's orbital plane); remarkable values are in italic	Rotational direction
Mercury	0° (though some scientists believe the planet is flipped over, so this value may be 180°)	7.01°	prograde
Venus	*177.3°*	3.39°	retrograde
Earth	23.45°	0° (by definition)	prograde
Mars	25.2°	1.85°	prograde
Jupiter	3.12°	1.30°	prograde
Saturn	26.73°	2.48°	prograde
Uranus	*97.6°*	0.77°	retrograde
Neptune	29.56°	1.77°	prograde
Pluto (now categorized as a dwarf planet)	*122.5°*	*17.16°*	retrograde

have the same length ("equinox" means equal night), occurring where the plane of the planet's equator intersects its orbital plane. The angle between the vernal equinox γ and the ascending node *N* is called the longitude of the ascending node. Mercury's longitude of the ascending node is 48.331°.

ω **argument of the perigee** The argument of the perigee is the angle (in the body's orbit plane) between the ascending node *N* and perihelion *P,* measured in the direction of the body's orbit. Mercury's argument of the perigee is 77.456°.

The complexity of the six measurements shown starting on page 127, demonstrates the extreme attention to detail that is necessary when moving from simple theory ("every orbit is an ellipse")to measuring the movements of actual orbiting planets. Because of the gradual changes in orbits over time caused by gravitational interactions of many bodies and by changes within each planet, natural orbits are complex, evolving motions. To plan with such accuracy a space mission such as the recent one that involve the Mars Exploration Rovers, each of which landed perfectly in their targets, the mission planners must be masters of orbital parameters.

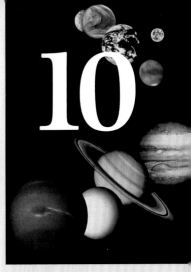

Mercury's Interior: A Huge Core

Venus, the Earth, and Mars are all thought to have formed from similar materials. Their iron cores take up similar fractions of the planets, and their silicate mantles melt to produce similar kinds of volcanic rocks. Mercury, on the other hand, may have been formed from a different bulk composition, or it may have formed under different conditions than the other terrestrial planets. The planet has a huge iron core, either indicating that the planet contains at least twice the iron content of the other terrestrial planets or that virtually all the iron from the bulk composition was pulled into its core, leaving its mantle almost iron-free. At the same time, the planet shows no recent volcanic activity, and so its interior can be assumed to be stationary (not convecting). The lack of volcanic activity is usually taken to mean that the planet has largely finished losing its internal heat. Mercury, however, has a small magnetic field. Magnetic fields are generally accepted to be caused by fluid movements in the outer core caused by heat loss. Somehow Mercury has created a balance that allows the generation of a magnetic field in the absence of mantle movements.

COMPOSITION

Mercury's average density is 341 pounds per cubic feet (5,430 kg/m^3), just less than the densest planet, Earth, at 347 pounds per cubic feet (5,515 kg/m^3). The planet's high density was first discovered by measuring the surprising acceleration of the Mariner mission toward Mercury, in the grip of the planet's strangely strong gravity field. Earth is a much larger planet, and so its interior pressure is much higher, pressing the material into much denser phases. With the effects of pressure taken away, Mercury's density is actually much higher than the Earth's and is therefore the densest planet in the solar system. The high density of the planet is though to imply that it contains a lot of iron—more, by proportion, than any other planet. Iron is the most common dense inner solar system element, and it is likely to be responsible for high density in Mercury.

If Mercury's extra density is due to iron content, then Mercury has a core that is 60 percent or more by mass, the largest core relative to planetary radius of any planet in the solar system. Mercury's core is probably 1,120 to 1,180 miles (1,800 to 1,900 km) in radius, nearly 75 percent of the planet's diameter. This is at least twice the metal content of Venus, Earth, or Mars (see the sidebar "Interior Structure of the Terrestrial Planets" opposite).

Why would Mercury have such a huge core relative to its size? Current models for planetary accretion suggest that any terrestrial planet should form with a larger percentage of silicates, which would make up a thick mantle above the core, as they do on Venus, Earth, and Mars (see the sidebar "Accretion and Heating: Why Are Some Solar System Objects Round and Others Irregular?" on page 137). Mercury, then, may have lost most of its silicate mantle in some catastrophic event after its early formation. The simplest candidate for this event is a giant impact: If a large body struck Mercury more or less directly, then its iron would combine with Mercury's into an unusually large core, and much of Mercury's silicate mantle could have been lost to space. The impacting body may also have been made mainly of metal, like an iron meteorite. In

INTERIOR STRUCTURE OF THE TERRESTRIAL PLANETS

The outermost layer of the terrestrial planets is the *crust*, made up of one or more of the following: igneous rocks (rocks that were once hot enough to be completely molten), metamorphic rocks (rocks that have been changed from their original state by heat or pressure, but were never liquid), and sedimentary rocks (rocks that are made of mineral grains that were transported by water or air). Sedimentary rocks, such as shale and limestone, can only be made at the surface of the planet, by surface processes such as rivers, glaciers, oceans, and wind. Sedimentary rocks make up the majority of rock outcrops at the surface of the Earth, and they may also exist on Mars. Igneous rocks make up the majority of the crust on Mars and on Venus, and probably on Mercury, though its surface is not well known because of the difficulty in taking good images of a body so close to the Sun. Igneous rocks predominate on Venus and probably Mercury because water is the main driving force for the formation of sedimentary rocks, and those planets are dry. Mars alone has sedimentary rocks similar to those on Earth. Plate tectonics on Earth is the main process that creates metamorphic rocks, which are commonly made by burial under growing mountains as tectonic plates collide or drive under each other. Since neither surface water nor plate tectonics exist on Venus or Mercury, they would be expected to be covered almost exclusively with igneous rocks.

Radioactive decay of atoms throughout the Earth and other planets produces heat, and the interior of the Earth and most other planets is hotter than the surface. Heat radiates away from the planet into space, and the planet is cooling through time. If the planet had only the heat from its initial formation, it can be calculated that planets the size of Earth and smaller, including Mars, would have completely cooled by this time. Scientists can measure heat flowing out of the Earth, however, by placing thermal measuring devices in holes dug deeply into the soil, and they know that heat flux (the amount of heat moving through a unit of surface area in a unit of time) is different in different parts of the world. Heat flux in areas of active volcanism, for example, is higher than heat flux in quiet areas. It is possible to calculate the likely internal temperatures of the Earth based on heat flux at the surface. This leads to the conclusion that the Earth's shallow interior, not much deeper than the hard, cold crust mankind lives upon, is at 2,190 to 2,640°F (1,200 to 1,450°C). Similar calculations can be made for other planets remotely, but without the precision of the answers for the Earth.

(continues)

(continued)

Rocks at temperatures like those in Earth's mantle are able to flow over geologic time. They are not liquid, but there is enough energy in the atoms of the crystals that the crystals can deform and "creep" in response to pressure, given thousands or millions of years (for more, see the sidebar "Rheology, or How Solids Can Flow" on page 181 in chapter 14). The interior of the Earth is moving in this way, in giant circulation patterns driven by heat escaping toward the surface and radiating into space. This movement in response to heat is called convection.

Plate tectonics, the movement of the brittle outside of the Earth, is caused in part by these internal convective movements, but largely by the pull of oceanic plates descending into the mantle at *subduction zones*. At the surface, this movement is only one or two inches (a few centimeters) a year. Scientists are constantly looking for evidence for plate tectonics on other planets and, for the most part, not finding it; apparently other terrestrial planets have not experienced plate tectonics, likely because they have insufficient surface water, which lubricates plate movement and allows the mantle to flow more easily. There may be some ice plate tectonics on Europa, but there is nothing in the solar system like the complex plate configurations and movements on the Earth. On Mars there may be some evidence for plate tectonics that ended early in the planet's history, left recorded in a few regions of the crust that have retained a magnetic field. Mars and the other terrestrial planets and the Moon are all considered *one-plate planets,* where their crust and upper mantle have cooled into a stiff shell that moves as a unit. Without plate tectonics, there are no volcanic arcs such as Japan or the Cascades, and there are no *mid-ocean ridges* at which new oceanic crust is produced. Surface features on one-plate planets are therefore different from those on Earth.

Below the crust and above the core, the planet's material is called the mantle. The uppermost mantle is too cool to be able to flow, except over many millions of years, and so it moves as a unit with the crust. Together, these two cool, connected layers

this scenario, the metal meteorite would combine with the early, small proto-Mercury, creating a planet with an unusually large iron core. Alternatively, the silicate mantle could have been removed by vaporization in a burst of heat from the early Sun. A third possibility is that there may have been strong compositional gradients in the early solar system and that in fact Mercury formed with the iron-rich composition are called the *lithosphere*. Beneath the lithosphere, the remaining mantle might be hot enough to flow. This is certainly true on the Earth and is probably the case on the other terrestrial planets. The mantles of terrestrial planets are thought to be mainly made of minerals based on silicon atoms. The most common minerals at shallow depths in the mantle are olivine (also known as the semiprecious gem peridot) and pyroxene at shallow depths, which then convert to other minerals at the higher pressures of the deep interior. Mantles on other differentiated terrestrial planets are thought to be similar.

Based on an analysis of the bulk "silicate Earth" (the mantle and crust, made mostly of minerals based on silicon atoms) compared to the composition of primitive meteorites that represent the material the inner planets were made of, the silicate Earth is clearly missing a lot of iron and some nickel. Models of planetary formation also show that the heat of *accretion* (the initial formation of the planet) will cause iron to melt and sink into the deep interior of the Earth. The core of the Earth, then, is made of iron with some nickel and a few percent of other elements. The other terrestrial planets almost certainly have iron cores, and even the Moon probably has a tiny iron core with a radius of a few hundred kilometers at most.

This is the structure of the Earth, used as the starting point in understanding the structures of other terrestrial planets: The outermost cool, thin veneer of the Earth is the crust. The crust is coupled to the coolest, uppermost mantle, and together they are called the lithosphere. Under the lithosphere is the convecting mantle, and beneath that, the core. The outer core is liquid metal, and the inner core is solid metal.

How the crusts formed seems to differ among the planets, as does the composition of the mantle (though thought to be always silicate) and core (though thought to be always iron-dominated), and the heat and convective activity of the mantle. Theorizing about the degree of these differences and the reasons for their existence is a large part of planetary geology.

it now seems to possess. Finally, Mercury could have differentiated in a particularly oxygen-poor environment. Without oxygen, iron will preferentially form a metal and sink into the core, rather than forming iron oxide and combining into silicate mantle materials. In this scenario, Mercury could have started with the same bulk composition and ended with its current structure without having endured a giant impact.

These models may be distinguishable on the basis of crustal composition. The MESSENGER mission, launched by NASA on August 3, 2004, will measure the crustal compositions with spectrometers while in orbit around Mercury. If the mantle was removed by solar heat, then the crustal composition should be unusually rich in elements that do not vaporize easily, such as aluminum, titanium, and magnesium, and poor in volatile elements such as sodium, potassium, and even iron. If the mantle was removed by impact, then the remaining crust should have compositions more similar to what is seen on the Earth and Mars.

Much of what is known about the composition of the Moon comes from sample returns from the American Apollo and Soviet Luna missions, which together brought back more than 440 pounds (200 kg) of lunar material, all of which has been pored over and analyzed in great detail. Though there are no samples from Mars missions, there are more than 30 meteorites that have come from Mars, thrown off in violent impacts and sent through space to eventually land on Earth. These samples have been invaluable in beginning to make some hypotheses about the composition of the Martian interior, since many are volcanic rocks that melted from the planet's mantle. Now there are also remote-sensing data from planetary orbiting missions on the compositions of the surface of the Moon and Mars. The remote-sensing data indicate the concentrations of certain radioactive trace elements on the surface, as well as concentrations of titanium, iron, and even the existence of certain mineral phases, such as olivine, pyroxene, and plagioclase. All this data can be combined to make some initial inferences about the bulk compositions of the planets' mantles and also about processes that led to the formation of their crusts and, in some cases, about the specific compositions of the mantle at depth.

For Mercury, almost none of this data is available. There are no meteorites identified as having come from Mercury, though it is theoretically possible for pieces of Mercury expelled from the planet by energetic meteorite impacts to travel to Earth, though it is about 100 times less likely for meteorites to arrive

(continues on page 142)

ACCRETION AND HEATING: WHY ARE SOME SOLAR SYSTEM OBJECTS ROUND AND OTHERS IRREGULAR?

There are three main characteristics of a body that determine whether it will become round.

The first is its *viscosity*, that is, its ability to flow. Fluid bodies can be round because of surface tension, no matter their size; self-gravitation does not play a role. The force bonding together the molecules on the outside of a fluid drop pull the surface into the smallest possible area, which is a sphere. This is also the case with gaseous planets, like Uranus. Solid material, like rock, can flow slowly if it is hot, so heat is an important aspect of viscosity. When planets are formed, it is thought that they start as agglomerations of small bodies, and that more and more small bodies collide or are attracted gravitationally, making the main body larger and larger. The heat contributed by colliding planetesimals significantly helps along the transformation of the original pile of rubble into a spherical planet: The loss of their kinetic energy (more on this at the end of this sidebar) acts to heat up the main body. The hotter the main body, the easier it is for the material to flow into a sphere in response to its growing gravitational field.

The second main characteristic is density. Solid round bodies obtain their shape from gravity, which acts equally in all directions and therefore works to make a body a sphere. The same volume of a very dense material will create a stronger gravitational field than a less dense material, and the stronger the gravity of the object, the more likely it is to pull itself into a sphere.

The third characteristic is mass, which is really another aspect of density. If the object is made of low-density material, there just has to be a lot more of it to make the gravitational field required to make it round.

Bodies that are too small to heat up enough to allow any flow, or to have a large enough internal gravitational field, may retain irregular outlines. Their shapes are determined by mechanical strength and response to outside forces such as meteorite impacts, rather than by their own self-gravity. In general the largest asteroids, including all 100 or so that have diameters greater than 60 miles (100 km), and the larger moons, are round from self-gravity. Most asteroids and moons with diameters larger than six miles (10 km) are round, but not all of them, depending on their composition and the manner of their creation.

(continues)

(continued)

There is another stage of planetary evolution after attainment of a spherical shape: internal differentiation. All asteroids and the terrestrial planets probably started out made of primitive materials, such as the class of asteroids and meteorites called CI or enstatite chondrites. The planets and some of the larger asteroids then became compositionally stratified in their interiors, a process called differentiation. In a *differentiated body,* heavy metals, mainly iron with some nickel and other minor impurities in the case of terrestrial planets, and rocky and icy material in the case of the gaseous planets, have sunk to the middle of the body, forming a core. Terrestrial planets are therefore made up, in a rough sense, of concentric shells of materials with different compositions. The outermost shell is a crust, made mainly of material that has melted from the interior and risen buoyantly up to the surface. The mantle is made of silicate minerals, and the core is mainly of iron. The gas giant outer planets are similarly made of shells of material, though they are gaseous materials on the outside and rocky or icy in the interior. Planets with systematic shells like these are called differentiated planets. Their concentric spherical layers differ in terms of composition, heat, density, and even motion, and planets that are differentiated are more or less spherical. All the planets in the solar system seem to be thoroughly differentiated internally, with the possible exception of Pluto and Charon. What data there is for these two bodies indicates that they may not be fully differentiated.

Some bodies in the solar system, though, are not differentiated; the material they are made of is still in a more primitive state, and the body may not be spherical. Undifferentiated bodies in the asteroid belt have their metal component still mixed through their silicate portions; it has not separated and flowed into the interior to form a core.

Among asteroids, the sizes of bodies that differentiated vary widely. Iron meteorites, thought to be the differentiated cores of rocky bodies that have since been shattered, consist of crystals that grow to different sizes directly depending upon their cooling rate, which in turn depends upon the size of the body that is cooling. Crystal sizes in iron meteorites indicate parent bodies from six to 30 miles (10 to 50 km) or more in diameter. Vesta, an asteroid with a basaltic crust and a diameter of 326 miles (525 km), seems to be the largest surviving differentiated body in the asteroid belt. Though the asteroid Ceres, an unevenly-shaped asteroid approximately 577 by 596 miles (930 by 960 km), is much larger than Vesta, it seems from spectroscopic analyses to be largely undifferentiated. It is thought that the higher percentages of volatiles available at the distance of Ceres's orbit may have helped cool the asteroid faster and prevented the buildup of heat required for differentiation. It is also believed that Ceres and Vesta are among the last surviving "protoplanets," and that almost all asteroids of smaller size are the shattered remains of larger bodies.

Where does the heat for differentiation come from? The larger asteroids generated enough internal heat from radioactive decay to melt (at least partially) and differentiate (for more on radioactive decay, see the sidebar "Elements and Isotopes" on page 10 in chapter 1). Generally bodies larger than about 300 miles (500 km) in diameter are needed in order to be insulated enough to trap the heat from radioactive decay so that melting can occur. If the body is too small, it cools too fast and no differentiation can take place.

A source for heat to create differentiation, and perhaps the main source, is the heat of accretion. When smaller bodies, often called planetesimals, are colliding and sticking together, creating a single larger body (perhaps a planet), they are said to be accreting. Eventually the larger body may even have enough gravity itself to begin altering the paths of passing planetesimals and attracting them to it. In any case, the process of accretion adds tremendous heat to the body, by the transformation of the kinetic energy of the planetesimals into heat in the larger body. To understand kinetic energy, start with momentum, called p, and defined as the product of a body's mass m and its velocity v:

$$p = mv$$

Sir Isaac Newton called momentum "quality of movement." The greater the mass of the object, the greater its momentum is, and likewise, the greater its velocity, the greater its momentum is. A change in momentum creates a force, such as a person feels when something bumps into her. The object that bumps into her experiences a change in momentum because it has suddenly slowed down, and she experiences it as a force. The reason she feels more force when someone tosses a full soda to her than when they toss an empty soda can to her is that the full can has a greater mass, and therefore momentum, than the empty can, and when it hits her it loses all its momentum, transferring to her a greater force.

How does this relate to heating by accretion? Those incoming planetesimals have momentum due to their mass and velocity, and when they crash into the larger body,

(continues)

(continued)

their momentum is converted into energy, in this case, heat. The energy of the body, created by its mass and velocity, is called its kinetic energy. Kinetic energy is the total effect of changing momentum of a body, in this case, as its velocity slows down to zero. Kinetic energy is expressed in terms of mass *m* and velocity *v*:

$$K = \frac{1}{2}mv^2$$

Students of calculus might note that kinetic energy is the integral of momentum with respect to velocity:

$$K = \int mvdv = \frac{1}{2}mv^2$$

The kinetic energy is converted from mass and velocity into heat energy when it strikes the growing body. This energy, and therefore heat, is considerable, and if accretion occurs fast enough, the larger body can be heated all the way to melting by accretional kinetic energy. If the larger body is melted even partially, it will differentiate.

How is energy transfigured into heat, and how is heat transformed into melting? To transfer energy into heat, the type of material has to be taken into consideration. Heat capacity describes how a material's temperature changes in response to added energy. Some materials go up in temperature easily in response to energy, while others take more energy to get hotter. Silicate minerals have a heat capacity of 245.2 cal/°lb (1,256.1 J/°kg). What this means is that 245.2 calories of energy are required to raise the temperature of one pound of silicate material one degree. Here is a sample calculation. A planetesimal is about to impact a larger body, and the planetesimal is a kilometer in radius. It would weigh roughly 3.7 × 10¹³ lb (1.7 × 10¹³ kg), if its density were about 250 lb/ft³ (4,000 kg/m³). If it were traveling at 6 miles per second (10 km/s), then its kinetic energy would be

$$K = \frac{1}{2}mv^2 = \left(1.7 \times 10^{13}\,kg\right)\left(10,000\,m/sec\right)^2$$
$$= 8.5 \times 10^{20}\,J = 2 \times 10^{20}\,cal.$$

Using the heat capacity, the temperature change created by an impact of this example planetesimal can be calculated:

$$\frac{8.5 \times 10^{20}\,^\circ kg}{1,256.1 J\,/\,^\circ kg} = 6.8 \times 10^{17}\,^\circ kg = 8.3 \times 10^{17}\,^\circ lb$$

The question now becomes, how much mass is going to be heated by the impact? According to this calculation, the example planetesimal creates heat on impact sufficient to heat one pound of material by $8.3 \times 10^{17}\,^\circ F$ (or one kilogram by $6.8 \times 10^{17}\,^\circ C$), but of course it will actually heat more material by lesser amounts. To calculate how many degrees of heating could be done to a given mass, divide the results of the previous calculation by the mass to be heated.

The impact would, of course, heat a large region of the target body as well as the impactor itself. How widespread is the influence of this impact? How deeply does it heat, and how widely. Of course, the material closest to the impact will receive most of the energy, and the energy input will go down with distance from the impact, until finally the material is completely unheated. What is the pattern of energy dispersal? Energy dispersal is not well understood even by scientists who study impactors.

Here is a simpler question: If all the energy were put into melting the impacted material, how much could it melt? To melt a silicate completely requires that its temperature be raised to about $2,700^\circ F$ ($1,500^\circ C$), as a rough estimate, so here is the mass of material that can be completely melted by this example impact:

$$\frac{6.8 \times 10^{17}\,^\circ kg}{1,500^\circ} = 4.5 \times 10^{14}\,kg = 9.9 \times 10^{14}\,lb$$

This means that the impactor can melt about 25 times its own mass ($4.5 \times 10^{14}/1.7 \times 10^{13} = 26$). Of course this is a rough calculation, but it does show how effective accretion can be in heating up a growing body, and how it can therefore help the body to attain a spherical shape and to internally differentiate into different compositional shells.

(continued from page 136)

on Earth from Mercury than from Mars. Since the only space mission to Mercury was *Mariner 10,* which simply flew by the planet, there are no samples whatsoever from the planet.

All the data on compositions of Mercury comes from the MESSENGER mission orbiter and from ground-based reflectance spectrometry. Radiation bounced off the planet and observed on Earth shows that certain wavelengths have unexpectedly low intensities compared to their neighboring wavelengths. This low intensity indicates that material on the planet's surface absorbed the specific wavelength in question. By looking at the reflectance spectra of minerals on Earth, the specific wavelengths that they absorb most efficiently can be measured and then compared to the spectra obtained from other planets.

Reflectance spectra from Mercury indicate that the planet's surface is poor in iron oxide. Data collected from Earth-based observation and by the three flybys of *Mariner 10* show that Mercury's surface is low in iron-bearing silicates, containing between 0 and 3–4 wt% FeO in the minerals on the planet's surface. Observers have detected the presence of calcic plagioclase feldspar and low-FeO pyroxene, similar to the crust on parts of the Moon. Recent measurements by the flybys of Mercury *MESSENGER* are consistent with these ground-based observations and limit total iron content to be less than 6 wt%, with iron oxide in silicates at less than 2–3 wt%. This percentage of iron oxide in the minerals in the crust is astonishingly low and must be telling a story about the planet's formation. There may also be metallic iron or titanium grains in the crust: Recent observations indicate the presence of a possible global darkening agent, thought to be an opaque oxide, a non-silicate mineral.

Reflectance spectra from parts of Mercury indicate that the surface may be even lower in iron than the Moon's, which was already one of the lowest-iron surfaces known in the terrestrial planets. On the Moon, the presence of the feldspar-rich pale highlands rocks (anorthosites, named after a type of feldspar) is considered one of the main lines of evidence that the Moon was fully molten early in its history and crystallized slowly enough to allow the buoyant feldspar to float up to the surface. Feldspar on Mercury may tell a similar story about early planetary development.

MAGNETIC FIELD

Mercury has a magnetic field similar to Venus's, and about 0.1 percent as strong as Earth's. Mercury's magnetic field was a complete surprise when the *Mariner 10* craft discovered it in 1974. Mercury's magnetic field was only roughly measured by the *Mariner 10* craft and will have to await the arrival of the MESSENGER mission to be better described, but it seems to be a relatively simple dipole field, like Earth's. A dipole magnetic field is a two-poled system like the Earth's, with magnetic field lines flowing out of the south magnetic pole and into the north magnetic pole, and compasses on Mercury would point to the north pole of the planet (there are other, more complex configurations possible for magnetic fields, which are detected on Jupiter and the Sun).

There is a prevalent idea for why terrestrial planets have magnetic fields, and though this idea is fairly well accepted by scientists, it is not thoroughly proven. On the Earth, it is known clearly that the outer core is liquid metal, almost entirely iron but with some nickel and also some small percentage of lighter elements (the exact composition is a topic of great argumentation at the moment in the scientific community). The idea for forming the magnetic field is that a planet's liquid outer core convects like boiling oatmeal around the solid inner core, and the moving currents of metal act like electrical currents, creating a magnetic field around them. The electrical to magnetic transition is simple because every electrical current creates a magnetic field spiraling around itself; even the electrical wires in your house have magnetic fields around them. Electricity and magnetism are inseparable forces and always exist together.

The more innovative part of the theory concerns the convection of the liquid core: The liquid core is moving because it is carrying heat away from the inner core of the planet. Heat from the inner core conducts into the lowest part of the outer core, and that heated material expands slightly from the energy of the heating. Because it has expanded a tiny fraction, it is now less dense than the unheated liquid next to it, and so it begins to rise through the radius of the outer core. When the heated material reaches the boundary with the mantle, it loses its heat by conducting it to the cooler mantle, and so it loses its extra buoyancy and sinks again. Many packages of material are going through this process of convection all at once, and together they form complex currents. It is common to describe convecting liquid as boiling oatmeal, but the liquid in the outer core is thought to be much less viscous (in other words, "thinner" and more fluid) than oatmeal. The convective currents are therefore thought to be much more complex and very rapidly moving.

Sir Joseph Larmour, an Irish physicist and mathematician, first proposed the hypothesis that the Earth's active magnetic field might be explained by the way the moving fluid iron in Earth's outer core mimics electrical currents and the fact that every electric current has an associated, enveloping magnetic field. The combination of convective currents and a spinning inner and outer core is called the dynamo effect. If the fluid motion is fast, large, and conductive enough, then a magnetic field can not only be created, but also carried and deformed by the moving fluid (this is also what happens in the Sun). This theory works well for the Earth and for the Sun and even for Jupiter and Saturn, though they are thought to have a dynamo made of metallic hydrogen, not iron.

The theory is more difficult, potentially, for Mercury. Convection in the outer core cannot go on indefinitely because it is the process of moving heat out of the inner core and into the mantle, and then the mantle moves the heat out of the surface of the planet and into space. Over time, the inner, solid core grows, as heat is lost from the outer core and more of it freezes into a solid, and eventually the planet has cooled enough that the dynamo is no longer active, and the planet no longer has a magnetic field. The Earth's field is still very active. Strong magnetism remaining in Mars's crust shows that it once had a magnetic field, but now the planet has none.

Mercury, though much smaller than Mars, still has a magnetic field. Many scientists thought it should have cooled completely by now and therefore a dynamo in the outer core was impossible. Before *Mariner* measured a field around Mercury, it was widely assumed in the scientific community that no field could be present. In addition, when heat is moved from the outer core into the mantle, the mantle may be heated enough that it, too begins to convect. When the mantle convects, it can move hot material close enough to the surface that it melts through pressure release, and this creates volcanic eruptions on the planet's surface. Since as far as can be told with the photos from *Mariner 10* and from radar imaging from Earth, Mercury has not been volcanically active for a long time; in fact, its volcanic activity stopped before even the Moon's did. Together, Mercury's small size and apparent lack of volcanic activity argue against a magnetic field, and yet it has one. The exceptional size of its core may contribute to its continued field, but no one has any supporting data at the moment for theories that involve the large size of Mercury's core.

Another possibility suggested was that Mercury has no dynamo, and its magnetic field is entirely due to magnetic minerals in its crust that were magnetized eons ago when the planet had an active dynamo. Some minerals, like magnetite, can hold a magnetic field: When they crystallize from a melt (such as a volcanic lava flow) in the presence of the Earth's magnetic field, they retain the record of that field indefinitely, even if the Earth's field changes. If the minerals are reheated above a certain temperature, they lose the field. In this way, Earth scientists can reconstruct what the Earth's magnetic field was like in the past, by measuring the magnetic fields retained in minerals that formed in the past. On Mercury, the theory says, minerals in its crust may have become magnetized and retained their magnetization through the time since the magnetic field of the planet died, and it is their magnetism that *Mariner* measured.

This theory requires some special circumstances. If a planet has a crust of uniform thickness covering its surface and the crust is more or less uniformly magnetized, then the magnetic field produced by the crust effectively cancels itself out, and no magnetic field can be detected by a nearby spacecraft. To create a magnetic field that is detectable outside the planet, a magnetic crust has to be nonuniform. On Mercury, a nonuniform crust could have been caused by impact cratering, which both thins the crust and heats it locally to the point that the magnetic minerals lose their fields. The resonance of Mercury with the Sun may also cause the magnetic field to be nonuniform because of the two especially hot spots caused by heat from the Sun: This extra heat could also remove the magnetization from the crust.

Work by Jean-Luc Margot at Cornell University in 2007 showed that Mercury definitively still has a molted outer core. By taking detailed measurements of the spin of Mercury, Margot was able to determine that Mercury's crust and mantle rotates in a way not perfectly bound to its inner core: A liquid outer core acts as a lubricant. Then, in 2008, *MESSENGER* data showed that Mercury's magnetic field is created by a planetary dynamo, created in the planet's interior, and not just the leftover signals of magnetized rocks left in the planet's crust. Now Mercury is known to have an interior dynamo, likely in the planet's liquid outer core as it is on the Earth, and this dynamo is producing an ongoing magnetic field for the planet.

How can there be a strong present interior magnetic field but no volcanism? This is a paradox because planetary magnetic fields are thought to be caused by an inner, solid iron core rotating inside a liquid outer core, as described above. If this is so, then the outer core has to be hot enough to melt iron. Heat is necessarily conducted from that hot core to the mantle just above it, so why is Mercury's mantle apparently not convecting and melting near the surface, the way Earth's is? One possibility is that Mercury's field is produced in a dynamo in a liquid outer core, but the mantle is not transferring enough heat to create melting in the mantle. One possibility for retaining a liquid outer core over time is if the outer core contains more sulfur. Sulfur is easily mixed into iron, and it lowers the melting temperature and the density of the liquid iron considerably, allowing it to remain molten for far longer and at lower temperatures.

Jeremy Bloxham, a scientist at Harvard University, and his colleague Sabine Stanley (now at the Massachusetts Institute of Technology) suggest that Mercury's field might be caused by convection in a very thin liquid shell around its core. If the core has largely solidified and only a small volume of liquid metal remains, heat flow out of the core may still be large enough to create a magnetic field while being too small to drive mantle flow and create volcanism.

With the new data from *MESSENGER* better models can be made, better hypotheses to explain this paradoxical planetary interior. The questions remain how the planet's outer core is still hot enough to be liquid and why there appears to be no active volcanism.

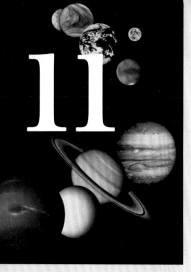

Visible Mercury

Before 2008, when *MESSENGER* made its first flyby of the planet, scientists had better images of even distant planets such as Saturn than they had of Mercury. In general, from what can be seen, Mercury has an ancient, heavily cratered surface, much like the Moon's. The image of Mercury on page 98 is from *Mariner 10* on March 29, 1974. This picture is assembled from a number of separate images that were taken while the spacecraft was 3,340,000 miles (5,380,000 km) away.

Mercury's surface, as photographed by *Mariner 10,* seems to consist of four major terrain types: ancient, heavily cratered areas; intercrater plains; smooth, young plains; and lastly, a chaotic region that lies on the opposite side of the planet from an immense impact crater named Caloris Basin. Mercury's surface is known to be ancient because of the high cratering rate it records. Scientists are fairly sure that there was more material bombarding the planets early in the solar system. If the planets accreted from a nebula, as is widely accepted, then it stands to reason that there were more stray bodies orbiting near the terrestrial planets early in the solar system and that their population has been gradually depleted as they fall

This surface mosaic of Mercury, assembled from photos taken by Mariner 10, shows the ancient cratered surface of the planet. (NASA/ Mariner/JPL)

into the Sun or crash into planets. Over time, the surfaces of the terrestrial planets collect more impact craters, though the rate of cratering was highest early in solar system development. Mercury's heavily cratered surface indicates that no later processes, such as volcanism, have obliterated its cratering record. Though some of Mercury's surface is designated as young plains, they are only young in comparison with the rest of the planet.

CRATERS

Like the Moon and Mars, Mercury has ancient areas on its surface covered by craters. This is the most extensive type of terrain photographed by *Mariner 10*. The photomosaic shown below includes Mercury's north pole near the top of the image. Some heavily cratered regions are shown. Based on knowledge of the Moon and the density of the craters seen on Mercury, these surfaces are thought to be 4.1–4.2 billion years old (see the sidebar "The Late Heavy Bombardment" on page 155). Recently radar observations of Mercury from the Arecibo Observatory have spotted unusual echoes from the south and north poles, which have been interpreted by some scientists as signals from ice deposits in the floors of some permanently

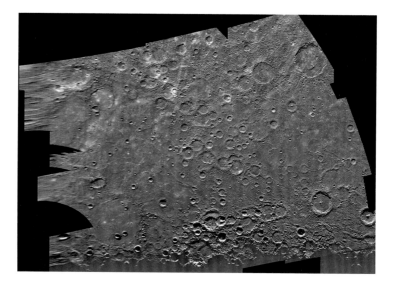

Mercury's Borealis quadrangle includes the planet's north pole near the top of the image, which is a mosaic of images taken by Mariner 10. (NASA/ JPL/Mariner 10)

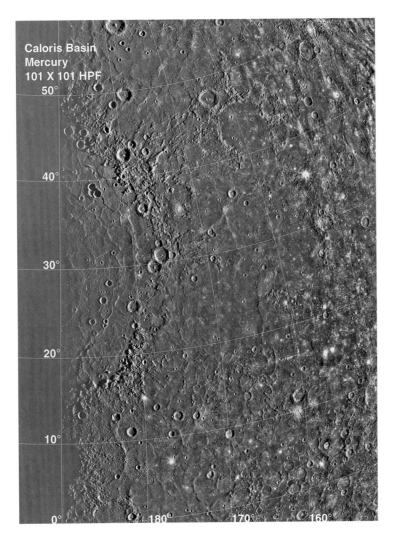

Caloris Basin
Mercury
101 X 101 HPF
50°
40°
30°
20°
10°
0° 180° 170° 160°

The right half of Mercury's largest impact crater, the Caloris Basin, lies on the left side of this photomosaic. Mariner 10 achieved a 0.6-mile (1-km) per pixel resolution when it passed the planet in 1974. (NASA/JPL/ Mariner 10)

shadowed craters. If it is water, it is thought to have come from cometary impacts.

Caloris Basin is both the youngest and the largest impact crater on Mercury. At 800 miles (1,300 km) in diameter, it is almost as large as Hellas Basin on Mars, which is also the youngest and, at 870 miles (1,400 km) in diameter, the largest giant impact on Mars. The right half of Caloris Basin is shown along the left side of the photo above, a mosaic of images taken by *Mariner 10*. This photo shows the concentric rings of a complex crater along with ancient streamers of crater *ejecta*. While

This false color image of Caloris Basin taken by MESSENGER makes a stark contrast with the earlier image by Mariner 10 shown above. (NASA/JPL)

Mars's Hellas has opposite it the immense Tharsis rise, a volcanic complex including the largest volcano in the solar system, opposite Mercury's Caloris is simply chaotic, jumbled terrain hills and faults. Though it is most intuitive to assume that the shock energy of the impact that produced Caloris traveled away from the impact and was focused on the other side of the planets, where all the wave fronts converged (shown in the figure on page 153), there is no well-developed theory of the effect giant impacts have on the antipodal side of their planets.

SMOOTH YOUNG PLAINS

The smooth plains appear to be the youngest terrain on Mercury, and they make up about 40 percent of the area photographed by *Mariner 10*. The photomosaic on page 154 from *Mariner 10* is of the southern half of Mercury's Shakespeare quadrangle, named for the ancient Shakespeare crater located

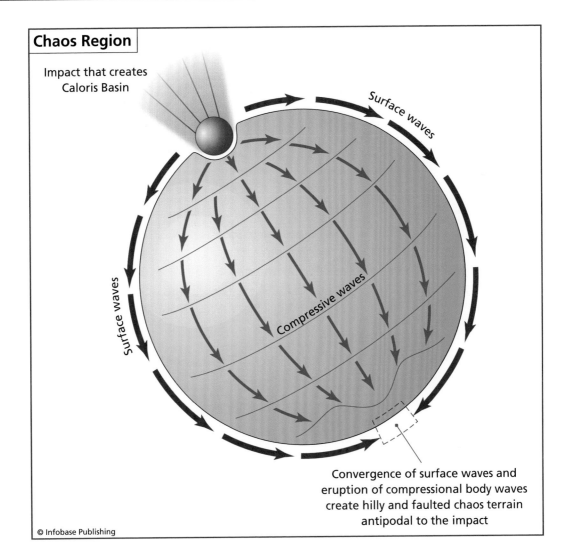

Chaos Region

Impact that creates
Caloris Basin

Surface waves

Surface waves

Compressive waves

Convergence of surface waves and
eruption of compressional body waves
create hilly and faulted chaos terrain
antipodal to the impact

© Infobase Publishing

on the upper edge to the left of center. This portion of the quadrangle covers the Mercurian surface from 20° to 45° north latitude and from 90° to 180° longitude. Bright ejecta rays radiating away from craters cut across and are superimposed on all other surface features, indicating that the source craters are the youngest topographic features on the surface of Mercury. Other parts of this quadrangle are almost bare of craters. These plains could be the result of resurfacing by volcanic activity, since this is the most common process for creating smooth plains in the terrestrial planets. The action of water

The chaos region antipodal to Caloris Basin may have been caused by the convergence of shock waves generated by the impact that formed the basin.

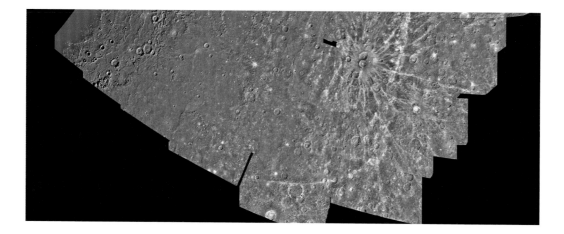

Mercury's Shakespeare quadrangle, named for the ancient crater on the upper edge of the mosaic to the left of center, stretches from 20° to 45° north latitude and from 90° to 180° longitude. (NASA/JPL/Mariner 10)

can create flat plains, such as those in the Northern Hemisphere of Mars, which are thought to be the basin bottoms of oceans dried up long ago. Mercury's obvious lack of water and its immense temperatures courtesy of the Sun make volcanic activity the most likely resurfacing process.

Though these are called young plains, they are only "young" in comparison to the ancient cratered areas. The better-known geologic history of the Moon and models of the early solar system show that there was a period of intense bombardment of the early planets, up to about 3.8 billion years ago. From studying the surfaces of other planets it is thought that even aside from the Late Heavy Bombardment, which was a particularly intense cratering period, cratering rates have subsided over time in the inner solar system (see the sidebar "The Late Heavy Bombardment" on page 155). Geologists who study cratering in images from other planets (often this discipline is called photogeology) have produced graphs of cratering rates versus time, as best they can without radiometric dates for planetary surfaces other than the Moon's. These curves allow us to make estimates of the ages of terrain that has craters. Even the smooth young plains of Mercury have some craters, and judging from cratering rates, they were formed about 3.7 billion years ago. These are immensely aged when compared to surface materials on Earth, most of which are younger than 500 million years, but they are still a young feature on the very old surface of Mercury.

THE LATE HEAVY BOMBARDMENT

There was a period of time early in solar system development when all the celestial bodies in the inner solar system were repeatedly impacted by large bolides. This high-activity period might be anticipated by thinking about how the planets formed, accreting from smaller bodies into larger and larger bodies, and so it may seem intuitive that there would be a time even after most of the planets formed when there was still enough material left over in the early solar system to continue bombarding and cratering the early planets.

Beyond this theory, though, there is visible evidence on Mercury, the Moon, and Mars in the form of ancient surfaces that are far more heavily cratered than any fresher surface on the planet (Venus, on the other hand, has been resurfaced by volcanic activity, and plate tectonics and surface weathering have wiped out all record of early impacts on Earth). The giant basins on the Moon, filled with dark basalt and visible to the eye from Earth, are left over from that early period of heavy impacts, called the Late Heavy Bombardment.

Dating rocks from the Moon using radioactive isotopes and carefully determining the age relationships of different craters' ejecta blankets indicate that the lunar Late Heavy Bombardment lasted until about 3.8 billion years ago. Some scientists believe that the Late Heavy Bombardment was a specific period of very heavy impact activity that lasted from about 4.2 to 3.8 billion years ago, after a pause in bombardment following initial planetary formation at about 4.56 billion years ago, while other scientists believe that the Late Heavy Bombardment was the tail end of a continuously decreasing rate of bombardment that began at the beginning of the solar system.

In this continual bombardment model, the last giant impacts from 4.2 to 3.8 billion years ago simply erased the evidence of all the earlier bombardment. If, alternatively, the Late Heavy Bombardment was a discrete event, then some reason for the sudden invasion of the inner solar system by giant bolides must be discovered. Were they bodies perturbed from the outer solar system by the giant planets there? If they came from the outer solar system, then more of the material was likely to be water-rich cometary material. If as much as 25 percent of the Late Heavy Bombardment was cometary material, it would have contributed enough water to the Earth to create its oceans. If this model is correct for placing water on the Earth, then a further quandary must be solved: Why didn't Venus receive as much water, or if it did, where did the water go?

The lava flows seem, from remote sensing, to contain only about 3 percent iron oxide, much less than in terrestrial lava flows. From years of laboratory experiments on how rocks melt, it is known that about the same amount of iron goes into the melt as stays behind in the rock. These experiments indicate, therefore, that Mercury's mantle contains only about 3 percent iron oxide, much less than the Earth's and especially less than Mars's mantle, which is thought to contain about 18 percent iron oxide. Mercury, the Earth, and Mars all formed in the inner solar system and should differ only slightly and systematically in bulk composition, so how can Mercury have so little iron in its silicate mantle? Mercury's large core may have left the mantle depleted in iron.

The volcanic history of the planet remains uncertain, since better-resolved photos are needed to clearly determine the relationships among surface features, and the rest of the planet must also be photographed. What can be seen of Mer-

Mercury's Michelangelo Quadrangle, near the planet's south pole, shows bright crater ejecta rays that lie across other surface features, indicating that the craters formed more recently than the other features. (NASA/JPL/ Mariner 10)

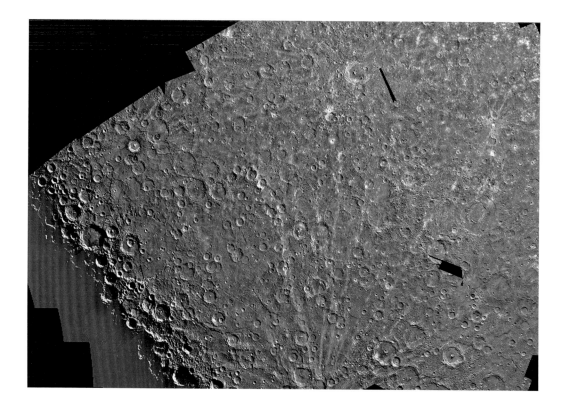

cury in the existing photographs indicates that volcanism seems to have ended early in Mercury's history, leaving the very old, cratered surfaces pristine. These clean, old surfaces prove that Mercury's geologic activity ceased earlier than any other planet; Venus, Earth, and Mars have all had their crusts completely resurfaced by geologic activity, wiping away the cratering record of the early, violent solar system. Though the mechanism that caused the volcanic activity of Mercury is unknown, researchers have noted that these smooth young plains are much like the volcanic pools on the Moon, visible from the Earth as dark surfaces in impact basins. The volcanic activity on the two planets happened at about the same time, but even on the much better studied Moon, it is not agreed why the large volcanic flows, called mare basalts, occurred ("mare" means ocean, one of their first interpretations).

All the other features on Mercury are cut across by Mercury's most predominant surface feature, called lobate scarps (curved cliffs that meet in relatively sharp angles, creating a scalloped shape). The scarps are between 12 and 300 miles (20 and 500 km) long, and each is hundred of yards in height: These are huge surface features. They can be sinuous when viewed from above, but generally they form smooth arcs. The scarps are approximately evenly distributed across the planet's surface and trend in all directions; they are not parallel or in sets. Analysis of three large scarps (which on Mercury are called "rupes")—Adventure Rupes, Resolution Rupes, and Discovery Rupes—indicate that they are formed by thrust faults. A thrust fault is one in which the land surface has been pressed together laterally, so that one side of the fault moves up and over the other. The scarps are therefore asymmetric in cross section, with a more shallowly sloping side and a steeper, cliff-like side. Discovery Rupes is 220 miles (350 km) long and has a maximum height of about two miles (3 km).

The Michelangelo Quadrangle, which lies in Mercury's southern polar region, contains several large lobate scarps in the lower left side of the image in the figure below. The scarps here cut through existing surface features, including several

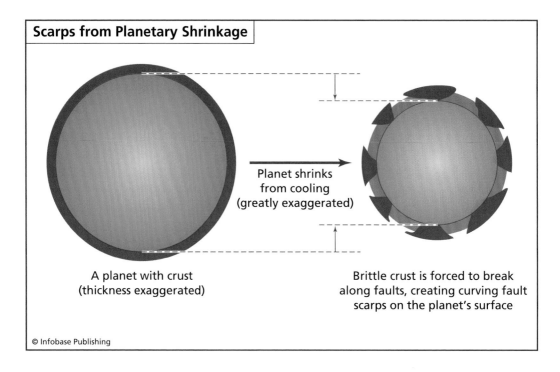

Scarps from Planetary Shrinkage

Planet shrinks
from cooling
(greatly exaggerated)

A planet with crust
(thickness exaggerated)

Brittle crust is forced to break
along faults, creating curving fault
scarps on the planet's surface

© Infobase Publishing

Scarps (cliffs formed by vertical movement of faults) may be created by planetary shrinkage, possibly the result of cooling.

impact craters, indicating that the scarps formed after the features they cut.

Thrust faults indicate that the surface of the planet was in compression, possibly caused when the planet's interior cooled and shrank, early in its history. The mechanism for forming thrust faults through planetary shrinkage is shown in the figure above. These scarps pass through both volcanic and cratered terrain, so they cannot be older than the volcanic plains, at about 3.7 billion years. Remember that the age of the solar system is about 4.56 billion years, so if cooling and shrinking caused these scarps, the planet was apparently still cooling and shrinking over a half billion years after its formation, according to the estimates made by examining the photographs of the surface. Measuring the scarps and adding their effect across the surface of the planet has led some researchers to state that the scarps represent a 0.5–1 percent shrinkage of the planet, which means that Mercury's radius shrank by one to two kilometers. Why the planet would relatively suddenly cool and shrink a half billion years after its initial formation is not well understood.

SURFACE CONDITIONS, ATMOSPHERE, AND WEATHER

Mercury has almost no atmosphere; its atmosphere is 10^{13} times less dense than ours (that is a million billion times less dense). Mercury is thought to have lost its atmosphere because of the high temperatures near the Sun, because of its weak magnetic field that allows the solar wind to strip away gases, and because of its relatively weak gravity. Because of its very thin atmosphere and relatively low gravity, the atmospheric pressure at the surface of Mercury is 10^{-15} atm, which is 10^{15} times less than Earth's atmospheric pressure. With such a thin atmosphere, Mercury has no weather in the common sense, but it is certainly bombarded by storms and material expelled from the Sun. The atmosphere consists partly of solar wind, mainly helium and hydrogen nuclei or atoms, but it also contains a significant proportion of sodium, potassium, and calcium, atoms that could only have come from its own crust. The atmospheric composition seems to change significantly with time, as a function of local time on Mercury, distance from the Sun, and level of solar activity.

The mosaic of images of Mercury's surface shown in the figure at right was taken by *Mariner 10* as it passed from the dark side of the planet. The dark and bright parts of the planet lie in stark comparison, symbolizing the intense energy input the Sun provides the planet.

Mercury's average surface temperature is 243°F (117°C), but over the course of a Mercurian day, the surface temperature ranges from 889°F to −297°F (467°C to −183°C),

This photomosaic image of Mercury was taken as Mariner 10 was outbound from the planet. The north pole is at the top of the image and, because of the angle of imaging, the equator is about two-thirds down the image. (NASA/JPL/Mariner 10)

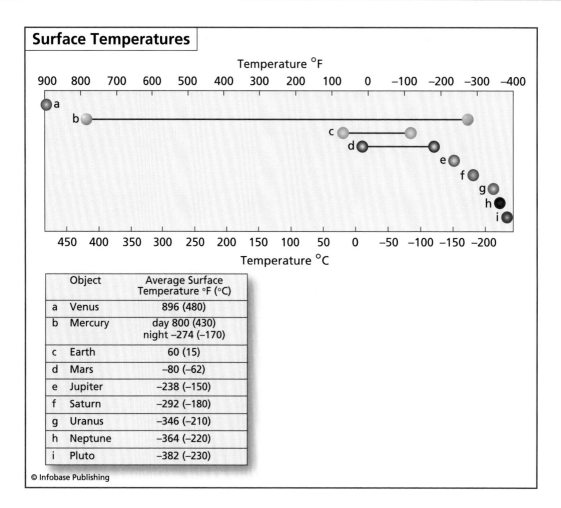

Surface Temperatures

	Object	Average Surface Temperature °F (°C)
a	Venus	896 (480)
b	Mercury	day 800 (430) night −274 (−170)
c	Earth	60 (15)
d	Mars	−80 (−62)
e	Jupiter	−238 (−150)
f	Saturn	−292 (−180)
g	Uranus	−346 (−210)
h	Neptune	−364 (−220)
i	Pluto	−382 (−230)

© Infobase Publishing

The surface temperature ranges of each of the planets and dwarf planets graphed here show that Mercury has by far the widest range of surface temperatures, though Venus has the hottest surface temperature, while Pluto, unsurprisingly, has the coldest.

the largest range in surface temperature of any planet. During a single day, the temperature rises high enough to melt lead and plunge low enough to freeze carbon-dioxide gas. The immense temperature range on Mercury is compared to those on other planets in the figure on this page; no other planet approaches the temperature extremes of Mercury. The surface temperature of Mercury is also influenced by its strange orbital resonance: Since it orbits the Sun in a 3:2 resonance, Mercury has two spots on its equator that are especially hot because they face the Sun more often than the rest of the equator. Mercury also has, therefore, two especially cold spots, placed between the hot ones.

Mercury's ancient surface appears to have been most recently covered by volcanism about 3.7 billion years ago. The craters and scarps resemble the ancient surface of the Moon. Like the Moon, Mercury has no atmosphere and so is naked to the radiative effects of the Sun. The planet's surface is bombarded by the solar wind and cosmic rays, heated intensely during the day and frozen at night. The high pressure, constant heat, and acidic environment of Mercury's neighbor Venus is an immense challenge to the engineers who design landing spacecraft, but Mercury's intense radiation and huge temperature swings may produce an even larger challenge. To date there has been no attempted landing on Mercury.

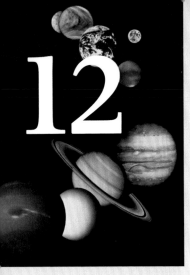

Missions
to Mercury

Space missions largely drive planetary science. While images and data provide ways to answer questions about planets, they also stimulate further questions about the planets, entice scientists into studying those planets, and create further interest and research. New ideas spring from data returned by each mission. For Mercury, information was sparse until the MESSENGER mission. Most of what is known came from the Mariner 10 mission in the mid-1970s, and little had been added to it. Earth-based telescopes cannot see Mercury well because of its closeness to the Sun.

Scientists have made theoretical models of Mercury's formation and current state, but models are unsatisfying unless there is mission data against which to check their predictions. In the space community, this is called "ground truth." The missions to the Moon showed how far off scientists' models could be from ground truth; some prominent and reputable scientists thought the surface of the Moon would be a sea of dust so fine and light that the landers would sink into it, never to be seen again. Fortunately this model proved to be far from ground truth for the Moon.

MESSENGER's data has already changed our view of Mercury. Its interior structure and dynamics are a particular focus, since the planet has a magnetic field but apparently no volcanic activity. Studies of its sparse exosphere show that the surface of the planet is being blasted off, atom by atom, and blown away in the solar wind. Its surface appears to record events from the earliest evolution of the planets. As the mission continues, new hypotheses will be made to explain the data the mission collects, and this least studied and most enigmatic planet will begin to reveal its secrets.

Mariner 10 1973
American

Mariner 10 was the only mission to Mercury before the 21st century. *Mariner 10* was the seventh successful launch in the Mariner series, the first spacecraft to use the gravitational pull of one planet (Venus) to reach another (Mercury), and the first mission to visit two planets. The other Mariner missions visited Venus, the closest planet to Earth and the most obvious space target after the Moon. Little *Mariner* measured only about 1 by 0.5 by 0.5 yards (~1 by 0.5 by 0.5 meters) and carried two large solar panels in addition to its scientific equipment. The spacecraft also carried the all-important parabolic antenna mounted on a boom, with which to send information back to Earth.

Various failures and errors in the spacecraft en route worried the mission scientists, though the measurements taken on the mission have been invaluable to science. The protective cover for an experiment to measure electrons emitted from the Sun did not fully open after launch, and so the instrument could not be used. The heaters for the television cameras failed, so the cameras were left on to prevent low temperatures from damaging the optics. *Mariner 10* used an instrument that locked onto background stars as part of its navigation system. Ten days after launch this star-tracker locked onto a shiny flake of paint that had come off the spacecraft and thus lost its lock on the guide star Canopus. An automated safety protocol recovered Canopus, but paint flakes continued to trouble the mission throughout its flight. These "bright particle distractions" increased to about 10 per week as the spacecraft approached Mercury.

Despite these problems, *Mariner 10* made three successive flybys of Mercury in 1973 and 1974, after a gravity-assist from Venus. The mission's scientific objectives were to measure characteristics of Mercury's atmosphere and surface and to make similar measurements for Venus. The mission also took measurements of the interplanetary medium. *Mariner 10* acquired the first high-resolution images of Mercury, taking 12,000 images covering about 45 percent of the planet's surface. The first feature that could be seen on the planet as *Mariner 10* approached turned out to be a bright, young crater, which was named Kuiper after the brilliant planetary scientist Gerard Kuiper who had died some months before. The mission discovered Caloris Basin, which is not resolvable from Earth, the scarps on Mercury's surface, and the chaotic terrain antipodal to the giant Caloris Basin. *Mariner* revealed that Mercury has a magnetic field and a very thin atmosphere.

MESSENGER 2004
United States

MESSENGER, a NASA mission launched on August 3, 2004, is investigating Mercury's surface and geologic history, geochemistry, internal structure, and magnetic field. *MESSENGER* is an acronym for MErcury, Surface, Space ENvironment, GEochemistry, and Ranging. *MESSENGER* carries imaging systems, gamma-ray, neutron, and X-ray spectrometers for remote geochemical sensing, a magnetometer, a laser altimeter, an ultraviolet-visible-infrared spectrometer to detect atmospheric composition and map mineralogy on the surface, and a plasma spectrometer to measure particles in the magnetosphere. The mission took a complex and lengthy trip from Earth to Mercury, beginning with entering solar orbit, flying back by the Earth after a year in space, passing Venus twice, once in 2006 and once in 2007, and finally making its first flyby of Mercury in January 2008. The second Mercury flyby was October 2008, and the third September 2009. Finally, the craft will enter Mercury orbit in March 2011. *MESSENGER* will collect data from Mercury orbit for one Earth year. The mission will produce global compositional maps, global imaging maps at 250 m/pixel, topographic profiles, gravity and magnetic field measurements and models, and a measurement of volatiles in the permanently shadowed craters at the poles.

BepiColombo

BepiColombo, scheduled for launch in 2013, should reach Mercury in 2019. The mission consists of two orbiters: The *Mercury Planetary Orbiter* to be built by the European Space Agency, and the *Mercury Magnetospheric Orbiter,* to be built by the Japanese Space Agency. *BepiColombo* will make accurate measurements of the movement of the center of mass of Mercury (the point inside the planet that has equal amounts of mass in each radial direction from it). The movement of the center of mass of the planet is important because it records the forces on the planet from the Sun's gravity and, to a much lesser degree, the gravity fields of the other planets, but most interestingly because it records the relativistic influence of the Sun on Mercury. This was Einstein's prediction: that mass actually bends space around itself. This can only be observed when near very large masses. Mercury exhibits movements that are only attributable to the relativistic effects of the Sun, but BepiColombo will measure its movements with an accuracy several orders of magnitude better than previously possible. Its other mission objectives include observations of the origin and evolution of a planet close to its parent star, of its thin exosphere, its magnetic field, and polar deposits.

These two missions are the focus of huge hopes in the scientific community. Mercury is a difficult planet to reach and a difficult planet to observe, and as this section has demonstrated, there are many holes in mankind's knowledge of this nearest neighbor to the Sun. Mercury may appear on its surface like the Moon, but its strange interior composition and structure make it the anomaly among the terrestrial planets. Like all exceptions to the rule, understanding Mercury may help scientists understand planetary formation in ways that Venus, Earth, and Mars cannot.

PART FOUR

VENUS

Venus: Fast Facts about a Planet in Orbit

Venus, Earth's closest neighbor, sometimes shines brightly enough to cast shadows on Earth. The planet shines from the west after sunset and from the east after sunrise. The clear shining of the planet both in the morning and evening caused the ancient Greeks to believe for some time that the brilliance was caused by two separate heavenly objects, which they called Vesper (evening) and Phosphor (morning). The planet's brightness made it an obvious target for observations starting in the 17th century with the invention of the telescope, but its seemingly blank surface posed a conundrum for astronomers. Early astronomers were able to discern dark patches. Several, including Francesco Fontana, a Roman Italian architect and theorist who lived from 1668 to 1708, and Giovanni Cassini, the Genoan astronomer who lived from 1625 to 1712, created maps of Venus based on these dark and bright patches, which they labeled seas and continents.

Venus is covered with dense clouds that make direct photographic imaging in visible light, such as can be done of the Moon, impossible. Not until 1761 did anyone postulate that the planet had a thick atmosphere. At that time, Mikhail Lomonosov, a scientist at the St. Petersburg Observatory, saw an unusual refraction of sunlight from the planet. The figure

More than a decade of radar observations of Venus are compiled in this false-color map of its surface, centered at 180°E longitude. Colors are added to represent surface elevations. (JPL/NASA/Magellan/MIT/USGS)

on page 171 shows four views of Venus as seen by *Galileo* at distances of 1.4–2 million miles (2.24–3.2 million km). The top two images were taken four and five days after *Galileo*'s closest approach to the planet. The bottom two images were taken on day six, two hours apart. These violet light images show the dynamic cloud patterns and movements that always dominate the atmosphere of the planet. These clouds never part and are exceptionally dense, so the surface of the planet is never visible to the eye.

Seeing the surface of the planet requires radar imaging. The wavelengths of radar can pass through Venus's clouds and bounce off its surface. Characteristics of the surface change the waves when they bounce, so when they return to the spacecraft, its instruments can use the changes in the waves to make images of the surface (see the sidebar "Remote Sensing" on page 79 in chapter 5). A bright radar image is created by a higher percentage of the radar signal being bounced back to the detector, which can be caused by several things. The surface being examined may be at a higher altitude, so there is less atmosphere for the signal to pass through (though variations in altitude are slight on Venus, a difference of even a few kilometers can make a difference in reflection of up to 25 percent). The roughness of the surface also influences its reflectivity, as does the composition of the surface.

Venus is Earth's closest twin in terms of size, composition, and distance from the Sun (see the sidebar "Fundamental

Clouds on Venus taken by Galileo in violet light over three days show the dynamic atmospheric movements on the planet. (NASA/Galileo/JPL)

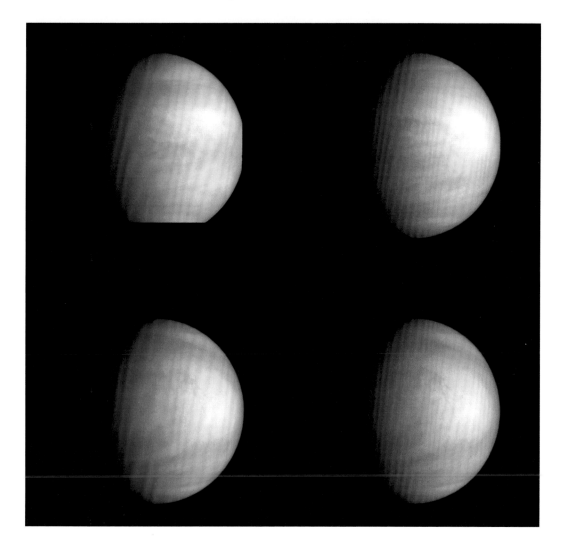

The complex surface of Venus, created by radar imaging, was created by a wide variety of volcanic and tectonic processes, as well as by impact cratering. The false color is based on photographs taken by the Soviet Venera 13 and 14 missions. (NASA/ Magellan/Pioneer/JPL)

Information about Venus" on page 174). Despite their similar beginnings, the planets have evolved into very different states, as already evidenced by Venus's thick atmosphere and strange surface features.

The figure above is a complete radar image of one side of Venus, showing its widely varied surface, which carries chasms, faults, craters, volcanoes, and enigmatic channels that may have been formed by swiftly flowing magma. The light colors in the radar image occur where the radar waves are reflected intensely, generally implying rough terrain. Smooth terrain remains dark. These tones, therefore, correspond to terrain types, and not to composition or anything relating to surface color as it would appear to human eyes.

Each planet and some other bodies in the solar system (the Sun and certain asteroids) have been given a symbol as a shorthand in scientific writing. The symbol for Venus is shown in the illustration on page 173.

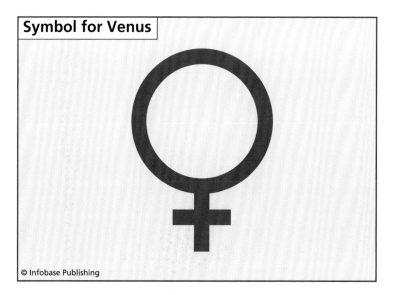

Symbol for Venus

© Infobase Publishing

Many solar system objects have simple symbols; this is the symbol for Venus.

Because Venus orbits between the Earth and the Sun, it displays phases when viewed from the Earth, similar to those of the Moon. When Venus is between the Earth and Sun it shows its unlit face to the Earth but only during the Earth's daytime, and so it is seldom seen. When Venus is opposite the Sun from the Earth, it is in full light when viewed from the Earth; between these stages Venus shows partially lit faces like the Moon's phases. Because Venus is always within 46° of the Sun when viewed from the Earth, it can only be seen in the morning and the evening.

Venus rotates on its axis in a retrograde sense, that is, in the opposite direction from the Earth's rotation. Venus's day length is therefore listed as a negative number in the table "Venus's Orbit," on page 176. On Venus, the Sun rises in the west and sets in the east. Its rotation, though, is unusually slow, and the planet completes a revolution around the Sun (a Venusian year) before it completes a rotation on its axis (a Venusian day). The simplest way to measure the rotational period of a planet is to watch surface features move across the disk of the planet. For three centuries astronomers attempted to measure Venus's rotational period this way. Confused by both thick clouds and retrograde rotation, attempts resulted in estimates from 23 hours to 225 days. Only the advent of radar observations in the late 1950s and 1960s made the measurement possible.

There are three main theories for Venus's retrograde rotation. The first two theories stand upon the idea that the planet's retrograde rotation is likely the result of its rotation axis being tipped almost 180° from the vertical. Venus almost certainly began rotating normally as a result of forming from the rotating planetary nebula, but because the planet has been almost completely tipped over, the planet appears to be rotating in the opposite direction. Some astronomers believe that high internal frication and turbulence in its atmosphere caused the planet to flip over; others believe that some cata-

FUNDAMENTAL INFORMATION ABOUT VENUS

Venus's radius is almost identical to the Earth's, being only about 5 percent shorter (see the table below. The slight discrepancy in radius means that its volume is about 12 percent less than the Earth's. Because Venus's density is comparable to the Earth's, but its volume is slightly less, its gravitational field is also slightly weaker. In all these respects, though, Venus is still the most similar to Earth of all the planets. Measuring a planet's mass is most easily done when the planet has a moon orbiting it. The speed and radius of the moon's orbit depends upon the mass of the planet it is orbiting. Venus has no moons and as a result its mass was not known with great accuracy until *Mariner 10* flew past it and experienced the planet's gravitational pull.

Though Venus closely resembles the Earth in its bulk physical characteristics, its rotational and orbital characteristics are entirely different, as are its surface conditions. Venus's exceptionally slow rotation also means that it experiences only weak forces from spinning and so has no discernible equatorial bulge. Unlike faster-spinning planets, Venus is virtually spherical. In addition to being virtually spherical as an overall shape, Venus also has little surface *relief* (differences in elevation, especially hills or mountains). Nearly 90 percent of the planet lies within six-tenths of a mile (1 km) of the average level.

strophic event such as a giant meteorite impact knocked the planet over.

A third theory has been proposed by French astronomers Alexandre Correia and Jacques Laskar of the CNRS Institute of Celestial Mechanics, who argue that chaotic effects could have reversed the planet's spin while its rotation axis remained stationary. These scientists created large computer models of planets with different atmospheric tides, gravitational forces, internal friction, and obliquities. For the rotation axis of Venus to flip, Correia and Laskar calculated that the planet's equator must once have had a high obliquity. Although this widely accepted idea is still possible, Correia and Laskar calculated

FUNDAMENTAL FACTS ABOUT VENUS

equatorial radius	3,760.4 miles (6,051.8 km), or 0.949 of the Earth's
ellipticity ([equatorial radius—polar radius]/polar radius)	0, meaning the planet is almost a perfect sphere, outside of surface features
volume	2.23×10^{11} cubic miles (9.284×10^{11} km³), 0.88 times Earth's volume
mass	1.07×10^{25} pounds (4.87×10^{24} kg), or 0.814 times Earth
average density	330 pounds per cubic feet (5,240 kg/m³), comparable to Earth
acceleration of gravity on the surface at the equator	29 feet per second squared (8.87 m/s²), 0.9 times Earth
magnetic field strength at the surface	about 2×10^{-9} Tesla, or 5×10^{-5} times the Earth's field
rings	0
moons	0

VENUS'S ORBIT	
rotation on its axis ("day")	–243 Earth days
rotation speed at equator	0.29 miles per second (0.47 km/s)
rotation direction	retrograde (clockwise when viewed from above the North Pole; opposite direction to Earth's spin)
sidereal period ("year")	224.7 days ("day" longer than "year")
orbital velocity (average)	21.75 miles per second (35.02 km/s)
sunlight travel time (average)	6 minutes and 1 second to reach Venus
average distance from the Sun	67,239,750 miles (108,208,930 km,) or 0.723 AU
perihelion	66,952,000 miles (107,476,000 km), or 0.718 AU from the Sun
aphelion	67,695,000 miles (108,942,000 km), or 0.728 AU from the Sun
orbital eccentricity	0.006773°
orbital inclination to the ecliptic	3.39°
obliquity (inclination of equator to orbit)	177.3° (because the rotation axis is within 3° of the vertical, Venus has no discernible seasons)

that chaotic behavior in the atmosphere of Venus could have slowed and then reversed the rotation of Venus without a high initial obliquity. Venus therefore may have flipped its rotation axis to produce its retrograde rotation, or its rotation may have slowed and reversed as a result of atmospheric turbulence. Together, Venus's slow retrograde rotation and its intense surface conditions cause the planet to differ significantly from the Earth despite their similar sizes, compositions, and distances from the Sun.

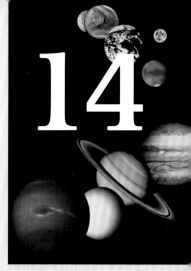

The Interior
of Venus

The brief lifetime of instruments on Venus's inhospitable surface means that few relevant measurements have been made that shed light on Venus's interior. Because Venus formed near the Earth in the solar nebula it is expected to have a similar bulk composition, but all other calculations of its internal structure and conditions need to be made from orbital data. The rocks on the surface of Venus are thought to be exclusively volcanic. The compositions of several surface rocks were measured by the *Venera 13, Venera 14,* and *Vega 2* mission craft and found to be strikingly similar to terrestrial basaltic volcanic lavas. Because the composition of a volcanic rock is directly dependent upon the material from which it melted, the similar compositions of Venusian volcanic rocks implies that Venus's mantle consists of a material similar to Earth's.

Venus's mantle (see the sidebar "Interior Structure of the Terrestrial Planets" on page 133 in chapter 10) is almost certainly made from the same iron- and magnesium-rich minerals that the Earth's is, since they almost certainly have similar bulk compositions and exist over a similar pressure range. The upper mantle of the planet is thought to reach from about 44 to 300 miles (70 to 480 km) in depth. The predominant mantle mineral is olivine ($(Mg, Fe)_2SiO_4$), *clinopyroxene* ($(Ca,Mg,Fe,Al)_2(Si,Al)_2O_6$), orthopyroxene ($(Mg, Fe)SiO_3$), and one of several minerals that contains alumina, which cannot fit into the other three minerals in any great amount. The aluminous minerals change according to pressure. At the shallowest depths and lowest pressures, the aluminous mineral is plagioclase. At greater depths, the plagioclase ($NaAlSi_3O_8$ to $CaAl_2Si_2O_8$) transforms into spinel ($MgAl_2O_4$), and then at greater depths, into the beautiful mineral *garnet* ($(Ca,Mg,Fe Mn)_3(Al,Fe,Cr,Ti)_2(SiO_4)3$).

Because of this mineralogy, the mantle is an exceptionally beautiful material: The olivine is a bright olive green, usually making up more than 50 percent of the rock, and the remainder are black orthopyroxenes, bottle-green clinopyroxenes, and brilliant ruby-colored garnets.

The more pressure placed on a material, the closer the atoms are forced together. Crystalline substances, like the minerals that make up rocks, are generally close to incompressible. The crystal lattices are stiff and are able to withstand large pressures without changing their shapes or allowing their atoms to press more closely together (though pressure may cause defects, such as empty spaces or offsets in the crystal lattice, to migrate through the crystal, creating the creep phenomenon that leads to the ability of the mantle to flow). Raising temperature along with pressure enhances the crystal's ability to change its properties. By raising temperature, the atoms in the crystal lattices vibrate faster and are more able to move out of position. As pressure and temperature are raised, the material eventually reaches a point where its current crystal structure is no longer stable, and it metamorphoses into a new, more compact crystal structure. The first such transformations in the mantle are in the aluminous phases, which transform from plagioclase to spinel to garnet with increasing pressure. These comprise only a small percentage of the mantle, though, and their transformations do not change the way *seismic waves* travel through Venus in any significant way. Olivine makes up the majority of the mantle, and when it transforms to a different crystal structure, the seismic properties of the mantle are significantly changed.

Within the upper mantle, as pressure increases with depth, olivine transforms to a higher-pressure phase called γ-olivine, and the pyroxene and garnet minerals transform into a garnet-like mineral with lower silica, called majorite. The big transformation occurs at higher pressure when γ-olivine transforms to perovskite. The pressures and temperatures for these transformations have been measured experimentally in high-pressure laboratory devices, so their positions in the Venusian mantle can be inferred. Below about 600 miles (1,000 km) in depth, the Venusian mantle probably consists of perovskite, which persists down to the core-mantle boundary. Based on information about the planet's overall mass and assumptions about its bulk compositions, scientists have calculated that Venus has an iron core about 1,863 miles (3,000 km) in radius, similar to Earth's.

Temperatures in Venus's interior are less well constrained. Clearly the mantle had to be hot enough to melt in the fairly recent past, since Venus's surface has fewer craters than would be expected for an old surface. Its surface has been covered by volcanic flows, obliterating the craters. On Earth, ongoing volcanism is caused by plate tectonics, but there is apparently no plate tectonic movement on Venus now. Venus is thought to be a one-plate planet, that is, its lithosphere forms a complete shell around the planet and moves little with respect to itself. Venus's craters are also distributed very evenly across the planet's surface, meaning that there is no part of its surface significantly older or younger than any other. There is no other body in the solar system with a completely even distribution of craters, implying a surface with a single age. While Venus's crust can be seen in radar and has been measured by spacecraft, the depth of the planet's stiff lithosphere is a matter of great debate. The lithosphere consists of the brittle crust and the coolest portions of the upper mantle. Some researchers believe that the lithosphere is thin, perhaps 19–113 miles (30–182 km) thick, while others believe it may be as much as 180 miles (300 km) thick. The thickness of the lithosphere has a great effect on the ability of the planet to transfer heat from its interior to its surface, and so the lithospheric thickness will constrain the temperature and amount of movement in the planet's interior.

Venus is also large enough that it must still retain some heat from its formation (a smaller planet would have radiated the heat into space by now), and it also has internal heat sources in the form of radioactive elements. This heat necessarily lowers the viscosity of the mantle and may allow it to flow (see the following sidebar "Rheology, or How Solids Can Flow" on page 181). While the Earth loses its internal heat through processes of plate tectonics, Venus may lose it primarily through volcanism. If portions of deep, hot mantle begin to flow upward, they may form rising plumes that melt as they reach lower pressures. This can be a source of volcanism. Rising distinct plumes may form some of the curious surface features discussed in the next section, in particular, the large semicircular features known as coronae.

A close inspection of volcanic features on Venus has lead some researchers to believe that volcanic resurfacing of Venus has been periodic. Heat may build up in the interior for a period of time, and then at some threshold, volcanism may commence. Don Turcotte, a professor of earth science at Cornell University, suggested in the mid-1990s that when heat builds up sufficiently inside the static shell of Venus's lithosphere, the entire lithosphere breaks up and sinks into the Venusian interior, to be replaced with a fresh volcanic crust. Marc Parmentier and Paul Hess of Brown University have a similar theory. This catastrophic method for resurfacing Venus was initially shocking to the geologic community, which inherently prefers gradual change to models that require sudden disturbances. Dan McKenzie, Royal Society Professor of Earth Sciences at the University of Cambridge, disagrees with the catastrophic model. He suggests that Venus has a thin lithosphere and that heat escapes continuously, more in the way it does on Earth. These entirely opposing theories probably can not be reconciled without further missions to the planet.

Venus's exceptionally weak magnetic field also has implications for heat loss from the planet and for internal temperatures.

RHEOLOGY, OR HOW SOLIDS CAN FLOW

Rheology is the study of how materials deform, and the word is also used to describe the behavior of a specific material, as in "the rheology of ice on Ganymede." Both ice and rock, though they are solids, behave like liquids over long periods of time when they are warm or under pressure. They can both flow without melting, following the same laws of motion that govern fluid flow of liquids or gases, though the timescale is much longer. The key to solid flow is viscosity, the material's resistance to flowing.

Water has a very low viscosity: It takes no time at all to flow under the pull of gravity, as it does in sinks and streams and so on. Air has lower viscosity still. The viscosities of honey and molasses are higher. The higher the viscosity, the slower the flow. Obviously, the viscosities of ice and rock are much higher than those of water and molasses, and so it takes these materials far longer to flow. The viscosity of water at room temperature is about 0.001 Pas (pascal seconds), and the viscosity of honey is about 1,900 Pas. By comparison, the viscosity of window glass at room temperature is about 10^{27} Pas, the viscosity of warm rocks in the Earth's upper mantle is about 10^{19} Pas.

The viscosity of fluids can be measured easily in a laboratory. The liquid being measured is put in a container, and a plate is placed on its surface. The liquid sticks to the bottom of the plate, and when the plate is moved, the liquid is sheared (pulled to the side). Viscosity is literally the relationship between shear stress σ and the rate of deformation ε. Shear stress is pressure in the plane of a surface of the material, like pulling a spatula across the top brownie batter.

$$\eta = \frac{\sigma}{\varepsilon}.$$

The higher the shear stress needed to cause the liquid to deform (flow), the higher the viscosity of the liquid.

The viscosity of different materials changes according to temperature, pressure, and sometimes shear stress. The viscosity of water is lowered by temperature and raised by pressure, but shear stress does not affect it. Honey has a similar viscosity relation with temperature: The hotter the honey, the lower its viscosity. Honey is 200 times less viscous at 160°F (70°C) than it is at 57°F (14°C). For glass, imagine its behavior at the glasshouse. Glass is technically a liquid even at room temperature, because its molecules are not organized into crystals. The flowing glass the glassblower works with is

(continues)

(continued)

simply the result of high temperatures creating low viscosity. In rock-forming minerals, temperature drastically lowers viscosity, pressure raises it moderately, and shear stress lowers it, as shown in the accompanying figure.

Latex house paint is a good example of a material with shear-stress dependent viscosity. When painting it on with the brush, the brush applies shear stress to the paint,

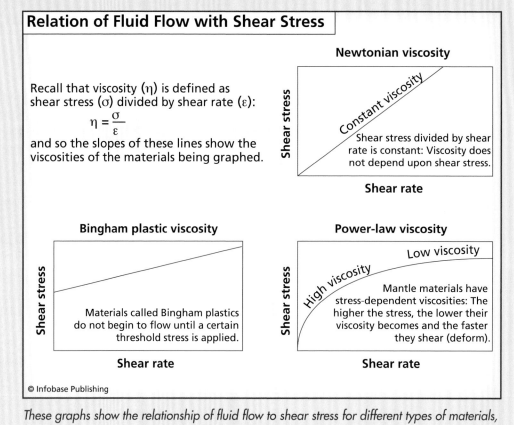

Relation of Fluid Flow with Shear Stress

Recall that viscosity (η) is defined as shear stress (σ) divided by shear rate (ε):

$$\eta = \frac{\sigma}{\varepsilon}$$

and so the slopes of these lines show the viscosities of the materials being graphed.

Newtonian viscosity

Constant viscosity

Shear stress divided by shear rate is constant: Viscosity does not depend upon shear stress.

Bingham plastic viscosity

Materials called Bingham plastics do not begin to flow until a certain threshold stress is applied.

Power-law viscosity

Low viscosity

High viscosity

Mantle materials have stress-dependent viscosities: The higher the stress, the lower their viscosity becomes and the faster they shear (deform).

© Infobase Publishing

These graphs show the relationship of fluid flow to shear stress for different types of materials, showing how viscosity can change in the material with increased shear stress.

Venus's magnetic field is only about $2 = 10^{-9}$ Tesla, or $5 = 10^{-5}$ times the Earth's. To make a magnetic field, the planet's liquid outer core needs to be convecting rapidly and twisting as the planet rotates. Venus is likely to have a liquid outer core, but its predicted dynamo field is 100 times larger than what and its viscosity goes down. This allows the paint to be brushed on evenly. As soon as the shear stress is removed, the paint becomes more viscous and resists dripping. This is a material property that the paint companies purposefully give the paint to make it perform better. Materials that flow more easily when under shear stress but then return to a high viscosity when undisturbed are called thixotropic. Some strange materials, called dilatent materials, actually obtain higher viscosity when placed under shear stress. The most common example of a dilatent material is a mixture of cornstarch and water. This mixture can be poured like a fluid and will flow slowly when left alone, but when pressed it immediately becomes hard, stops flowing, and cracks in a brittle manner. The viscosities of other materials do not change with stress: Their shear rate (flow rate) increases exactly with shear stress, maintaining a constant viscosity.

Temperature is by far the most important control on viscosity. Inside the Earth's upper mantle, where temperatures vary from about 2,000°F (1,100°C) to 2,500°F (1,400°C), the solid rocks are as much as 10 or 20 orders of magnitude less viscous than they are at room temperature. They are still solid, crystalline materials, but given enough time, they can flow like a thick liquid. The mantle flows for a number of reasons. Heating in the planet's interior makes warmer pieces of mantle move upward buoyantly, and parts that have cooled near the surface are denser and sink. The plates are also moving over the surface of the planet, dragging the upper mantle with them (this exerts shear stress on the upper mantle). The mantle flows in response to these and other forces at the rate of about one to four inches per year (2 to 10 cm per year).

Rocks on the planet's surface are much too cold to flow. If placed under pressure, cold, brittle surface rocks will fracture, not flow. Ice and hot rocks can flow because of their viscosities. Fluids flow by molecules sliding past each other, but the flow of solids is more complicated. The individual mineral grains in the mantle may flow by "dislocation creep," in which flaws in the crystals migrate across the crystals and effectively allow the crystal to deform or move slightly. This and other flow mechanisms for solids are called plastic deformations, since the crystals neither return to their original shape nor break.

is observed for the planet. Venus may have no solid inner core, if it is still much hotter than the Earth, and without the solid inner core no magnetic field is created. Perhaps Venus's slow rotation is insufficient to create a field, or perhaps so little heat is escaping from the planet that the outer core is not convecting. Despite the strong pieces of evidence about the internal conditions of Venus (the recent volcanic resurfacing and the lack of a magnetic field), no clear picture of its dynamic processes has emerged. If the thickness of its lithosphere were known, then the patterns and timing of volcanic resurfacing might be constrained. If new missions to Venus were able to measure the heat flow out of the planet, then both mantle and core dynamics would be better described. Barring future missions to the planet, its interior processes will remain a mystery.

Surface Conditions, Landforms, and Processes on Venus

Venus is always closer to the Sun than is the Earth, and so it receives more radiation from the Sun than does the Earth. Far less of that heat reaches the surface directly, though, because of the planet's thick atmosphere. Only 3 percent of the energy reaches the surface, while 70 percent of the energy is absorbed between about 40 and 50 miles (60 and 80 km) altitude, above the cloud layer, and the remaining energy is absorbed in and beneath the cloud layer. The hot atmosphere creates a hot planet surface. This process is known as the greenhouse effect, in which the Sun's energy is trapped within the atmosphere rather than reflected or radiated back into space.

The planet's hot surface is highly inhospitable to life, but radar images taken through the clouds show landforms similar to those on Earth and other planets. Though the planet's surface has little vertical relief, Venus has impact craters, mountains, plateaus, chasms, and volcanoes. In addition to the familiar features, it also has giant semicircular features called coronae, sometimes filled with volcanoes and always ringed with faults and scarps. These features may be the result of hot mantle plumes rising from the interior or of cool mantle drips sinking off the bottom of the planetary lithosphere. In either case they are unique to this one-plate planet.

Venus's rocky surface is covered with volcanic rocks. If it could be seen by a human eye, it is thought it would appear reddish orange. The color is probably not due to oxidized iron and dust, as it is on Mars, but by sunlight altered in color by passage through Venus's atmosphere. Sunlight is highly scattered by the thick atmosphere and mostly reddish orange light reaches the surface.

ATMOSPHERE AND WEATHER

The existence of Venus's atmosphere was first determined in 1761 by Mikhail Lomonosov, a scientist at the St. Petersburg Observatory. He prepared to watch Venus pass in front of the Sun from the vantage of the Earth and saw a bright ring of refracted light form in front of the planet as it approached the Sun. This bright ring, which he called a "hair-thin luminescence," could only be explained by the presence of a thick atmosphere.

The first measurements of Venus's atmospheric temperature were made in 1923 and 1924 at the Mount Wilson and Lowell Observatories. Astronomers used infrared radiation emitted by Venus at wavelengths of nine to 13 microns (an interval that passes successfully through the Earth's atmosphere) to estimate temperature and concluded that the planet was −10°F to 27°F (−23°C to −3°C) on its night side and 116°F to 135°F (47°C to 57°C) on its day side. These measurements were severely limited by the narrow wavelength of measurement; any current values show that there is virtually no temperature variation between the day and night sides. The currently accepted average temperatures are −27°F (−33°C) on the night side and −36°F (−38°C) on the day side.

The steadiness of the temperatures at the top of Venus's atmosphere reflects the steadiness of temperatures at the planet's surface, though the values are significantly different. Until the mid-20th century, there was no way to measure conditions on the planet's surface, and two main theories predominated: Venus was either a warm and humid place like Earth around 300 million years ago, or the planet was covered with water oceans. Neither theory turned out to be accurate.

Though Venus rotates once every 243 Earth days, its atmosphere is driven by exceptionally high winds. At the surface there is almost no wind. The craft that measured surface wind speeds typically found less than about one mile per hour. Above the clouds, however, there is a high-speed "jet stream" that blows from west to east at about 190–250 miles per hour (300–400 km/h). This wind is fastest at the equator and slows toward the poles, often creating a distinctive pattern in the clouds. The pattern of circulation and reasons for its severity are not well explained.

As soon as measurements were made showing that Venus's atmosphere consisted largely of carbon dioxide (CO_2), scientists hypothesized that the planet's surface temperature was high due to retained heat through the greenhouse effect of the atmosphere. The main constituents of Venus's atmosphere are listed in the table below. Venus's average surface temperature is now known to be 855°F (457°C), far hotter even than Mercury despite its greater distance from the Sun. Greenhouse heating is thought to be responsible for 515°F (285°C) of heating. Venus receives twice the solar heat that the Earth does, but by comparison, Earth's greenhouse heating is only 58°F (31°C).

Along with the high temperatures, Venus's thick atmosphere creates high surface pressure. At the rock surface of the planet, the pressure is 90 atmospheres, 90 times the value on Earth. At 38 miles (60 km) height the temperature is 80°F (27°C), and the pressure is about five atmospheres. These values rise continuously to the planet's surface. At the surface only gentle winds exist, and no rain of any kind (all the acid rain is at higher altitudes in the atmosphere). Nonetheless, a visitor to Venus would be simultaneously roasted, crushed, and asphyxiated.

There are two main categories of theories for the formation of a planetary atmosphere: the accretion hypothesis, stating that the atmosphere came from gases trapped in the original accreting planetesimals that made up the planet, and the capture hypothesis, that the atmosphere came from early solar nebula, or from solar wind, or from comets that impacted the Earth after its formation. There are now better computer models for the formation of the planets, and they indicate that

ATMOSPHERIC CONSTITUENTS ON VENUS

Constituent	Chemical symbol	Fraction	Fraction on Earth	Fraction on Mars
carbon dioxide	CO_2	0.965	345 ppm	0.95
nitrogen	N_2	0.035	0.7808	0.027
hydrochloride	HCl	0.4 ppm	~0	~0
hydrofluoride	HF	0.01 ppm	~0	~0
hydrogen sulfide	H_2S	0.008	~0	~0
sulfur dioxide	SO_2	150 ppm	~0	~0
water	H_2O	100 ppm	0.3 to 0.04 ppm	300 ppm
argon	Ar	70 ppm	0.0093	0.016
carbon monoxide	CO	40 ppm	100 ppb	700 ppm
oxygen	O_2	[LT]20 ppm	0.2095	0.013
neon	Ne	5 ppm	18 ppm	2.5 ppm
krypton	Kr	4 ppm	1 ppm	0.3 ppm

(Note: ppm means parts per million; 1 ppm is equal to 0.000001 or 1×10^{-6}.)

within a few tens of millions of years after core formation the terrestrial planets should have been completely solid and should have formed an early crust. These formation models indicate that there was so much heat during accretion and solidification that there is a good chance that most of the volatiles (gases and liquids) were lost from the early planet into space. This weakens the accretion hypotheses for atmospheric formation.

At about 1 million years after its formation, the Sun probably went through a special stage of its evolution, called the T-Tauri stage. During the T-Tauri stage, the early star's contraction slows or ends, and a strong outflow of charged particles is released. It has long been thought that this outflow would have been strong enough to sweep away all the gaseous atmospheres of the inner solar system planets, and it had been thought that this is the compelling evidence that the inner planets had to obtain their gaseous atmospheres by later additions, such as from comets, or from later outgassing of their interiors. Recently, however, evidence from images of T-Tauri stars elsewhere in the solar system indicates that the T-Tauri stage may happen before significant planets have been formed and that the flux is strongest from the star's poles and not in its equatorial plane. Recent models and work on extinct isotopic systems indicate that the cores of the Earth, Mars, and the Moon all formed within about 15 million years of the beginning of the solar system, but even this early formation may have been long after the Sun's T-Tauri stage. Now, therefore, both the ages of formation of the planets and the direction of flux during the T-Tauri stage indicate that the evolution of the Sun may not have much influence on the formation or retention of atmospheres in the terrestrial planets.

Some researchers, like Kevin Zahnle at the NASA Ames Research Center, think that the early Earth was accreted from both rocky planetesimals and icy cometary matter. In this model, huge quantities of water were added to the early Earth, so much so that the vast amounts lost to space during the heat and atmospheric disruption of giant impacts, and the evaporation into space due to the large quantities of accretional heat still present in the early Earth, still left plenty of water to form oceans. Even if the Earth was accreted entirely from ordinary chondrite meteoritic material, it would have started with about one-tenth of a percent of water by weight (0.1 percent, the amount naturally existing in ordinary chondrites), and this is still two to four times as much water as the Earth is thought to have today (though the amount of water in oceans and in ice on the surface of the Earth is well known, the amount of water existing in trace amounts in deep minerals in the Earth's interior is not known).

Since Venus probably formed with about the same quantity of water as did the Earth, some explanation has to be sought for how it lost its water. Currently the scientific community believes that the water on Venus may have been lost from the atmosphere by dissociation by solar radiation: Strong solar radiation broke the water molecules and the hydrogen went into space while oxygen bonded with surface rocks. Venus today has a striking lack of hydrogen, supporting this hypothesis.

Venus's lack of water has tremendous implications for its surface conditions. Carbon dioxide, the main constituent in its atmosphere, creates its exceptionally high surface temperatures. The same quantity of carbon dioxide is present on the Earth, but on Earth it is bound into carbonate rocks (predominantly limestones) that are deposited in the oceans. If all the limestone on Earth were converted into gas in the atmosphere, then Earth would have the same stifling greenhouse heat that Venus has. Without oceans and with a highly acidic environment, Venus's carbon dioxide remains in its atmosphere.

The atmospheres on different planets have strikingly similar structures, caused by their temperature profiles. The lowest layer of the atmosphere begins at the planetary surface and is known as the *troposphere*. In the troposphere, temperature falls with increasing height above the planet. On Venus, the troposphere reaches from the surface to about 40 miles (70 km) in height. On some planets the atmospheric temperatures reach a sharp minimum at the top of the troposphere, but on Venus the available data indicate the temperature reach a broad minimum in a region called the stratomesosphere. The stratomesosphere extends to 81 miles (130 km), where the temperature reaches a minimum of about −99°F (−73°C). In the overlying region, known as the *thermosphere,* temperature rises slightly to about 260°F (130°C). This high temperature in the upper atmosphere is much less than the still-unexplained hot thermospheres and *exospheres* of the gas giant planets, where temperatures rise to as high as 34°F (530°C).

Venus's great atmospheric feature is concentrated clouds and rain of sulfuric acid (H_2SO_4) from 30 to 45 miles (50 to 70 km) altitude in a dense, continuous blanket completely covering the planet. A wide variety of exotic and toxic compounds, including arsenic sulfide, tin chloride, and mercury and lead compounds, are probably present in trace amounts in the sulfuric acid clouds. Above the clouds lies a haze to an altitude of about 50 miles (80 km). Between the altitudes of about 20 and 30 miles (30 and 50 km), there is a subcloud haze. Below about 20 miles (30 km) in the atmosphere, the temperature is too high, and the acids evaporate back into higher clouds. The lower atmosphere, then, is clear.

Though the lowermost and uppermost atmospheres on Venus are clear, the cloud layer is dense, complete, and permanent. Its thickness is indicated by a measurement called optical depth, which shows how opaque something is to radiation passing through it (see the following sidebar "Optical Depth" on page 192). Venus's clouds have an optical depth of 25. By comparison, most of the Earth's atmosphere (including clouds) have optical depths of 0.5 to 1.5.

An analysis of radiation from Venus at a range of frequencies from 1.385 to 22.46 GHz obtained by a giant Earth-based observatory called the Very Large Array allowed scientists in 2001 to make models of the composition and layering of the Venusian atmosphere (see Appendix 2, Light, Wavelength, and Radiation, and the sidebar "Remote Sensing," on page 79 in chapter 5). They found that the Venusian atmosphere contains 1–2.5 ppm of sulfuric acid (H_2SO_4) just below the cloud layer and 50 ppm of sulfur dioxide (SO_2) below the cloud layers. These measurements are much lower than the 180 ppm of sulfur dioxide measured by the *Pioneer* sounder probe when it visited Venus. This contradiction is probably not simply because of errors in measurement or data analysis, since both methods are precise and reliable. Similarly, in 1995 the *Hubble Space Telescope* took measurements that indicated only about 30 ppm of sulfur dioxide in Venus's atmosphere.

Some scientists think that this high variability is real and not an artifact of errors. These large variations in sulfur dioxide make some scientists suspect that volcanoes are active; they postulate that the sulfur dioxide content in Venus's atmosphere may rise from emissions of volcanic eruptions. Since Venus is thought by some to still be volcanically active, scientists are planning methods to measure volcanism there. By observing thermal emissions on Venus's night side, volcanic eruptions could be seen. Thermal emissions at a one micron wavelength from hot lava on the surface should go through the thick Venusian atmosphere without being absorbed or scattered and thus be visible on Earth. This is true, though, only for hot or large eruptions (a lava lake about a half mile [about 1 km] in diameter should be detectable if the lake is at least as hot as 2,280°F [1,250°C]; otherwise, the lake must be larger). Because lava cools rap-

OPTICAL DEPTH

Optical depth (usually denoted τ) gives a measure of how opaque a medium is to radiation passing through it. In the sense of planetary atmospheres, optical depth measures the degree to which atmospheric particles interact with light: Values of τ less than one mean very little sunlight is scattered by atmospheric particles or has its energy absorbed by them, and so light passes through the atmosphere to the planetary surface. Values of τ greater than one mean that much of the sunlight that strikes the planet's outer atmosphere is either absorbed or scattered by the atmosphere, and so does not reach the planet's surface. Values of τ greater than one for planets other than Earth also mean that it is hard for observers to see that planet's surface using an optical telescope.

Optical depth measurements use the variable z, meaning height above the planet's surface into its atmosphere. In the planetary sciences, τ is measured downward from the top of the atmosphere, and so τ increases as z decreases, so that at the planet's surface, τ is at its maximum, and z is zero. Each increment of τ is written as $d\tau$. This is differential notation, used in calculus, meaning an infinitesimal change in τ. The equation for optical depth also uses the variable κ (the Greek letter kappa) to stand for the opacity of the atmosphere, meaning the degree of light that can pass by the particular elemental makeup of the atmosphere. The Greek letter rho (ρ) stands for the density of the atmosphere, and dz, for infinitesimal change in z, height above the planet's surface.

$$d\tau = -\kappa\rho dz$$

Mathematical equations can be read just like English sentences. This one says, "Each tiny change in optical depth $(d\tau)$ can be calculated by multiplying its tiny change in height (dz) by the density of the atmosphere and its opacity, and then changing the sign of the result" (this sign change is just another way to say that optical depth τ increases as z decreases; they are opposite in sign).

idly, it will only be detectable for about one Earth day after its eruption—and only if it erupts on Venus's night side. This is less likely to happen than one might think, since Venus's day lasts about 122 Earth days. It has been estimated that only about 10 percent of volcanic eruptions on Venus could be detected in this way.

To measure the optical depth of the entire atmosphere, this equation can be used on each tiny increment of height (z) and the results summed (or calculus can be used to integrate the equation, creating a new equation that does all the summation in one step). Optical depth also helps explain why the Sun looks red at sunrise and sunset but white in the middle of the day. At sunrise and sunset the light from the Sun is passing horizontally through the atmosphere, and thus has the greatest distance to travel through the atmosphere to reach an observer's eyes. At midday the light from the Sun passes more or less straight from the top to the bottom of the atmosphere, which is a much shorter path through the atmosphere (and let us remember here that no one should ever look straight at the Sun, since the intensity of the light may damage their eyes).

Sunlight in the optical range consists of red, orange, yellow, green, blue, indigo, and violet light, in order from longest wavelength to shortest (for more information and explanations, see Appendix 2, Light, Wavelength, and Radiation). Light is scattered when it strikes something larger than itself, like a piece of dust, a huge molecule, or a drop of water, no matter how tiny, and bounces off in another direction. Violet light is the type most likely to be scattered in different directions as it passes through the atmosphere because of its short wavelength, thereby being shot away from the observer's line of sight and maybe even back into space. Red light is the least likely to be scattered, and therefore the most likely to pass through the longest distances of atmosphere on Earth and reach the observer's eye. This is why at sunset and sunrise the Sun appears red: Red light is the color most able to pass through the atmosphere and be seen. The more dust and water in the atmosphere, the more scattering occurs, so the more blue light is scattered away and the more red light comes through, the redder the Sun and sunset or sunrise appear.

SURFACE FEATURES

Venus's surface is well known through the radar altimetry data of the *Pioneer, Venera, Mariner,* and *Magellan* craft. Though Venus's surface is covered with interesting features, it has little relief. Ninety percent of the surface lies within six-tenths of a mile (1 km) of the average level of the surface, equivalent to a planetary radius of 3,782.2 miles (6,051.5 km). The total elevation range of the planet is only about eight miles (13 km), while on Earth the range is about 12 miles (20 km). Venus also has the longest channel found anywhere in the solar system, the Dali and Diana Chasma system, which is 4,588 miles (7,400 km) long and an average of 1.1 miles (1.8 km) wide. The Nile River on Earth is a close second at 4,184 miles (6,695 km) long, while the Grand Canyon is only 250 miles (400 km) long, and the great Vallis Marineris system on Mars is 2,400 miles (4,000 km) long.

All of the features on Venus are named after famous women and include lowland volcanic plains, faults, rolling uplands, and plateaus. The largest of the plateaus, Ishtar Terra and Aphrodite Terra, are on the scale of continents. The surface has relatively few impact craters and has apparently been

Images of Venus's surface are artificially colored according to surface elevations compiled from radar observations. Place-names are shown as approved by the International Astronomical Union. (JPL/NASA/Magellan/MIT/USGS)

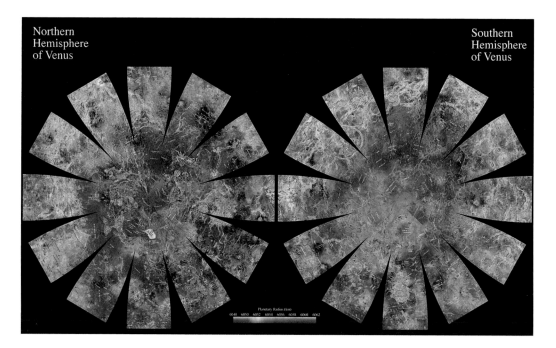

Northern Hemisphere of Venus

Southern Hemisphere of Venus

Planetary Radius (km)
6048 6050 6052 6054 6056 6058 6060 6062

Formation of a Graben

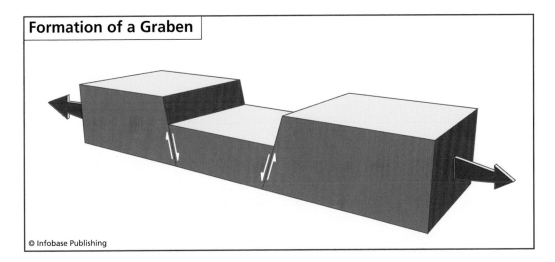

© Infobase Publishing

resurfaced by volcanic activity. Volcanoes on Venus come in several shapes and sizes, from small round domes to wide, shallow pancake-shaped mountains to the large round complex structures called coronae. Aside from the volcanic activity, Venus's thick atmosphere does serve to partially protect its surface from impacts; the thick atmosphere burns up small meteorites from friction and slows larger meteorites.

Careful assembly of a geologic map has allowed scientists to determine the order of geological events. Liz Rosenberg and George McGill, geologists at the University of Massachusetts at Amherst, assembled one for the vicinity of Pandrosos Dorsa. There they found *graben* cutting lava flows, so the lava flows had to have formed before the graben. Graben are long low areas formed by crustal extension. When the planet's crust is stretched, faults form that allow blocks to fall down relative to the original surface elevation, as shown in the figure above. Repeated graben in the American southwest form the Basin and Range region.

The complete sequence of geological events, pieced together by many scientists, is as follows: Belts of folds and fractures formed early in Venusian history, followed by tessera, then plains and shield volcanoes, then grabens, and then late belt fracturing. The tessera are areas with regular fracturing. (For more on names for planetary landforms, see the following sidebar "Fossa, Sulci, and Other Terms for Planetary Landforms" on page 196.)

(continues on page 199)

Graben, long, low areas bounded by faults, are formed by crustal extension.

FOSSA, SULCI, AND OTHER TERMS FOR PLANETARY LANDFORMS

On Earth the names for geological features often connote how they were formed and what they mean in terms of surface and planetary evolution. A caldera, for example, is a round depression formed by volcanic activity and generally encompassing volcanic vents. Though a round depression on another planet may remind a planetary geologist of a terrestrial caldera, it would be misleading to call that feature a caldera until its volcanic nature was proven. Images of other planets are not always clear and seldom include topography, so at times the details of the shape in question cannot be determined, making their definition even harder.

To avoid assigning causes to the shapes of landforms on other planets, scientists have resorted to creating a new series of names largely based on Latin, many of which are listed in the following table, that are used to describe planetary features. Some are used mainly on a single planet with unusual features, and others can be found throughout the solar system. Chaos terrain, for example, can be found on Mars, Mercury, and Jupiter's moon Europa. The Moon has a number of names for its exclusive use, including lacus, palus, rille, oceanus, and mare. New names for planetary objects must be submitted to and approved by the International Astronomical Union's (IAU) Working Group for Planetary System Nomenclature.

NOMENCLATURE FOR PLANETARY FEATURES

Feature	Description
astrum, astra	radial-patterned features on Venus
catena, catenae	chains of craters
chaos	distinctive area of broken terrain
chasma, chasmata	a deep, elongated, steep-sided valley or gorge
colles	small hills or knobs
corona, coronae	oval-shaped feature
crater, craters	a circular depression not necessarily created by impact
dorsum, dorsa	ridge

Feature	Description
facula, faculae	bright spot
fluctus	flow terrain
fossa, fossae	narrow, shallow, linear depression
labes	landslide
labyrinthus, labyrinthi	complex of intersecting valleys
lacus	small plain on the Moon; name means "lake"
lenticula, lenticulae	small dark spots on Europa (Latin for freckles); may be domes or pits
linea, lineae	a dark or bright elongate marking, may be curved or straight
macula, maculae	dark spot, may be irregular
mare, maria	large circular plain on the Moon; name means "sea"
mensa, mensae	a flat-topped hill with cliff-like edges
mons, montes	mountain
oceanus	a very large dark plain on the Moon; name means "ocean"
palus, paludes	small plain on the Moon; name means "swamp"
patera, paterae	an irregular crater
planitia, planitiae	low plain
planum, plana	plateau or high plain
reticulum, reticula	reticular (netlike) pattern on Venus
rille	narrow valley
rima, rimae	fissure on the Moon

(continues)

(continued)

NOMENCLATURE FOR PLANETARY FEATURES *(continued)*

Feature	Description
rupes	scarp
sinus	small rounded plain; name means "bay"
sulcus, sulci	subparallel furrows and ridges
terra, terrae	extensive land mass
tessera, tesserae	tile-like, polygonal terrain
tholus, tholi	small dome-shaped mountain or hill
undae	dunes
vallis, valles	valley
vastitas, vastitates	extensive plain

The IAU has designated categories of names from which to choose for each planetary body, and in some cases, for each type of feature on a given planetary body. On Mercury, craters are named for famous deceased artists of various stripes, while rupes are named for scientific expeditions. On Venus, craters larger than 12.4 miles (20 km) are named for famous women, and those smaller than 12.4 miles (20 km) are given common female first names. Colles are named for sea goddesses, dorsa are named for sky goddesses, fossae are named for goddesses of war, and fluctus are named for miscellaneous goddesses.

The gas giant planets do not have features permanent enough to merit a nomenclature of features, but some of their solid moons do. Io's features are named after characters from Dante's *Inferno*. Europa's features are named after characters from Celtic myth. Guidelines can become even more explicit: Features on the moon Mimas are named after people and places from Malory's *Le Morte d'Arthur* legends, Baines translation. A number of asteroids also have naming guidelines. Features on 253 Mathilde, for example, are named after the coalfields and basins of Earth.

(continued from page 195)

Craters

Venus's surface has about 1,000 craters, indicating that it was most recently resurfaced between 300 and 500 million years ago. Venus's surface is therefore one of the youngest in the solar system, along with the Earth and some active moons such as Io and Europa. While larger craters on Venus have a similar range of shapes to those on other planets, from bowl-shaped to complex, smaller craters are frequently irregular or complex. Venus's thick atmosphere affects the speed and integrity of bolides entering its atmosphere and creates a different range of sizes and shapes of craters than are found on other terrestrial planets. The odd shapes of smaller craters are interpreted as resulting from bolide breakup while passing through the thick atmosphere.

Complex craters account for about 96 percent of all craters on Venus with diameters larger than about nine miles (15 km).

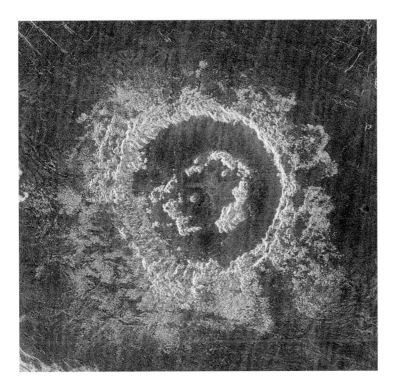

Barton crater, 31 miles (50 km) in diameter, is an excellent example of a complex crater on Venus. (NASA/Magellan/JPL)

Complex craters are thought to be formed by the impact of a large intact bolide with a speed that has not been strongly effected by its passage through the dense Venusian atmosphere. Complex craters are characterized by circular rims, terraced inner wall slopes, well-developed ejecta deposits, and flat floors with a central peak or peak ring. Barton crater (named after Clara Barton, founder of the Red Cross), shown in a radar image on page 199, is a good example of a complex crater. Barton crater has two rings and a central peak and is 31 miles (50 km) in diameter.

The largest known crater on Venus is Mead crater, 168 miles (280 km) in diameter. Mead is named for Margaret Mead, the American anthropologist who lived from 1901 to 1978. Mead is a good example of a complex crater, as shown in the radar image below. The crater shows multiple rings but no central peak. The peak may be obscured by the flat, radar-bright material filling the crater's center. This bright

Mead crater, at 168 miles (280 km) in diameter, is Venus's largest known crater. (NASA/Magellan)

filling may be melted surface material from the energy of the impactor, or it may be volcanic magma produced deeper in Venus from impact-related internal changes, which then erupted into the crater.

Irregular craters make up about 60 percent of the craters with diameters less than about nine miles (15 km). The second class of Venusian craters, irregular craters, are thought to form as the result of the impact of bolides that have been fragmented during their passage through the atmosphere. Irregular craters are characterized by irregular rims and hummocky or multiple floors. The dense atmosphere also slows smaller meteorites sufficiently so that they cannot produce craters when they strike the surface. There are virtually no impact craters smaller than two miles (3 km) on the surface of Venus.

Run-out flows from Howe, Danilova, and Aglaonice Craters on Venus may be caused by the high atmospheric pressure compressing parts of the impact clouds near the surface of the planet. (NASA/ Magellan/JPL)

Venus's very thick atmosphere also may be responsible for an unusual feature of its craters. Venus's craters commonly have distinctive flows out from their edges, different from craters on other planets. When an asteroid or meteorite strikes a planetary surface, the impact is immensely powerful and hot, and a plume of vaporized material, consisting of part of the planetary surface as well as the impacting body, expands rapidly upward, much like the blast from an explosion. On the Moon, Mars, or other bodies with thin atmospheres, the vapor cloud rapidly expands and becomes less dense. On Venus, the atmosphere may be so dense itself that it contains the vapor cloud, which then condenses and runs out of the crater along the ground, rather than rising into the Venusian atmosphere and dispersing. Both laboratory experiments and computer modeling suggest this may be the case, as their results match what is seen on Venus, but proving a theory like this is nearly impossible, unless high-speed photos could be taken of the process actually occurring on the planet.

Crater Riley on Venus (NASA/JPL)

Howe Crater, shown in the combined altimetry and radar image on page 201; is two miles (37 km) in diameter. Howe

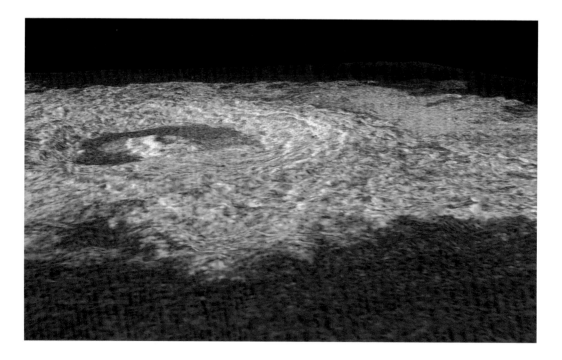

Crater is named for Julia Howe, the American biographer and poet. The crater in the background to the left of Howe is Danilova, 30 miles (48 km) in diameter and named for the Russian ballet dancer Maria Danilova. In the right background lies Aglaonice crater, named for an ancient Greek astronomer, with a diameter of 39 miles (63 km). All three of these craters show the run-out flows from their rims that are distinctive of craters on Venus.

Beneath and between Venus's scanty impact record stand immense floods of volcanism and a series of fascinating structural features, including numerous volcanoes, lava plains, and plateaus. Over them all are printed the effects of crustal compression and extension, in the form of faults and folds.

Faults and Folds

Venus's surface has ample evidence of strong crustal deformation in the form of linear faults and folds. In places the faults are aligned roughly in parallel; in other places they are randomly oriented into what is called chaos terrain; in still others, the fault sets intersect at angles and form patterns similar to a tiled floor. This final pattern, called tesserae, may form shapes from narrow diamonds to squares. The polygons in tesserated areas have diameters of a half to 15 miles (1 to 25 km), with an average of about 1.3 miles (2 km).

Tesserae regions are thought to be the oldest visible crust on Venus. They stand higher than the surrounding volcanic plains, as shown in the radar image on page 204, and comprise about 15 percent of the surface of Venus. The right-hand side of the image shows a large region of tesserae, while on the left a bright volcanic flow has approached the tessera across the plain. The age sequence in this image is therefore, from oldest to youngest, the bright, highly fractured tesserar highlands, the dark lowland volcanic seas, and the recent bright volcanic flow. This image was taken in the Eistla Regio in Venus's Northern Hemisphere, at about 1° south latitude and 37° east longitude.

Debra Buczkowski and George McGill, scientists at the University of Massachusetts at Amherst, have used detailed radar maps of Venus from the Magellan mission to more clearly understand these early Venusian features. By examining the

Tesserae (right) and a volcanic flow (left) are both clearly visible in this radar image of Venus's surface. Tesserae regions are thought to be some of the oldest crust on the planet, while the younger volcanic flows sweep onto them. (NASA/ Magellan/JPL)

patterns of radar reflection the linear crustal features can be identified as folds (which rise above the surrounding surface and indicate that the crust was compressed) or graben (which fall beneath the surrounding surface and indicate extension). In some regions, in particular around a volcano called Imini Mons, radial ridges surround the volcano and are superimposed on an earlier linear set of folds (called wrinkle ridges) along with a few graben. The researchers found that the pressure of magma in a chamber beneath the volcano, combined with a regional compressive state in the crust, is sufficient to create radial ridges around the volcano in addition to the regional linear sets. Using computer models such as these based on careful examination of regional geological radar images, scientists can actually recreate some of the tectonic settings of the planet's distant past.

Plateaus and Mountains

Venus has two giant plateaus, similar in size to terrestrial continents: the Aphrodite Terra and the Ishtar Terra. The Ishtar Terra is the largest of Venus's plateaus. At 3,200 miles (5,000 km) wide Ishtar Terra is larger than the continental United States. The plateau is surrounded by steep flanks and mountain ranges, and the western half of Ishtar Terra is an unusually smooth and even area named the Lakshmi Planum. The Lakshmi Planum itself is about the size of Tibet.

The four major mountain ranges of Venus—Maxwell Montes, Frejya Montes, Akna Montes, and Danu Montes—all surround the Lakshmi Planum. Maxwell Montes is on the east coast, Akna Montes on the west coast, Frejya Montes to the north, and Danu Montes in a portion of the south. The center of Ishtar Terra is split by the Maxwell Montes, mountains 7.5 miles (12 km) high. The Maxwell Montes are the highest mountains on Venus and 1.5 times as high as Mt. Everest on Earth.

The Lakshmi Planum shows bright and dark volcanic flows (radar brightness corresponds to surface roughness) and dark patches that are thought to be formed by impactors that break up in the atmosphere before forming craters. (NASA/Magellan/JPL)

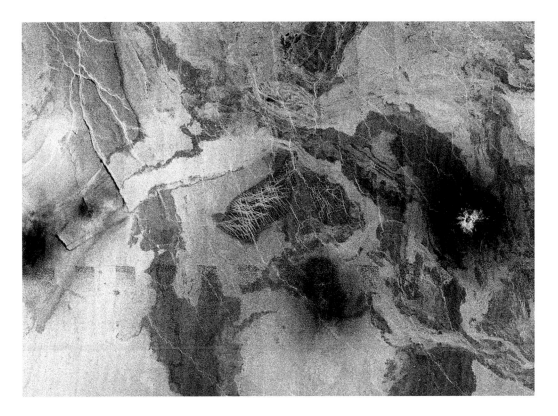

The *Magellan* image shown in the figure on page 205 is 180 miles (300 km) in width and 138 miles (230 km) in height and is centered at 55° north latitude, 348.5° longitude, in the eastern Lakshmi Planum. This part of the Lakshmi Planum is relatively flat and composed of many lava flows. On top of the lava flows are three dark splotches, created by impactors that broke up in the thick atmosphere before creating a crater.

The terrae on Venus are distinct and striking features that are intriguing to structural geologists. Though there are hypotheses for the formation of the large plateaus that involve large-scale mantle flow, there is no one leading idea.

Volcanoes

The surface of Venus displays more than 1,000 volcanic centers. There are about 170 large shield volcanoes similar to Hawaii on Earth, up to several hundred miles across and 2.5 miles (4 km) high. Many of the almost 1,000 smaller shield volcanoes appear in clusters. These smaller shield volcanoes appear in a number of unusual shapes. Some flat-topped, steep-sided circular shield volcanoes intermediate in size have been dubbed "pancake domes." Other shield volcanoes of intermediate size have radiating faults that resemble the legs on an insect, leading to their being informally called "ticks."

Together the activity of these many volcanoes have produced more than 200 large flow fields, areas completely covered with multiple lava flows. Widespread volcanism resurfaced the planet and is thought to have ended 300–500 million years ago. So much resurfacing occurred that most of the planet's impact craters were buried, and now the planet has fewer than 1,000 craters on its surface.

Volcanic plains make up about 80 percent of Venus's surface. An example of the flat, featureless resurfaced volcanic plains is shown in the *Magellan* radar image on page 207. A small grouping of volcanoes on the left create a shield volcano. Scalloped dome volcanoes appear on the right; the scalloped look arises from faulting around the edges of the volcano. The farthest right feature is a volcanic caldera. The image area is 303 by 193 miles (489 by 311 km).

Many of the small shield volcanoes have ridges both beneath them and cutting through their shields. The shields form a thin, widespread veneer. Analyses of data from *Venera 9* and *10* and *Vega 1* and *2* landing sites indicate that the shield plains with wrinkle ridges probably consist of tholeiitic lava, the same kind of dark, easily flowing lava that is erupted at Hawaii on Earth. Because the volcanic lava on Venus apparently flowed so easily, some scientists think it contained water, which reduces the viscosity of lava. There may be a water-bearing mineral shallow in Venus's lithosphere that melts easily, erupting low-viscosity melts across Venus's surface. The lava could have contained little silica and much calcium carbonate, a combination that produces a lava that flows easily at

Venus's lava plains are flat and among the youngest surface features on the planet. Centered on 10°N latitude, 301°E longitude, this image shows in its center small bright bumps that are a clustering of volcanoes called a shield field. On the right is a scalloped dome volcano, about 16 miles (25 km) in diameter. The lobe-shaped patterns around this volcano may be lava flows or debris flows. Further still to the right is a volcanic caldera, a crater formed when an emptied lava chamber collapses downward and inward. (NASA/Magellan/JPL)

the high surface temperatures of the planet. Maat Mons is the largest volcano on Venus and stands five miles (8 km) above surroundings. The volcano has dark flows to its east, probably representing low-viscosity lava that cooled with a smooth surface. Other flows from the volcano are bright, probably indicating a rough flow that reflects radar well. The differences in reflectivity may represent different magma compositions, an important clue to internal processes in Venus.

Photos from the surface of Venus taken by *Venera 14* show many thin horizontal layers of rock near the landing site. Each layer is only a couple of inches in thickness. Though some scientists have suggested these may be sedimentary layers, perhaps a more likely possibility is that the layers are volcanic tuffs. Tuffs are consolidated layers of volcanic ash, laid down by air falls. Along with the compositional data on the lava flows sent back by Venus landers, these thin volcanic layers show that volcanic activity on Venus is similar to that on the Earth, though apparently more voluminous.

Venus is probably still volcanically active, and some scientists regularly search for radar data that show hot fresh volcanic flows on the planet. Whether Venus's surface is resurfaced continuously or periodically, humankind has a chance to see active volcanism on a planet other than Earth.

Coronae and Arachnoids

Coronae are large, roughly circular features, some with domes in their centers and some with depressed features like calderas. They were first recognized by Soviet radar images from early missions, a great accomplishment considering the technology available. Coronae all have roughly circular rims, sometimes in series, and sometimes accompanied by domes, plateaus, depressions, moats, chasms, or volcanic flows. Arachnoids are also complex combinations of faulting and volcanism. They are smaller than coronae, at 30–140 miles (50–230 km) in diameter, with a central volcanic feature surrounded by a complex network of fractures. There are about 210 coronae and 270 arachnoids in total on Venus.

The combinations of faulting and volcanism differ among coronae. Quetzalpetlatl is among the largest of the coronae, with a diameter of 500 miles (800 km). There appears to have been abundant volcanism at the site, and the formation has a moat and a rim at its edge. Another corona, Heng-O, has a diameter of 680 miles (1,100 km) and outer rim heights of 0.25–1 mile (0.4–1.6 km) but no recent volcanic activity.

Artemis, by far the largest corona, has a diameter of 1,615 miles (2,600 km), large enough to reach from Colorado to California, were it on Earth. Artemis contains complex systems of fractures, numerous flows and small volcanoes, and at least two impact craters, the larger of which is located in the lower left (southwest) quadrant of the feature as shown in the radar image below. The fractures that define the edge of Artemis, called Artemis Chasma, form steep troughs with raised rims approximately 75 miles (120 km) wide and with as much as 1.6 miles (2.5 km) of relief from the rim crest to the bottom of the trough. Lava plains are tilted away in all directions. The stripes in the image are simply missing data. The coronae

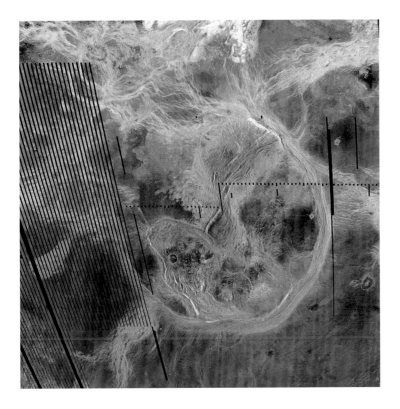

Artemis is by far Venus's largest corona, consisting of a complex system of faults and volcanic features 1,615 miles (2,500 km) in diameter. (NASA/Magellan/JPL)

appear to have started to form long before the regional plains and to have continued long after.

The image on page 211 shows two coronae, the Bahet and Onateh. This large image is a mosaic taken around 49° north latitude and 2° east longitude. Bahet, on the left, is 138 by 90 miles (230 by 150 km). Onateh is larger, at about 210 miles (350 km) in diameter. This large image was taken with a resolution of 400 feet (120 m) per pixel, allowing detailed examination of the surface. Each corona is surrounded by rings of troughs and ridges.

There are a number of theories for the formation of coronae. The original theories postulated that a hot, rising plume of mantle material from inside Venus rose and pushed against the bottom of Venus's lithosphere (see the sidebar "Interior Structure of the Terrestrial Planets" on page 133 in chapter 10). A hot, buoyant plume would push up on the lithosphere, causing it to rise in a dome. When the plume subsides, the dome will subside, but the surface will show radial fractures and ring-shaped ridges, typical of the coronae seen on Venus.

Other studies using computer-based numerical modeling by Sue Smrekar, Ellen Stofan, and Trudi Hoogenboom, scientists at the Jet Propulsion Laboratory, and Gregory Houseman, a scientist at the University of Leeds, have shown that these features can be made by a process called gravitational instability. In this scenario, the lower lithosphere drips from the upper lithosphere and crust and sinks into the Venusian mantle. During the dripping and sinking process, the surface of the planet is first pulled down (causing radial fractures) and then relaxes back to close to its original height, causing ring-shaped ridges. These researchers have been able to reproduce most of the complex and variable coronae topography by combinations of warm upwellings and the stresses of gravitational instability.

Channels

Channels are common on Venus's plains and are thought to be created by flowing lava. The extremely hot and caustic surface conditions of Venus make flowing water impossible, but they allow lava to remain heated and flow for much longer distances than it can on Earth. Normal silica-rich lava is an unlikely candidate, though, because of the extreme volumes and low viscosities required to form channels of such length. The composition of the fluid that carved Venus's channels remains a mystery.

In the image on page 212, the right-hand side is covered with a polygonal terrain, while running up the left side is a 370-mile (600-km) segment of the largest channel on Venus, the Dali and Diana Chasma system. The Dali and Diana Chasma system consist of deep troughs that extend for 4,588 miles (7,400 km). The Nile River, Earth's longest river, is 3,470 miles (5,584 km) from Lake Victoria to the Mediterranean Sea. Though much deeper than this channel on Venus, Valles Marineris on Mars is only 2,800 miles (4,200 km) long. The Dali and Diana Chasma system is therefore the longest channel in the solar system.

The image of Baltis Vallis on page 212 is 285 miles square (460 km square) and thus can show only a portion of this immense channel. The channel was initially discovered in data from the Soviet *Venera 15-16* orbiters, which detected more than 1,000 kilometers (620 miles) of the channel in spite

Bahet and Onateh coronae appear to be connected by a series of faults. Coronae are thought to be formed by some combination of rising mantle plumes and sinking lithospheric drips. (NASA/Magellan/JPL)

Polygonal terrain is crossed by a portion of the Baltis Vallis channel, believed to have been carved by a river of low-viscosity flowing lava. (NASA/Magellan/JPL)

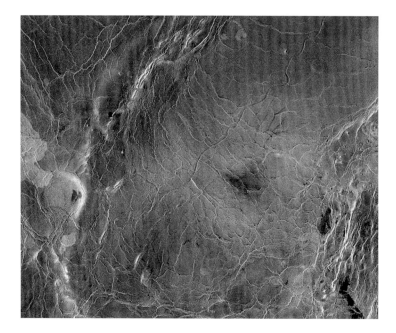

of their coarse one kilometer resolution. About 375 miles (600 km) of Baltis Vallis is visible here, beginning near the right side of the top edge of the image and winding diagonally toward the bottom left of the image. This image also shows a large region of polygonal terrain, where the surface of Venus has been broken into regular patterns by faulting.

A long, radar-dark sinuous channel that particularly resembles Earth water channels is shown in the *Magellan* image on page 213. The Venusian channels, however, are far less tightly sinuous than those on Earth, and the Venus channels are commonly associated with dark units that appear to be volcanic flows. Even this narrow, well-defined channel was almost certainly produced by flowing liquid lava.

Though Venus's thick and continuous cloud cover foiled for centuries the attempts of astronomers to see its surface, the development of radar in the 20th century made imaging Venus possible. Through the intense efforts of the Soviets (outlined in the next chapter) and the immensely successful Mariner and Magellan missions, almost the whole planet has now been mapped. Venus has a young volcanic surface and few impact craters. The planet carries an immense number of

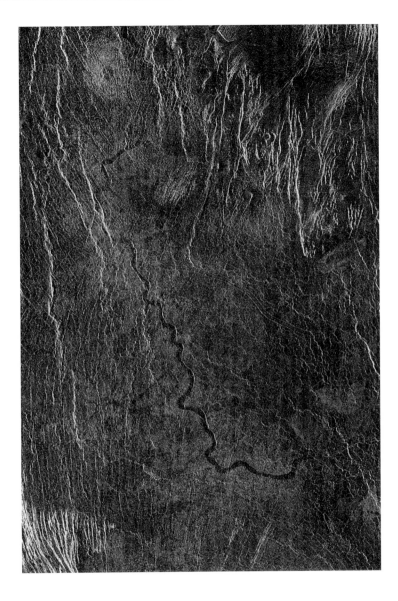

This dark Venusian channel shows the wide curves of a lava river rather than the tight bends of a water channel. (NASA/ Magellan/JPL)

volcanoes, perhaps more than the total on Earth, including those in oceanic plates. Though it has no plate tectonics, curious features called coronae may indicate patterns of mantle convection that have pulled down or pushed up the crust and created faulted volcanic provinces. Venus is almost certainly still volcanically active.

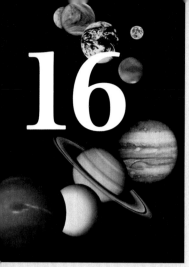

16

Missions to Venus

Both the United States and the Soviet Union have sent probes to Venus as listed in the following table. The major Soviet mission was named Venera (meaning Venus), and the American missions were named Mariner. There were many Venera missions, including seven that analyzed rock compositions. The Soviets suffered great disappointments in their Mars missions and had a crushing series of Venus mission failures. Eventually their Venusian missions, begun the year after their first attempt to reach Mars, were spectacularly successful and marked a series of firsts in space science. In general, intense pressure and hurricane-force winds destroy all probes within an hour, but in 1982 a *Venera* probe went to the surface and survived 127 minutes. Much of the information on Venus comes from the long and intense efforts of the Soviets, summarized in this table along with American missions. In addition to the missions in this table, *Cassini-Huygens* and *Galileo* flew past Venus and returned information on dust, magnetism, lower-atmosphere maps, and camera images. Some notable missions are written about in more detail in the table below.

PAST AND POSSIBLE FUTURE MISSIONS TO VENUS

Launch date	Mission craft	Country	Comments
February 4, 1961	Sputnik 7	USSR	The final rocket stage failed
February 12, 1961	Venera 1	USSR	Flyby; communication lost
July 22, 1962	Mariner 1	U.S.	Destroyed just after launch
August 25, 1962	Sputnik 19	USSR	Final rocket stage failed and craft reentered Earth's atmosphere
August 27, 1962	Mariner 2	U.S.	First successful flyby
September 1, 1962	Sputnik 20	USSR	Final rocket stage failed
September 12, 1962	Sputnik 21	USSR	Third rocket stage exploded shortly after liftoff
February 19, 1964	Venera 1964A	USSR	Rocket failed to reach Earth orbit
March 1, 1964	Venera 1964B	USSR	Rocket failed to reach Earth orbit
March 27, 1964	Cosmos 27	USSR	Final rocket stage failed
April 2, 1964	Zond 1	USSR	Communications lost on the way to Venus
November 12, 1965	Venera 2	USSR	Flyby, but communications lost before closest approach
November 16, 1965	Venera 3	USSR	Entry probe; first spacecraft to land on another planet, but no data returned
November 23, 1965	Venera 1965A	USSR	Attempted Venus flyby
June 12, 1967	Venera 4	USSR	Flyby with descent vehicle; first successful Venus probe
June 14, 1967	Mariner 5	U.S.	Flyby with descent vehicle
June 17, 1967	Cosmos 167	USSR	Final rocket stage failed
January 5, 1969	Venera 5	USSR	Flyby with descent vehicle

(continues)

PAST AND POSSIBLE FUTURE MISSIONS TO VENUS
(continued)

Launch date	Mission craft	Country	Comments
January 10, 1969	Venera 6	USSR	Flyby with descent vehicle
August 17, 1970	Venera 7	USSR	Flyby and soft lander; first mission to return data from the surface of another planet
August 22, 1970	Cosmos 359	USSR	Final rocket stage failed
March 27, 1972	Venera 8	USSR	Flyby and soft lander
March 31, 1972	Cosmos 482	USSR	Final rocket stage failed
November 3, 1973	Mariner 10	U.S.	Flyby and soft lander
June 8, 1975	Venera 9	USSR	Flyby and soft lander; returned first photograph of the surface of another planet
June 14, 1975	Venera 10	USSR	Orbiter and lander pair
May 20, 1978	Pioneer Venus Orbiter (Pioneer Venus 1)	U.S.	Satellite and soft lander
August 8, 1978	Pioneer Venus bus and probes (Pioneer Venus 2)	U.S.	Orbiter and four probes
September 9, 1978	Venera 11	USSR	Flyby and lander
September 14, 1978	Venera 12	USSR	Flyby and lander
October 30, 1981	Venera 13	USSR	Flyby and lander; first color images of Venus
November 4, 1981	Venera 14	USSR	Flyby and lander
June 2, 1983	Venera 15	USSR	Orbiter; joint mission with Venera 16 lasted 8 months
June 7, 1983	Venera 16	USSR	Orbiter
December 15, 1984	Vega 1	USSR	Flyby and lander

Launch date	Mission craft	Country	Comments
December 21, 1984	Vega 2	USSR	Flyby and lander
May 4, 1989	Magellan	U.S.	Orbiter
August 3, 2004	MESSENGER	U.S.	Mercury mission that flew by Venus twice on its way to Mercury
November 9, 2005	Venus Express	E.S.A.	Venus orbiter

Venera 1 1961
Soviet

This first attempted flight to Venus lost communications after 14 days and passed within 62,000 miles (100,000 km) from the planet without communicating any data back to Earth.

Mariner 2 1962
American

This was the first spacecraft approach to another planet. *Mariner 2* confirmed the intensity of Venus's surface conditions, measuring surface temperatures as high as 800°F (428°C) and detected no magnetic field or water vapor in the atmosphere. It passed 21,581 miles (34,752 km) above the planet. Contact with the mission was lost on January 3, 1963.

Venera 4 1967
Soviet

This was the first mission to successfully send back information about the Venusian atmosphere. The craft dropped probes into the atmosphere before parachuting into the nighttime side of Venus and measured temperature, pressure, and density in the atmosphere up to a height of 16 miles (26 km). Data from the probe indicated that more than 90 percent of the Venusian atmosphere consists of carbon dioxide. Temperature and pressure increased steadily as the probe parachuted toward Venus's surface, until the temperature reached 503°F (262°C) and 18 atmospheres of pressure. The casing of the probe was designed to withstand pressure as high as 18 atmospheres and apparently the engineering was precise, since transmissions ceased at that point. Initially a misreading from the altimeter made scientists believe that the probe had reached the surface but measurements made the next day from the *Mariner 5* spacecraft indicated that the surface pressures and temperatures were far higher.

Venera 5 and Venera 6 1969
Soviet

Like *Venera 4, Venera 5* parachuted a probe into the Venusian atmosphere and obtained almost one hour's worth of measurements, until the probe failed at 10 miles (16 km) height. *Venera 6* also reached the surface using a parachute and returned 51 minutes of data. The *Venera 6* probe also failed before it reached the surface.

Venera 7 1970
Soviet

The *Venera 7* probe achieved the first controlled landing of a spacecraft on another planet. The probe was expected to take 60 minutes to reach the surface but took only 35 minutes; a harder than expected impact may have damaged the probe. For 23 minutes after landing on the night side the probe transmitted information, including compositional information about the atmosphere. The surface temperature was measured at 887°F (475°C).

Venera 8 1972
Soviet

Venera 8 made the first soft landing on the day side of Venus. The temperature was measured at 880°F (470°C), and measurements of wind velocity, surface radioactivity, and pressure were also made. The probe transmitted data for 50 minutes and measured the light intensity on the surface in preparation for the surface photographs returned by the next four Venera missions.

Mariner 10 1974
American

Mariner 10 took the first close-up photos of Venus. It passed within 3,580 miles (5,760 km) of the surface and took 3,000 photographs, including the first of spiral clouds. The craft transmitted television images of Venus's clouds in the infrared spectrum. *Mariner 10* went on to be the first probe to pass Mercury, on March 29, 1974, taking 2,300 photographs covering 40 percent of the planet's surface.

Venera 9 1975
Soviet

Venera 9 took the first pictures of Venus's surface and made the first measurements of the structure and physical properties of the clouds. The lander also took measurements of the surface rocks, the gravitational field, and wind speed.

Pioneer Venus 1 1978
American

Pioneer Venus 1 was an orbiter, carrying 17 experiments, including the first radar, ultraviolet, and infrared observations. Its highly elliptical orbit brought it within 120 miles (200 km) of the planet's surface. *Pioneer Venus 1* orbited the planet until August 1992, when it fell into and burned up in Venus's atmosphere.

Magellan 1989
American

During its five-year mission *Magellan* mapped 99 percent of Venus's surface with radar, down to objects 390 feet (120 m) across, and crashed into the planet for a final bout of data collection. The mission lasted from its August 10, 1990, Venus orbital insertion until October 12, 1994, when its signal was lost.

MESSENGER 2004
American

Though *MESSENGER* is primarily a mission to Mercury, it flew by Venus twice, once in October 2006 and again in June 2007. The two flybys were at 1,859 miles (2,992 km) and 210 miles (338 km) respectively and sent back valuable color images to Earth.

Venus Express 2005
European Space Agency

This European Space Agency Venus orbiter launched in November 2005 on a Soyuz-Fregat booster from the Baikonur Cosmodrome in Kazakhstan. The mission is based on the *Mars Express* craft plan. After 153 days in transit, the craft entered an orbit that took it over the poles of the planet and collected data to help scientists understand the extreme wind speeds on the planet, as well as other questions concerning the atmosphere and its circulation. The primary mission lasted 500 Earth days (2 Venusian days), and its success and the robustness of the craft have allowed it to pursue two extended missions, operating the spacecraft until 2012.

Planet-C (Venus Climate Orbiter)

This Japanese Space Agency mission is scheduled for launch in May 2010. Like *Venus Express, Planet-C* will be an orbiter and will look for evidence of volcanic activity and lightning.

BepiColombo

Though primarily planned as a Mercury orbiter and lander, this European Space Agency mission may fly by Venus.

The great efforts made by the Soviets and also by the Americans to reach and make measurements on Venus have produced an invaluable data set, including almost complete radar mapping of the surface, atmospheric composition, structure, and dynamics, and surface compositions and conditions. As with all planetary data sets, far more questions have been created in the wake of the few that have been answered. As space missions to Mars and the Moon have continued, and *MESSENGER* has sent so much information back about Mercury, our understanding of Venus is again lagging behind the other planets. Increased interest in Venus missions by NASA may mean more orbiters and probes in the next 10 years.

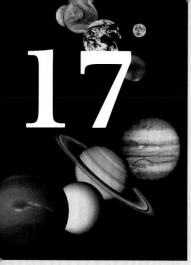

Conclusions: The Known and the Unknown

The three bodies covered in this book, the Sun, Mercury, and Venus, could hardly be more different despite their proximity in the solar system. Each is the subject of great study at the present time, and each has posed its own special problems for observing and for spacecraft. The Sun, of course, has the dual challenge of its great gravity and its intense heat and radiation. No craft can approach closely. Mercury shares those dangers because of its own proximity to the Sun: Spacecraft that visit Mercury have to avoid being pulled into the Sun and have to be prepared for the intense radiative environment. Venus, on the other hand, is covered with dense clouds of acid and has a crushing surface pressure. Though the planets Mercury and Venus are among Earth's closest neighbors and might teach scientists the most about how the Earth itself formed, the challenges of learning about Mercury and Venus have made Mars a more enticing target. Some of the largest outstanding questions about the Sun, Mercury, and Venus are listed here.

1. **Why does the Sun become hotter the farther above the radiative zone one goes?**
   Temperatures in most planets become cooler and cooler with distance from the core. Most planets retain heat in

their interiors both from the initial heat of formation of the solar system and from decay of radioactive elements. Surely the Sun should have a similar structure, with its intense inner heat caused by its own nuclear reactions. In the deep parts of the Sun, the material does cool with distance from the core: Though the temperature at the top of the radiative zone is still in the millions of degrees, by the time material reaches the edge of the convective zone, the temperature has fallen to about 11,000°F (6,000°C).

Above the convective zone lies the photosphere, only 310 miles (500 km) thick, but with a steady average temperature of 9,900°F (5,500°C). From this low, temperatures then begin to rise through the chromosphere. In the top 300 miles (500 km) of the chromosphere, the temperature rises to 36,000°F (20,000°C). Above the chromosphere, temperatures in the transition zone are even more extreme. The transition zone is just tens of kilometers thick, but its temperature rises from 36,000°F (20,000°C) on its inside edge to 3,600,000°F (2,000,000°C) at its outside edge. Above the transition zone, the bright loops of active regions in the corona can be as hot as 7,200,000°F (4,000,000°C), while huge, slow arches of quiet regions with weak fields are often only about 1,800,000°F (1,000,000°C).

In the distance from the photosphere, the layer of the Sun that is seen in visible light, to the thin, broad corona, the Sun's temperature has risen from 9,900°F (5,500°C) to 7,200,000°F (4,000,000°C), almost 1,000 times as hot. There is currently no clear physical theory for how this is possible. The magnetic field can transfer energy without transferring material, which may allow heat to be moved out to the diffuse corona without requiring dense material transfer. The exact mechanism for changing magnetic field energy back into heat is unknown, though there are several complex hypotheses.

2. **What is the Sun made of in detail? What can its composition tell us about the protoplanetary disk?**
   The Sun contains almost all the mass of the solar system. By examining the wavelengths given off by its photosphere

and other outer layers, estimates have been made of its composition. Knowing its composition is critical to making models for the formation of the solar system, since the Sun almost certainly represents the bulk composition of the material available to make the planets. Knowing in detail the composition of the interior layers of the Sun will allow more accurate models for solar system formation as well as for dynamics of the interior of the Sun.

3. **What are the mechanics of formation of the many dynamic solar features, and how do they relate to accelerated particles and radiation?**
   Structures on the Sun, mainly from the corona, but also from the chromosphere, appear to rise from and to themselves effect the Sun's magnetic field lines. The most violent of these structures, solar flares and coronal mass ejections, are associated with magnetic storms on Earth, blackouts, and damage to satellites because of the energetic particles that stream out into space from the structures themselves.

   Solar flares consisting of plasma can be for short periods of time the hottest material on the Sun, at tens of millions of degrees, containing electrons and protons accelerated almost to the speed of light. They are often accompanied by X-ray and gamma-ray bursts. The superheated, supersonic material in the flare is thrown into space. Solar cosmic rays are also created in solar flares. Coronal mass ejections, on the other hand, occasionally reach out far enough to themselves collide with Earth and other planets. A large coronal mass ejection, covering 45° of the disk of the Sun, can send literally billions of tons of material at a million degrees flying out into space, fast enough to reach the Earth in four days. Violent and gigantic as they are, coronal mass ejections occur three to five times a day at peak.

   Though recent missions sent to study the Sun have gathered data on the formation and evolution of these structures, exactly how the evolving cycles of the Sun and movement of its magnetic field create these structures is not understood. Aside from their gorgeous appearance and dramatic speeds, their devastating effect on technology makes them a natural target for further study. They are tied in ways that are not well understood to the movement and activity of the Sun's magnetic field. The magnetic field can be measured and tracked, and scientists know it changes from dipole to quadrupole to octupole and switches alignment from north pole to south pole during times of high solar activity, but the internal mechanisms that cause these changes are not understood.

4. **What processes of planetary formation led to the high percentage of metal in Mercury?**
   Mercury's high average density implies that it has at least twice as much iron as the other terrestrial planets. Because Venus, Earth, and Mars have similar iron contents, Mercury's very high iron content is a conundrum. There are several potential answers, and data from the MESSENGER and BepiColombo missions may help discriminate among them. First, Mercury may have formed as a larger planet, with a ratio of iron to silicate material similar to the rest of the terrestrial planets, and had much of its silicate mantle removed either by giant impacts or by intense radiation from the Sun. Alternatively, the material that Mercury formed from may have been enriched with iron, perhaps by solar radiation removing lighter elements to greater radii from the Sun. Finally, all of Mercury's initial iron budget may have sunk into its core, leaving none in its mantle (the mantles of the other terrestrial planets are rich in iron).

5. **What is the geologic history of Mercury?**
   Mariner was able to photograph less than half of Mercury's surface. Full coverage of the planet at much higher resolution, along with magnetic measurements, compositional measurements, and other data are needed to start to unravel the geologic history of the planet. Apparently there was partial resurfacing of the planet at some point in the planet's history more recent than the Late Heavy Bombardment. The surface is also covered with scarps that seem to imply the planet contracted, probably from cooling, at least 500 million years after its formation. This is

also an unexpected result, since the planet should have cooled earlier. The timing and processes of the events that shaped the planet are not yet determined, but the pieces of information gathered so far are interesting and enigmatic.

6. **What are the nature and origin of Mercury's magnetic field?**

The discovery of a planetary magnetic field for Mercury, albeit a small one, was a huge surprise when *Mariner 10* passed the planet in 1973 and 1974. Planetary magnetic fields are thought only to be created by rapid convection in a fluid layer above a solid layer in a planet. For the terrestrial planets, this is the liquid outer core convecting around the solid inner core, acting as electric currents and creating attendant magnetic fields. In the case of the gas giant planets, it is thought that rapidly flowing metallic hydrogen may cause their magnetic fields. Mercury, being a very small planet, should no longer have had a magnetic field. Its field may be caused by a liquid outer core, kept liquid through a means not yet understood, or it could be the result of magnetized minerals remaining in Mercury's crust long after the planet's inherent field has died away or the field could be created in more exotic ways. There is no leading theory at the present moment.

7. **What are the exact compositions of the highly radar-reflective materials detected in craters near Mercury's poles? Are they really deposits of water ice?**

Only a few years ago, bright materials were spotted in high-latitude craters on Mercury, where the surface is always in shadow. Researchers hypothesize that these bright deposits are water ice, perhaps left there by cometary impacts and remaining only in the dark shadows, protected from the Sun's energy. Recently similar deposits have also been found on the Moon and are also thought to be water ice. If these two planets really have water ice on them, it overthrows the long-held belief that they are both completely dry. In the case of Mercury, the existence of water ice anywhere on a planet that reaches 840°F (450°C) at the height of each day would indicate an astonishing range of conditions existing at once on such a small, hot planet.

8. **What are the sources of the volatiles measured in Mercury's atmosphere, and how are their cycles in the atmosphere controlled?**

It was a surprise to discover recently that Mercury has elements in its atmosphere other than helium and hydrogen, which it obtains from the solar wind. Iron, calcium, sodium, and other elements apparently from the crust of the planet sublimate into the atmosphere in amounts that vary according to a number of cycles, including day time, orbital point, and temperature. Such a strange atmosphere is not found on any other planet, and the mechanisms for the changing composition of the atmosphere are not understood.

9. **When and in what quantities were volatiles degassed from Venus's interior to its atmosphere? Where do they reside now?**

Venus now has only about 100 ppm of water in its atmosphere. The planet's intense surface conditions make the existence of liquid water impossible there, and surface rocks under those conditions can be shown to be baked entirely dry (and in the process made intensely hard and stiff). Since Venus probably formed with about the same quantity of water as did the Earth, some explanation has to be sought for how it lost its water. Currently the scientific community believes that the water on Venus may have been lost from the atmosphere by dissociation by solar radiation: Strong solar radiation broke the water molecules and the hydrogen went into space while oxygen bonded with surface rocks. Venus today has a striking lack of hydrogen, supporting this hypothesis.

Venus's lack of water has tremendous implications for its surface conditions. Carbon dioxide, the main constituent in its atmosphere, creates it exceptionally high surface temperatures. The same quantity of carbon dioxide is present on the Earth, but on Earth it is bound into carbonate rocks (predominantly limestones) that are deposited in the oceans. If all the limestone on Earth were converted into gas in the atmosphere, then Earth would have the same stifling greenhouse heat that Venus has. Without oceans and with a highly acidic environment, Venus's carbon dioxide remains in its atmosphere.

Since Venus and the Earth evolved from almost identical material in almost identical amounts, close to each other on the solar system, why did the two planets evolve in such different directions? If Venus lost its water early in its history, why did the Earth retain its water? These questions cannot be answered at the current time, but their answers may have great importance for the future of the Earth's climate as well.

10. What are the processes of tectonics on Venus, and did it ever experience plate tectonics?

On Earth, ongoing volcanism is caused by plate tectonics, but there is apparently no plate tectonic movement on Venus now. Venus is thought to be a one-plate planet, that is, its lithosphere forms a complete shell around the planet and moves little with respect to itself. Venus's craters are also distributed very evenly across the planet's surface, meaning that there is no part of its surface significantly older or younger than any other. There is no other body in the solar system with a completely even distribution of craters, implying a surface with a single age.

Venus's crust shows intriguing structures, such as coronae and shield volcanoes, that must be formed through mantle movements and volcanism. While Venus's crust can be seen in radar and has been measured by spacecraft, the depth of the planet's stiff lithosphere is a matter of great debate. The lithosphere consists of the brittle crust and the coolest portions of the upper mantle. Some researchers believe that the lithosphere is thin, perhaps 19–113 miles (30–182 km) thick, while others believe it may be as much as 180 miles (300 km) thick. The thickness of the lithosphere has a great effect on the ability of the planet to transfer heat from its interior to its surface, and so the lithospheric thickness will constrain the temperature and amount of movement in the planet's interior. While the Earth loses its internal heat through processes of plate tectonics, Venus may lose it primarily through volcanism.

A close inspection of volcanic features on Venus has led some researchers to believe that volcanic resurfacing of Venus has been periodic and not continuous. Heat may build up in the interior for a period of time, and then at some threshold volcanism may commence. When heat builds up sufficiently inside the static shell of Venus's lithosphere, the entire lithosphere might break up and sink into the Venusian interior, to be replaced with a fresh volcanic crust. This may constitute some variety of plate tectonics while it is occurring, though in the quiescent intervals the planet looks as static as Mars and Mercury, the other one-plate planets. There is little understanding of why and how Venus developed into this state of a single lithospheric plate combined with intense and ongoing volcanism. The lack of water may be a contributor, though that lack itself is not well understood.

The Sun's huge mass (greater than 99 percent of the total mass of the solar system) controls the orbits of all the planets and smaller bodies of the solar system, and its radiation and magnetic field dominate the space environments of the inner planets and define the size of the solar system itself. Its intense radiation production probably had a great effect on the formation and evolution of its two nearest planets, Mercury and Venus. In the heat of the Sun, Mercury had no chance to develop and retain an atmosphere, while Venus's thick atmosphere may have had its water boiled away, leaving only gases that trap heat onto the planet's surface. Venus's surface could not be less habitable: Its pressure is 90 times that on Earth, its temperature is high enough to melt lead, and its clouds are made of sulfuric acid. As the Sun evolves over the coming millions and billions of years, the climates of the Earth and Mars will also evolve. With increased understanding of processes on Venus and Mercury, humankind may be able to predict the coming changes and perhaps alter the effects civilization is having on the Earth's climate now.

APPENDIX 1:

Units and Measurements

FUNDAMENTAL UNITS

The system of measurements most commonly used in science is called both the SI (for Système International d'Unités) and the International System of Units (it is also sometimes called the MKS system). The SI system is based upon the metric units meter (abbreviated m), kilogram (kg), second (sec), kelvin (K), mole (mol), candela (cd), and ampere (A), used to measure length, time, mass, temperature, amount of a substance, light intensity, and electric current, respectively. This system was agreed upon in 1974 at an international general conference. There is another metric system, CGS, which stands for centimeter, gram, second; that system simply uses the hundredth of a meter (the centimeter) and the hundredth of the kilogram (the gram). The CGS system, formally introduced by the British Association for the Advancement of Science in 1874, is particularly useful to scientists making measurements of small quantities in laboratories, but it is less useful for space science. In this set, the SI system is used with the exception that temperatures will be presented in Celsius (C), instead of Kelvin. (The conversions between Celsius, Kelvin, and Fahrenheit temperatures are given below.) Often the standard unit of measure in the SI system, the meter, is too small when talking about the great distances in the solar system; kilometers (thousands of meters) or AU (astronomical units, defined below) will often be used instead of meters.

How is a unit defined? At one time a "meter" was defined as the length of a special metal ruler kept under strict conditions of temperature and humidity. That perfect meter could not be measured, however, without changing its temperature by opening the box, which would change its length, through thermal expansion or contraction. Today a meter is no longer defined according to a physical object; the only fundamental measurement that still is defined by a physical object is the kilogram. All of these units have had long and complex histories of attempts to define them. Some of the modern definitions, along with the use and abbreviation of each, are listed in the table here.

FUNDAMENTAL UNITS

Measurement	Unit	Symbol	Definition
length	meter	m	The meter is the distance traveled by light in a vacuum during 1/299,792,458 of a second.
time	second	sec	The second is defined as the period of time in which the oscillations of cesium atoms, under specified conditions, complete exactly 9,192,631,770 cycles. The length of a second was thought to be a constant before Einstein developed theories in physics that show that the closer to the speed of light an object is traveling, the slower time is for that object. For the velocities on Earth, time is quite accurately still considered a constant.
mass	kilogram	kg	The International Bureau of Weights and Measures keeps the world's standard kilogram in Paris, and that object is the definition of the kilogram.
temperature	kelvin	K	A degree in Kelvin (and Celsius) is 1/273.16 of the thermodynamic temperature of the triple point of water (the temperature at which, under one atmosphere pressure, water coexists as water vapor, liquid, and solid ice). In 1967, the General Conference on Weights and Measures defined this temperature as 273.16 kelvin.

(continues)

FUNDAMENTAL UNITS *(continued)*			
Measurement	**Unit**	**Symbol**	**Definition**
amount of a substance	mole	mol	The mole is the amount of a substance that contains as many units as there are atoms in 0.012 kilogram of carbon 12 (that is, Avogadro's number, or 6.02205×10^{23}). The units may be atoms, molecules, ions, or other particles.
electric current	ampere	A	The ampere is that constant current which, if maintained in two straight parallel conductors of infinite length, of negligible circular cross section, and placed one meter apart in a vacuum, would produce between these conductors a force equal to 2×10^{-7} newtons per meter of length.
light intensity	candela	cd	The candela is the luminous intensity of a source that emits monochromatic radiation with a wavelength of 555.17 nm and that has a radiant intensity of 1/683 watt per steradian. Normal human eyes are more sensitive to the yellow-green light of this wavelength than to any other.

Mass and weight are often confused. Weight is proportional to the force of gravity: Your weight on Earth is about six times your weight on the Moon because Earth's gravity is about six times that of the Moon's. Mass, on the other hand, is a quantity of matter, measured independently of gravity. In fact, weight has different units from mass: Weight is actually measured as a force (newtons, in SI, or pounds, in the English system).

The table "Fundamental Units" lists the fundamental units of the SI system. These are units that need to be defined in order to make other measurements. For example, the meter and the second are fundamental units (they are not based on any other units). To measure velocity, use a derived unit, meters per second (m/sec), a combination of fundamental units. Later in this section there is a list of common derived units.

The systems of temperature are capitalized (Fahrenheit, Celsius, and Kelvin), but the units are not (degree and kelvin). Unit abbreviations are capitalized only when they are named after a person, such as K for Lord Kelvin, or A for André-Marie Ampère. The units themselves are always lowercase, even when named for a person: one newton, or one N. Throughout these tables a small dot indicates multiplication, as in N · m, which means a newton (N) times a meter (m). A space between the symbols can also be used to indicate multiplication, as in N · m. When a small letter is placed in front of a symbol, it is a prefix meaning some multiplication factor. For example, J stands for the unit of energy called a joule, and a mJ indicates a millijoule, or 10^{-3} joules. The table of prefixes is given at the end of this section.

COMPARISONS AMONG KELVIN, CELSIUS, AND FAHRENHEIT

One kelvin represents the same temperature difference as 1°C, and the temperature in kelvins is always equal to 273.15 plus the temperature in degrees Celsius. The Celsius scale was designed around the behavior of water. The freezing point of water (at one atmosphere of pressure) was originally defined to be 0°C, while the boiling point is 100°C. The kelvin equals exactly 1.8°F.

To convert temperatures in the Fahrenheit scale to the Celsius scale, use the following equation, where F is degrees Fahrenheit, and C is degrees Celsius:

$$C = (F - 32)/1.8.$$

And to convert Celsius to Fahrenheit, use this equation:

$$F = 1.8C + 32.$$

To convert temperatures in the Celsius scale to the Kelvin scale, add 273.16. By convention, the degree symbol (°) is used for Celsius and Fahrenheit temperatures but not for temperatures given in Kelvin, for example, 0°C equals 273K.

What exactly is temperature? Qualitatively, it is a measurement of how hot something feels, and this definition is so easy to relate to that people seldom take it further. What is really happening in a substance as it gets hot or cold, and how does that change make temperature? When a fixed amount of energy is put into a substance, it heats up by an amount depending on what it is. The temperature of an object, then, has something to do with how the material responds to energy, and that response is called entropy. The entropy of a material (entropy is usually denoted S) is a measure of atomic wiggling and disorder of the atoms in the material. Formally, temperature is defined as

$$\frac{1}{T} = \left(\frac{dS}{dU} \right)_{N,}$$

meaning one over temperature (the reciprocal of temperature) is defined as the change in entropy (dS, in differential notation) per change in energy (dU), for a given number of atoms (N). What this means in less technical terms is that temperature is a measure of how much heat it takes to increase the entropy (atomic wiggling and disorder) of a substance. Some materials get hotter with less energy, and others require more to reach the same temperature.

The theoretical lower limit of temperature is $-459.67°F$ ($-273.15°C$, or 0K), known also as absolute zero. This is the temperature at which all atomic movement stops. The Prussian physicist Walther Nernst showed that it is impossible to actually reach absolute zero, though with laboratory methods using nuclear magnetization it is possible to reach $10^{-6}K$ (0.000001K).

USEFUL MEASURES OF DISTANCE

A *kilometer* is a thousand meters (see the table "International System Prefixes"), and a *light-year* is the distance light travels in a vacuum during one year (exactly 299,792,458 m/sec, but commonly rounded to 300,000,000 m/sec). A light-year, therefore, is the distance that light can travel in one year, or:

299,792,458 m/sec × 60 sec/min × 60 min/hr ×
24 hr/day × 365 days/yr = 9.4543 × 10^{15} m/yr.

For shorter distances, some astronomers use light minutes and even light seconds. A light minute is 17,998,775 km, and a light second is 299,812.59 km. The nearest star to Earth, Proxima Centauri, is 4.2 light-years away from the Sun. The next, Rigil Centaurs, is 4.3 light-years away.

An *angstrom* (10^{-10}m) is a unit of length most commonly used in nuclear or particle physics. Its symbol is Å. The diameter of an atom is about one angstrom (though each element and isotope is slightly different).

An astronomical unit (AU) is a unit of distance used by astronomers to measure distances in the solar system. One astronomical unit equals the average distance from the center of the Earth to the center of the Sun. The currently accepted value, made standard in 1996, is 149,597,870,691 meters, plus or minus 30 meters.

One kilometer equals 0.62 miles, and one mile equals 1.61 kilometers.

The following table gives the most commonly used of the units derived from the fundamental units above (there are many more derived units not listed here because they have been developed for specific situations and are little-used elsewhere; for example, in the metric world, the curvature of a railroad track is measured with a unit called "degree of curvature," defined as the angle between two points in a curving track that are separated by a chord of 20 meters).

Though the units are given in alphabetical order for ease of reference, many can fit into one of several broad categories: dimensional units (angle, area, volume), material properties (density, viscosity, thermal expansivity), properties of motion (velocity, acceleration, angular velocity), electrical properties (frequency, electric charge, electric potential, resistance, inductance, electric field strength), magnetic properties (magnetic field strength, magnetic flux, magnetic flux density), and properties of radioactivity (amount of radioactivity and effect of radioactivity).

DERIVED UNITS

Measurement	Unit symbol (derivation)	Comments
acceleration	unnamed (m/sec^2)	
angle	radian rad (m/m)	One radian is the angle centered in a circle that includes an arc of length equal to the radius. Since the circumference equals two pi times the radius, one radian equals $1/(2\ pi)$ of the circle, or approximately $57.296°$.
	steradian sr $(m^2/\ m^2)$	The steradian is a unit of solid angle. There are four pi steradians in a sphere. Thus one steradian equals about 0.079577 sphere, or about 3282.806 square degrees.
angular velocity	unnamed (rad/sec)	
area	unnamed (m^2)	
density	unnamed (kg/m^3)	Density is mass per volume. Lead is dense, styrofoam is not. Water has a density of one gram per cubic centimeter or 1,000 kilograms per cubic meter.
electric charge or electric flux	coulomb C $(A·sec)$	One coulomb is the amount of charge accumulated in one second by a current of one ampere. One coulomb is also the amount of charge on 6.241506×10^{18} electrons.
electric field strength	unnamed $[(kg·m)/(sec^3·A) \times V/m]$	Electric field strength is a measure of the intensity of an electric field at a particular location. A field strength of one V/m represents a potential difference of one volt between points separated by one meter.
electric potential, or electromotive force (often called voltage)	volt V $[(kg·m^2)/(sec^3·A) = J/C = W/A]$	Voltage is an expression of the potential difference in charge between two points in an electrical field. Electric potential is defined as the amount of potential energy present per unit of charge. One volt is a potential of one joule per coulomb of charge. The greater the voltage, the greater the flow of electrical current.

Measurement	Unit symbol (derivation)	Comments
energy, work, or heat	joule J [N·m (=kg·m^2/sec^2)]	
	electron volt eV	The electron volt, being so much smaller than the joule (one eV = 1.6 × 10^{-17} J), is useful for describing small systems.
force	newton N (kg·m/sec^2)	This unit is the equivalent to the pound in the English system, since the pound is a measure of force and not mass.
frequency	hertz Hz (cycles/sec)	Frequency is related to wavelength as follows: kilohertz × wavelength in meters = 300,000.
inductance	henry H (Wb/A)	Inductance is the amount of magnetic flux a material pro- duces for a given current of electricity. Metal wire with an electric current passing through it creates a magnetic field; different types of metal make magnetic fields with different strengths and therefore have different inductances.
magnetic field strength	unnamed (A/m)	Magnetic field strength is the force that a magnetic field exerts on a theoretical unit magnetic pole.
magnetic flux	weber Wb [(kg·m^2)/ (sec^2·A) = V·sec]	The magnetic flux across a perpendicular surface is the product of the magnetic flux density, in teslas, and the surface area, in square meters.
magnetic flux density	tesla T [kg/(sec^2·A) = Wb/m^2]	A magnetic field of one tesla is strong: The strongest artificial fields made in laboratories are about 20 teslas, and the Earth's magnetic flux density, at its surface, is about 50 microteslas (μT). Planetary magnetic fields are sometimes measured in gammas, which are nanoteslas (10^{-9} teslas).
momentum, or impulse	unnamed [N·sec (= kg m/sec)]	Momentum is a measure of moving mass: how much mass and how fast it is moving.
power	watt W [J/s (= (kg m^2)/sec^3)]	Power is the rate at which energy is spent. Power can be mechanical (as in horsepower) or electrical (a watt is produced by a current of one ampere flowing through an electric potential of one volt).

(continues)

DERIVED UNITS *(continued)*

Measurement	Unit symbol (derivation)	Comments
pressure, or stress	pascal Pa (N/m^2)	The high pressures inside planets are often measured in gigapascals (10^9 pascals), abbreviated GPa. ~10,000 atm = one GPa.
	atmosphere atm	The atmosphere is a handy unit because one atmosphere is approximately the pressure felt from the air at sea level on Earth; one standard atm = 101,325 Pa; one metric atm = 98,066 Pa; one atm ~ one bar.
radiation per unit mass receiving it	gray (J/kg)	The amount of radiation energy absorbed per kilogram of mass. One gray = 100 rads, an older unit.
radiation (effect of)	sievert Sv	This unit is meant to make comparable the biological effects of different doses and types of radiation. It is the energy of radiation received per kilogram, in grays, multiplied by a factor that takes into consideration the damage done by the particular type of radiation.
radioactivity (amount)	becquerel Bq	One atomic decay per second
	curie Ci	The curie is the older unit of measure but is still frequently seen. One Ci = 3.7×10^{10} Bq.
resistance	ohm Ω (V/A)	Resistance is a material's unwillingness to pass electric current. Materials with high resistance become hot rather than allowing the current to pass and can make excellent heaters.
thermal expansivity	unnamed (/°)	This unit is per degree, measuring the change in volume of a substance with the rise in temperature.
vacuum	torr	Vacuum is atmospheric pressure below one atm (one torr = 1/760 atm). Given a pool of mercury with a glass tube standing in it, one torr of pressure on the pool will press the mercury one millimeter up into the tube, where one standard atmosphere will push up 760 millimeters of mercury.

Measurement	Unit symbol (derivation)	Comments
velocity	unnamed (m/sec)	
viscosity	unnamed [Pa·sec (= kg/ (m·sec)]	Viscosity is a measure of resistance to flow. If a force of one newton is needed to move one square meter of the liquid or gas relative to a second layer one meter away at a speed of one meter per second, then its viscosity is one Pa·s, often simply written Pas or Pas. The cgs unit for viscosity is the poise, equal to 0.1Pa·s.
volume	cubic meter (m³)	

DEFINITIONS FOR ELECTRICITY AND MAGNETISM

When two objects in each other's vicinity have different electrical charges, an *electric field* exists between them. An electric field also forms around any single object that is electrically charged with respect to its environment. An object is negatively charged (−) if it has an excess of electrons relative to its surroundings. An object is positively charged (+) if it is deficient in electrons with respect to its surroundings.

An electric field has an effect on other charged objects in the vicinity. The field strength at a particular distance from an object is directly proportional to the electric charge of that object, in coulombs. The field strength is inversely proportional to the distance from a charged object.

Flux is the rate (per unit of time) in which something flowing crosses a surface perpendicular to the direction of flow.

An alternative expression for the intensity of an electric field is *electric flux density*. This refers to the number of lines of electric flux passing at right angles through a given surface area, usually one meter squared (1 m²). Electric flux density, like electric field strength, is directly proportional to the charge on the object. But flux density diminishes with distance according to the inverse-square law because it is specified in terms of a surface area (per meter squared) rather than a linear displacement (per meter).

A *magnetic field* is generated when electric charge carriers such as electrons move through space or within an electrical conductor. The geometric shapes of the magnetic flux lines produced by moving charge carriers (electric current) are similar to the shapes of the flux lines in an electrostatic field. But

INTERNATIONAL SYSTEM PREFIXES

SI prefix	Symbol	Multiplying factor
exa-	E	10^{18} = 1,000,000,000,000,000,000
peta-	P	10^{15} = 1,000,000,000,000,000
tera-	T	10^{12} = 1,000,000,000,000
giga-	G	10^{9} = 1,000,000,000
mega-	M	10^{6} = 1,000,000
kilo-	k	10^{3} = 1,000
hecto-	h	10^{2} = 100
deca-	da	10 = 10
deci-	d	10^{-1} = 0.1
centi-	c	10^{-2} = 0.01
milli-	m	10^{-3} = 0.001
micro-	μ or u	10^{-6} = 0.000,001
nano-	n	10^{-9} = 0.000,000,001
pico-	p	10^{-12} = 0.000,000,000,001
femto-	f	10^{-15} = 0.000,000,000,000,001
atto-	a	10^{-18} = 0.000,000,000,000,000,001

A note on nonmetric prefixes: In the United States, the word "billion" means the number 1,000,000,000, or 10^{9}. In most countries of Europe and Latin America, this number is called "one milliard" or "one thousand million," and "billion" means the number 1,000,000,000,000, or 10^{12}, which is what Americans call a "trillion." In this set, a billion is 10^{9}.

NAMES FOR LARGE NUMBERS

Number	American	European	SI prefix
10^9	billion	milliard	giga-
10^{12}	trillion	billion	tera-
10^{15}	quadrillion	billiard	peta-
10^{18}	quintillion	trillion	exa-
10^{21}	sextillion	trilliard	zetta-
10^{24}	septillion	quadrillion	yotta-
10^{27}	octillion	quadrilliard	
10^{30}	nonillion	quintillion	
10^{33}	decillion	quintilliard	
10^{36}	undecillion	sextillion	
10^{39}	duodecillion	sextilliard	
10^{42}	tredecillion	septillion	
10^{45}	quattuordecillion	septilliard	

This naming system is designed to expand indefinitely by factors of powers of three. Then, there is also the googol, the number 10^{100} (one followed by 100 zeroes). The googol was invented for fun by the eight-year-old nephew of the American mathematician Edward Kasner. The googolplex is 10^{googol}, or one followed by a googol of zeroes. Both it and the googol are numbers larger than the total number of atoms in the universe, thought to be about 10^{80}.

there are differences in the ways electrostatic and magnetic fields interact with the environment.

Electrostatic flux is impeded or blocked by metallic objects. *Magnetic flux* passes through most metals with little or no effect, with certain exceptions, notably iron and nickel. These two metals, and alloys and mixtures containing them, are known as ferromagnetic materials because they concentrate magnetic lines of flux.

Magnetic flux density and *magnetic force* are related to *magnetic field strength*. In general, the magnetic field strength diminishes with increasing distance from the axis of a magnetic dipole in which the flux field is stable. The function defining the rate at which this field-strength decrease occurs depends on the geometry of the magnetic lines of flux (the shape of the flux field).

PREFIXES

Adding a prefix to the name of that unit forms a multiple of a unit in the International System (see the table "International System Prefixes"). The prefixes change the magnitude of the unit by orders of 10 from 10^{18} to 10^{-18}.

Very small concentrations of chemicals are also measured in parts per million (ppm) or parts per billion (ppb), which mean just what they sound like: If there are four parts per million of lead in a rock (4 ppm), then out of every million atoms in that rock, on average four of them will be lead.

APPENDIX 2:

Light, Wavelength, and Radiation

Electromagnetic radiation is energy given off by matter, traveling in the form of waves or particles. Electromagnetic energy exists in a wide range of energy values, of which visible light is one small part of the total spectrum. The source of radiation may be the hot and therefore highly energized atoms of the Sun, pouring out radiation across a wide range of energy values, including of course visible light, and they may also be unstable (radioactive) elements giving off radiation as they decay.

Radiation is called "electromagnetic" because it moves as interlocked waves of electrical and magnetic fields. A wave is a disturbance traveling through space, transferring energy from one point to the next. In a vacuum, all electromagnetic radiation travels at the speed of light, 983,319,262 feet per second (299,792,458 m/sec, often approximated as 300,000,000 m/sec). Depending on the type of radiation, the waves have different wavelengths, energies, and frequencies (see the following figure). The wavelength is the distance between individual waves, from one peak to another. The frequency is the number of waves that pass a stationary point each second. Notice in the graphic how the wave undulates up and down from peaks to valleys to peaks. The time from one peak to the next peak is called one cycle. A single unit of frequency is equal to one cycle per second. Scientists refer to a single cycle as one hertz, which commemorates 19th-century German physicist Heinrich Hertz, whose discovery of electromagnetic waves led to the development of radio. The frequency of a wave is related to its energy: The higher the frequency of a

Electromagnetic Waves

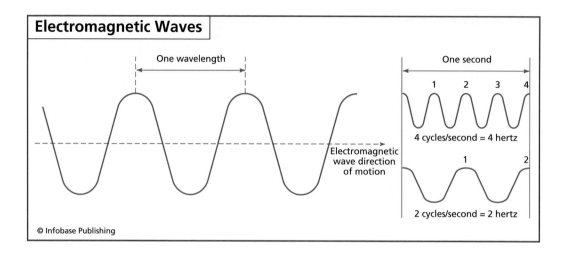

© Infobase Publishing

Each electromagnetic wave has a measurable wavelength and frequency.

wave, the higher its energy, though its speed in a vacuum does not change.

The smallest wavelength, highest energy and frequency electromagnetic waves are cosmic rays, then as wavelength increases and energy and frequency decrease, come gamma rays, then X-rays, then ultraviolet light, then visible light (moving from violet through indigo, blue, green, yellow, orange, and red), then infrared (divided into near, meaning near to visible, mid-, and far infrared), then microwaves, and then radio waves, which have the longest wavelengths and the lowest energy and frequency. The electromagnetic spectrum is shown in the accompanying figure and table.

As a wave travels and vibrates up and down with its characteristic wavelength, it can be imagined as vibrating up and down in a single plane, such as the plane of this sheet of paper in the case of the simple example in the figure here showing polarization. In nature, some waves change their polarization constantly so that their polarization sweeps through all angles, and they are said to be circularly polarized. In ordinary visible light, the waves are vibrating up and down in numerous random planes. Light can be shone through a special filter called a polarizing filter that blocks out all the light except that polarized in a certain direction, and the light that shines out the other side of the filter is then called polarized light.

Polarization is important in wireless communications systems such as radios, cell phones, and non-cable television. The orientation of the transmitting antenna creates the polarization of the radio waves transmitted by that antenna: A vertical antenna emits vertically polarized waves, and a horizontal antenna emits horizontally polarized waves. Similarly, a horizontal antenna is best at receiving horizontally polarized waves and a vertical antenna at vertically polarized waves. The best communications are obtained when the source and receiver antennas have the same polarization. This is why,

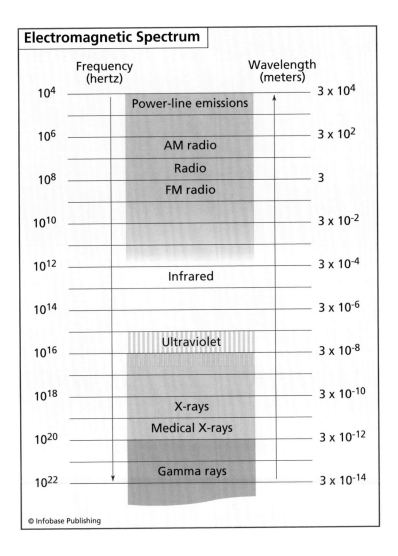

Electromagnetic Spectrum

Frequency (hertz) / Wavelength (meters)

Frequency (hertz)	Band	Wavelength (meters)
10^4	Power-line emissions	3×10^4
10^6	AM radio	3×10^2
10^8	Radio / FM radio	3
10^{10}		3×10^{-2}
10^{12}	Infrared	3×10^{-4}
10^{14}		3×10^{-6}
10^{16}	Ultraviolet	3×10^{-8}
10^{18}	X-rays	3×10^{-10}
10^{20}	Medical X-rays	3×10^{-12}
10^{22}	Gamma rays	3×10^{-14}

© Infobase Publishing

The electromagnetic spectrum ranges from cosmic rays at the shortest wavelengths to radio waves at the longest wavelengths.

when trying to adjust television antennas to get a better signal, having the two antennae at right angles to each other can maximize the chances of receiving a signal.

The human eye stops being able to detect radiation at wavelengths between 3,000 and 4,000 angstroms, which is deep violet—also the rough limit on transmissions through the atmosphere (see the table "Wavelengths and Frequencies of Visible Light"). (Three thousand to 4,000 angstroms is the same as 300–400 nm because an angstrom is 10^{-9} m, while the

Waves can be thought of as plane or circularly polarized.

Polarization

Plane polarization
(two wavelengths)

Circular polarization
(two wavelengths)

WAVELENGTHS AND FREQUENCIES OF VISIBLE LIGHT

Visible light color	Wavelength (in Å, angstroms)	Frequency (times 1014 Hz)
violet	4,000–4,600	7.5–6.5
indigo	4,600–4,750	6.5–6.3
blue	4,750–4,900	6.3–6.1
green	4,900–5,650	6.1–5.3
yellow	5,650–5,750	5.3–5.2
orange	5,750–6,000	5.2–5.0
red	6,000–8,000	5.0–3.7

prefix nano- or n means 10^{-10}; for more, see appendix 1, "Units and Measurements.") Of visible light, the colors red, orange, yellow, green, blue, indigo, and violet are listed in order from longest wavelength and lowest energy to shortest wavelength and highest energy. Sir Isaac Newton, the spectacular English physicist and mathematician, first found that a glass prism split sunlight into a rainbow of colors. He named this a "spectrum," after the Latin word for ghost.

If visible light strikes molecules of gas as it passes through the atmosphere, it may get absorbed as energy by the molecule. After a short amount of time, the molecule releases the light, most probably in a different direction. The color that is radiated is the same color that was absorbed. All the colors of visible light can be absorbed by atmospheric molecules, but the higher energy blue light is absorbed more often than the lower energy red light. This process is called Rayleigh scattering (named after Lord John Rayleigh, an English physicist who first described it in the 1870s).

The blue color of the sky is due to Rayleigh scattering. As light moves through the atmosphere, most of the longer wavelengths pass straight through: The air affects little of the red, orange, and yellow light. The gas molecules absorb much of the shorter wavelength blue light. The absorbed blue light is

WAVELENGTHS AND FREQUENCIES OF THE ELECTROMAGNETIC SPECTRUM

Energy	Frequency in hertz (Hz)	Wavelength in meters
cosmic rays	everything higher in energy than gamma rays	everything lower in wavelength than gamma rays
gamma rays	10^{20} to 10^{24}	less than 10^{-12} m
X-rays	10^{17} to 10^{20}	1 nm to 1 pm
ultraviolet	10^{15} to 10^{17}	400 nm to 1 nm
visible	4×10^{14} to 7.5×10^{14}	750 nm to 400 nm
near-infrared	1×10^{14} to 4×10^{14}	2.5 μm to 750 nm
infrared	10^{13} to 10^{14}	25 μm to 2.5 μm
microwaves	3×10^{11} to 10^{13}	1 mm to 25 μm
radio waves	less than 3×10^{11}	more than 1 mm

then radiated in different directions and is scattered all around the sky. Whichever direction you look, some of this scattered blue light reaches you. Since you see the blue light from everywhere overhead, the sky looks blue. Note also that there is a very different kind of scattering, in which the light is simply bounced off larger objects like pieces of dust and water droplets, rather than being absorbed by a molecule of gas in the atmosphere and then reemitted. This bouncing kind of scattering is responsible for red sunrises and sunsets.

Until the end of the 18th century, people thought that visible light was the only kind of light. The amazing amateur astronomer Frederick William Herschel (the discoverer of Uranus) discovered the first non-visible light, the infrared. He thought that each color of visible light had a different temperature and devised an experiment to measure the temperature of each color of light. The temperatures went up as the colors progressed from violet through red, and then Herschel decided to measure past red, where he found the highest temperature yet. This was the first demonstration that there was a kind of

COMMON USES FOR RADIO WAVES

User	Approximate frequency
AM radio	0.535×10^6 to 1.7×10^6Hz
baby monitors	49×10^6Hz
cordless phones	49×10^6Hz
	900×10^6Hz
	$2,400 \times 10^6$Hz
television channels 2 through 6	54×10^6 to 88×10^6Hz
radio-controlled planes	72×10^6Hz
radio-controlled cars	75×10^6Hz
FM radio	88×10^6 to 108×10^6Hz
television channels 7 through 13	174×10^6 to 220×10^6Hz
wildlife tracking collars	215×10^6Hz
cell phones	800×10^6Hz
	$2,400 \times 10^6$Hz
air traffic control radar	960×10^6Hz
	$1,215 \times 10^6$Hz
global positioning systems	$1,227 \times 10^6$Hz
	$1,575 \times 10^6$Hz
deep space radio	$2,300 \times 10^6$Hz

radiation that could not be seen by the human eye. Herschel originally named this range of radiation "calorific rays," but the name was later changed to infrared, meaning "below red." Infrared radiation has become an important way of sensing solar system objects and is also used in night-vision goggles and various other practical purposes.

At lower energies and longer wavelengths than the visible and infrared, microwaves are commonly used to transmit energy to food in microwave ovens, as well as for some communications, though radio waves are more common in this use. There is a wide range of frequencies in the radio spectrum, and they are used in many ways, as shown in the table "Common Uses for Radio Waves," including television, radio, and cell phone transmissions. Note that the frequency units are given in terms of 10^6 Hz, without correcting for each coefficient's additional factors of 10. This is because 10^6 Hz corresponds to the unit of megahertz (MHz), which is a commonly used unit of frequency.

Cosmic rays, gamma rays, and X-rays, the three highest-energy radiations, are known as ionizing radiation because they contain enough energy that, when they hit an atom, they may knock an electron off of it or otherwise change the atom's weight or structure. These ionizing radiations, then, are particularly dangerous to living things; for example, they can damage DNA molecules (though good use is made of them as well, to see into bodies with X-rays and to kill cancer cells with gamma rays). Luckily the atmosphere stops most ionizing radiation, but not all of it. Cosmic rays created by the Sun in solar flares, or sent off as a part of the solar wind, are relatively low energy. There are far more energetic cosmic rays, though, that come from distant stars through interstellar space. These are energetic enough to penetrate into an asteroid as deeply as a meter and can often make it through the atmosphere.

When an atom of a radioisotope decays, it gives off some of its excess energy as radiation in the form of X-rays, gamma rays, or fast-moving subatomic particles: alpha particles (two protons and two neutrons, bound together as an atomic *nucleus*), or beta particles (fast-moving electrons), or a combination of two or more of these products. If it decays with emission of an alpha or beta particle, it becomes a new element. These decay products can be described as gamma, beta, and alpha radiation. By decaying, the atom is progressing in one or more steps toward a stable state where it is no longer radioactive.

RADIOACTIVITY OF SELECTED OBJECTS AND MATERIALS

Object or material	Radioactivity
1 adult human (100 Bq/kg)	7,000 Bq
1 kg coffee	1,000 Bq
1 kg high-phosphate fertilizer	5,000 Bq
1 household smoke detector (with the element americium)	30,000 Bq
radioisotope source for cancer therapy	100 million million Bq
1 kg 50-year-old vitrified high-level nuclear waste	10 million million Bq
1 kg uranium ore (Canadian ore, 15% uranium)	25 million Bq
1 kg uranium ore (Australian ore, 0.3% uranium)	500,000 Bq
1 kg granite	1,000 Bq

The X-rays and gamma rays from decaying atoms are identical to those from other natural sources. Like other ionizing radiation, they can damage living tissue but can be blocked by lead sheets or by thick concrete. Alpha particles are much larger and can be blocked more quickly by other material; a sheet of paper or the outer layer of skin on your hand will stop them. If the atom that produces them is taken inside the body, however, such as when a person breathes in radon gas, the alpha particle can do damage to the lungs. Beta particles are more energetic and smaller and can penetrate a couple of centimeters into a person's body.

But why can both radioactive decay that is formed of subatomic particles and heat that travels as a wave of energy be considered radiation? One of Albert Einstein's great discoveries is called the photoelectric effect: Subatomic particles can all behave as either a wave or a particle. The smaller the particle, the more wavelike it is. The best example of this is light itself, which behaves almost entirely as a wave, but there is the particle equivalent for light, the massless photon. Even alpha particles, the largest decay product discussed here, can act like a wave, though their wavelike properties are much harder to detect.

The amount of radioactive material is given in becquerel (Bq), a measure that enables us to compare the typical radioactivity of some natural and other materials. A becquerel is one atomic decay per second. Radioactivity is still sometimes measured using a unit called a Curie; a Becquerel is 27×10^{-12} Curies. There are materials made mainly of radioactive elements, like uranium, but most materials are made mainly of stable atoms. Even materials made mainly of stable atoms, however, almost always have trace amounts of radioactive elements in them, and so even common objects give off some level of radiation, as shown in the following table.

Background radiation is all around us all the time. Naturally occurring radioactive elements are more common in some kinds of rocks than others; for example, *granite* carries more radioactive elements than does sandstone; therefore a person working in a bank built of granite will receive more radiation than someone who works in a wooden building. Similarly, the atmosphere absorbs cosmic rays, but the higher the elevation, the more cosmic-ray exposure there is. A person living in Denver or in the mountains of Tibet is exposed to more cosmic rays than someone living in Boston or in the Netherlands.

APPENDIX 3:

A List of All Known Moons

Though Mercury and Venus have no moons, the other planets in the solar system have at least one. Some moons, such as Earth's Moon and Jupiter's Galileans satellites, are thought to have formed at the same time as their accompanying planet. Many other moons appear simply to be captured asteroids; for at least half of Jupiter's moons, this seems to be the case. These small, irregular moons are difficult to detect from Earth, and so the lists given in the table below must be considered works in progress for the gas giant planets. More moons will certainly be discovered with longer observation and better instrumentation.

KNOWN MOONS OF ALL PLANETS						
Earth	**Mars**	**Jupiter**	**Saturn**	**Uranus**	**Neptune**	**Pluto**
1	**2**	**63**	**62**	**27**	**13**	**3**
1. Moon	1. Phobos	1. Metis	1. S/2009 S1	1. Cordelia	1. Naiad	1. Charon
	2. Diemos	2. Adrastea	2. Pan	2. Ophelia	2. Thalassa	2. Nix (P1)
		3. Amalthea	3. Daphnis	3. Bianca	3. Despina	3. Hydra
		4. Thebe	4. Atlas	4. Cressida	4. Galatea	(P2)
		5. Io	5. Prometheus	5. Desdemona	5. Larissa	
		6. Europa	6. Pandora	6. Juliet	6. Proteus	
		7. Ganymede	7. Epimetheus	7. Portia	7. Triton	
		8. Callisto	8. Janus	8. Rosalind	8. Nereid	
		9. Themisto	9. Aegaeon	9. Cupid (2003	9. Halimede	
		10. Leda	10. Mimas	U2)	(S/2002	
		11. Himalia	11. Methone	10. Belinda	N1)	

(continues)

KNOWN MOONS OF ALL PLANETS *(continued)*

Earth	Mars	Jupiter	Saturn	Uranus	Neptune	Pluto
		12. Lysithea	12. Anthe	11. Perdita	10. Sao	
		13. Elara	13. Pallene	(1986 U10)	(S/2002 N2)	
		14. S/2000 J11	14. Enceladus	12. Puck	11. Laomedeia	
		15. Carpo	15. Telesto	13. Mab (2003	(S/2002	
		(S/2003	16. Tethys	U1)	N3)	
		J20)	17. Calypso	14. Miranda	12. Psamathe	
		16. S/2003	18. Dione	15. Ariel	(S/2003	
		J12	19. Helene	16. Umbriel	N1)	
		17. Euporie	20. Polydeuces	17. Titania	13. Neso	
		18. S/2003 J3	21. Rhea	18. Oberon	(S/2002	
		19. S/2003 J18	22. Titan	19. Francisco	N4)	
		20. Orthosie	23. Hyperion	(2001 U3)		
		21. Euanthe	24. Iapetus	20. Caliban		
		22. Harpalyke	25. Kiviuq	21. Stephano		
		23. Praxidike	26. Ijiraq	22. Trinculo		
		24. Thyone	27. Phoebe	23. Sycorax		
		25. S/2003	28. Paaliaq	24. Margaret		
		J16	29. Skathi	(2003 U3)		
		26. Mneme	30. Albiorix	25. Prospero		
		(S/2003	31. S/2007	26. Setebos		
		J21)	S2	27. Ferdinand		
		27. Iocaste	32. Bebhionn	(2001 U2)		
		28. Helike	33. Erriapo			
		(S/2003 J6)	34. Siarnaq			
		29. Hermippe	35. Skoll			
		30. Thelxinoe	36. Tarvos			
		(S/2003	37. Tarqeq			
		J22)	38. Greip			
		31. Ananke	39. Hyrrokkin			
		32. S/2003	40. S/2004			
		J15	S13			
		33. Eurydome	41. S/2004			
		34. S/2003	S17			
		J17	42. Mundilfari			
		35. Pasithee	43. Jarnsaxa			
		36. S/2003	44. S/2006			
		J10	S1			

Earth	Mars	Jupiter	Saturn	Uranus	Neptune	Pluto
		37. Chaldene	45. Narvi			
		38. Isonoe	46. Bergelmir			
		39. Erinome	47. Suttungr			
		40. Kale	48. S/2004			
		41. Aitne	S12			
		42. Taygete	49. S/2004			
		43. Kallichore	S7			
		(S/2003	50. Hati			
		J11)	51. Bestla			
		44. Eukelade	52. Farbauti			
		(S/2003 J1)	53. Thrymyr			
		45. Arche	54. S/2007			
		(S/2002 J1)	S3			
		46. S/2003 J9	55. Aegir			
		47. Carme	56. S/2006			
		48. Kalyke	S3			
		49. Sponde	57. Kari			
		50. Magaclite	58. Fenrir			
		51. S/2003 J5	59. Surtur			
		52. S/2003	60. Ymir			
		J19	61. Loge			
		53. S/2003	62. Fornjot			
		J23				
		54. Hegemone				
		(S/2003 J8)				
		55. Pasiphae				
		56. Cyllene				
		(S/2003				
		J13)				
		57. S/2003 J4				
		58. Sinope				
		59. Aoede				
		(S/2003 J7)				
		60. Autonoe				
		61. Calirrhoe				
		62. Kore				
		(S/2003				
		J14)				
		63. S/2003 J2				

Glossary

accretion The accumulation of celestial gas, dust, or smaller bodies by gravitational attraction into a larger body, such as a planet or an asteroid

achondite A stony (silicate-based) meteorite that contains no chondrules; these originate in differentiated bodies and may be mantle material or lavas (see also chondrite and iron meteorite)

albedo The light reflected by an object as a fraction of the light shining on an object; mirrors have high albedo, while charcoal has low albedo

anorthite A calcium-rich plagioclase mineral with compositional formula $CaAl_2Si_2O_8$, significant for making up the majority of the rock anorthosite in the crust of the Moon

anticyclone An area of increased atmospheric pressure relative to the surrounding pressure field in the atmosphere, resulting in circular flow in a clockwise direction north of the equator and in a counterclockwise direction to the south

aphelion A distance; the farthest from the Sun an object travels in its orbit

apogee As for aphelion but for any orbital system (not confined to the Sun)

apparent magnitude The brightness of a celestial object as it would appear from a given distance—the lower the number, the brighter the object

atom The smallest quantity of an element that can take part in a chemical reaction; consists of a nucleus of protons and neutrons, surrounded by a cloud of electrons; each atom is about 10^{-10} meters in diameter, or one angstrom

atomic number The number of protons in an atom's nucleus

AU An AU is an astronomical unit, defined as the distance from the Sun to the Earth; approximately 93 million miles, or 150 million kilometers. For more information, refer to the UNITS AND MEASUREMENTS appendix

basalt A generally dark-colored extrusive igneous rock most commonly created by melting a planet's mantle; its low silica content indicates that it has not been significantly altered on its passage to the planet's surface

bolide An object falling into a planet's atmosphere, when a specific identification as a comet or asteroid cannot be made

bow shock The area of compression in a flowing fluid when it strikes an object or another fluid flowing at another rate; for example, the bow of a boat and the water, or the magnetic field of a planet and the flowing solar wind

breccia Material that has been shattered from grinding, as in a fault, or from impact, as by meteorites or other solar system bodies

CAIs Calcium-aluminum inclusions, small spheres of mineral grains found in chondritic meteorites and thought to be the first solids that formed in the protoplanetary disk

calcium-aluminum inclusion See **CAIs**

chondrite A class of meteorite thought to contain the most primitive material left from the solar nebula; named after their glassy, super-primitive inclusions called chondrules

chondrule Rounded, glassy, and crystalline bodies incorporated into the more primitive of meteorites; thought to be the condensed droplets of the earliest solar system materials

CI chondrite The class on chondrite meteorites with compositions most like the Sun, and therefore thought to be the oldest and least altered material in the solar system

clinopyroxene A common mineral in the mantle and igneous rocks, with compositional formula $((Ca,Mg,Fe,Al)_2(Si,Al)_2O_6)$

conjunction When the Sun is between the Earth and the planet or another body in question

convection Material circulation upward and downward in a gravity field caused by horizontal gradients in density; an example is the hot, less dense bubbles that form at the bottom of a pot, rise, and are replaced by cooler, denser sinking material

core The innermost material within a differentiated body; in a rocky planet this consists of iron-nickel metal, and in a gas planet this consists of the rocky innermost solids

Coriolis force The effect of movement on a rotating sphere; movement in the Northern Hemisphere curves to the right, while movement in the Southern Hemisphere curves to the left

craton The ancient, stable interior cores of the Earth's continents

crust The outermost layer of most differentiated bodies, often consisting of the least dense products of volcanic events or other buoyant material

cryovolcanism Non-silicate materials erupted from icy and gassy bodies in the cold outer solar system; for example, as suspected or seen on the moons Enceladus, Europa, Titan, and Triton

cubewano Any large Kuiper belt object orbiting between about 41 AU and 48 AU but not controlled by orbital resonances with Neptune; the odd name is derived from 1992 QB_1, the first Kuiper belt object found

cyclone An area in the atmosphere in which the pressures are lower than those of the surrounding region at the same level, resulting in circular motion in a counterclockwise direction north of the equator and in a clockwise direction to the south

debris disk A flattened, spinning disk of dust and gas around a star formed from collisions among bodies already accreted in an aging solar system

differential rotation Rotation at different rates at different latitudes, requiring a liquid or gassy body, such as the Sun or Jupiter

differentiated body A spherical body that has a structure of concentric spherical layers, differing in terms of composition, heat, density, and/or motion; caused by gravitational separations and heating events such as planetary accretion

dipole Two associated magnetic poles, one positive and one negative, creating a magnetic field

direct (prograde) Rotation or orbit in the same direction as the Earth's, that is, counterclockwise when viewed from above its North Pole

disk wind Magnetic fields that either pull material into the protostar or push it into the outer disk; these are thought to form at the inner edge of the disk where the protostar's magnetic field crosses the disk's magnetic field (also called "x-wind")

distributary River channels that branch from the main river channel, carrying flow away from the central channel; usually form fans of channels at a river's delta

eccentricity The amount by which an ellipse differs from a circle

ecliptic The imaginary plane that contains the Earth's orbit and from which the planes of other planets' orbits deviate slightly (Pluto the most, by 17 degrees); the ecliptic makes an angle of 7 degrees with the plane of the Sun's equator

ejecta Material thrown out of the site of a crater by the force of the impactor

element A family of atoms that all have the same number of positively charged particles in their nuclei (the center of the atom)

ellipticity The amount by which a planet's shape deviates from a sphere

equinox One of two points in a planet's orbit when day and night have the same length; vernal equinox occurs in Earth's spring and autumnal equinox in the fall

exosphere The uppermost layer of a planet's atmosphere

extrasolar Outside this solar system

faint young Sun paradox The apparent contradiction between the observation that the Sun gave off far less heat in its early years, and the likelihood that the Earth was still warm enough to host liquid water

garnet The red, green, or purple mineral that contains the majority of the aluminum in the Earth's upper mantle; its compositional formula is $((Ca,Mg,Fe\ Mn)_3(Al,Fe,Cr,Ti)_2(SiO_4)3)$

giant molecular cloud An interstellar cloud of dust and gas that is the birthplace of clusters of new stars as it collapses through its own gravity

graben A low area longer than it is wide and bounded from adjoining higher areas by faults; caused by extension in the crust

granite An intrusive igneous rock with high silica content and some minerals containing water; in this solar system thought to be found only on Earth

half-life The time it takes for half a population of an unstable isotope to decay

hydrogen burning The most basic process of nuclear fusion in the cores of stars that produces helium and radiation from hydrogen

igneous rock Rock that was once hot enough to be completely molten

impactor A generic term for the object striking and creating a crater in another body

inclination As commonly used in planetary science, the angle between the plane of a planet's orbit and the plane of the ecliptic

iron meteorite Meteorites that consist largely of iron-nickel metal; thought to be parts of the cores of smashed planetesimals from early solar system accretion

isotope Atoms with the same number of protons (and are therefore the same type of element) but different numbers of neutrons; may be stable or radioactive and occur in different relative abundances

lander A spacecraft designed to land on another solar system object rather than flying by, orbiting, or entering the atmosphere and then burning up or crashing

lithosphere The uppermost layer of a terrestrial planet consisting of stiff material that moves as one unit if there are plate tectonic forces and does not convect internally but transfers heat from the planet's interior through conduction

magnetic moment The torque (turning force) exerted on a magnet when it is placed in a magnetic field

magnetopause The surface between the magnetosheath and the magnetosphere of a planet

magnetosheath The compressed, heated portion of the solar wind where it piles up against a planetary magnetic field

magnetosphere The volume of a planet's magnetic field, shaped by the internal planetary source of the magnetism and by interactions with the solar wind

magnitude See APPARENT MAGNITUDE

mantle The spherical shell of a terrestrial planet between crust and core; thought to consist mainly of silicate minerals

mass number The number of protons plus neutrons in an atom's nucleus

mesosphere The atmospheric layer between the stratosphere and the thermosphere

metal 1) Material with high electrical conductivity in which the atomic nuclei are surrounded by a cloud of electrons, that is, metallic bonds, or 2) In astronomy, any element heavier than helium

metallicity The fraction of all elements heavier than hydrogen and helium in a star or protoplanetary disk; higher metallicity is thought to encourage the formation of planets

metamorphic rock Rock that has been changed from its original state by heat or pressure but was never liquid

mid-ocean ridge The line of active volcanism in oceanic basins from which two oceanic plates are produced, one moving away from each side of the ridge; only exist on Earth

mineral A naturally occurring inorganic substance having an orderly internal structure (usually crystalline) and characteristic chemical composition

nucleus The center of the atom, consisting of protons (positively charged) and neutrons (no electric charge); tiny in volume but makes up almost all the mass of the atom

nutation The slow wobble of a planet's rotation axis along a line of longitude, causing changes in the planet's obliquity

obliquity The angle between a planet's equatorial plane to its orbit plane

occultation The movement of one celestial body in front of another from a particular point of view; most commonly the movement of a planet in front of a star from the point of view of an Earth viewer

olivine Also known as the gem peridot, the green mineral that makes up the majority of the upper mantle; its compositional formula is $((Mg, Fe)_2SiO_4)$

one-plate planet A planet with lithosphere that forms a continuous spherical shell around the whole planet, not breaking into plates or moving with tectonics; Mercury, Venus, and Mars are examples

opposition When the Earth is between the Sun and the planet of interest

orbital period The time required for an object to make a complete circuit along its orbit

pallasite A type of iron meteorite that also contains the silicate mineral olivine, and is thought to be part of the region between the mantle and core in a differentiated planetesimal that was shattered in the early years of the solar system

parent body The larger body that has been broken to produce smaller pieces; large bodies in the asteroid belt are thought to be the parent bodies of meteorites that fall to Earth today

perigee As for perihelion but for any orbital system (not confined to the Sun)

perihelion   A distance; the closest approach to the Sun made in an object's orbit

planetary nebula   A shell of gas ejected from stars at the end of their lifetimes; unfortunately named in an era of primitive telescopes that could not discern the size and nature of these objects

planetesimal   The small, condensed bodies that formed early in the solar system and presumably accreted to make the planets; probably resembled comets or asteroids

plate tectonics   The movement of lithospheric plates relative to each other, only known on Earth

precession   The movement of a planet's axis of rotation that causes the axis to change its direction of tilt, much as the direction of the axis of a toy top rotates as it slows

primordial disk   Another name for a protoplanetary disk

prograde (direct)   Rotates or orbits in the same direction the Earth does, that is, counterclockwise when viewed from above its North Pole

proplyd   Abbreviation for a *protoplanetary disk*

protoplanetary disk   The flattened, spinning cloud of dust and gas surrounding a growing new star

protostar   The central mass of gas and dust in a newly forming solar system that will eventually begin thermonuclear fusion and become a star

radioactive   An atom prone to radiodecay

radio-decay   The conversion of an atom into a different atom or isotope through emission of energy or subatomic particles

red, reddened   A solar system body with a redder color in visible light, but more important, one that has increased albedo at low wavelengths (the "red" end of the spectrum)

reflectance spectra   The spectrum of radiation that bounces off a surface, for example, sunlight bouncing off the surface of as asteroid; the wavelengths with low intensities show the kinds of radiation absorbed rather than reflected by the surface, and indicate the composition of the surface materials

refractory   An element that requires unusually high temperatures in order to melt or evaporate; compare to volatile

relief (topographic relief)   The shapes of the surface of land; most especially the high parts such as hills or mountains

resonance   When the ratio of the orbital periods of two bodies is an integer; for example, if one moon orbits its planet once for every two times another moon orbits, the two are said to be in resonance

retrograde   Rotates or orbits in the opposite direction to Earth, that is, clockwise when viewed from above its North Pole

Roche limit   The radius around a given planet that a given satellite must be outside of in order to remain intact; within the Roche limit, the satellite's self-gravity will be overcome by gravitational tidal forces from the planet, and the satellite will be torn apart

rock   Material consisting of the aggregate of minerals

sedimentary rock   Rock made of mineral grains that were transported by water or air

seismic waves   Waves of energy propagating through a planet, caused by earthquakes or other impulsive forces, such as meteorite impacts and human-made explosions

semimajor axis   Half the widest diameter of an orbit

semiminor axis   Half the narrowest diameter of an orbit

silicate   A molecule, crystal, or compound made from the basic building block silica (SiO_2); the Earth's mantle is made of silicates, while its core is made of metals

spectrometer   An instrument that separates electromagnetic radiation, such as light, into wavelengths, creating a spectrum

stratosphere   The layer of the atmosphere located between the troposphere and the mesosphere, characterized by a slight temperature increase and absence of clouds

subduction Movement of one lithospheric plate beneath another

subduction zone A compressive boundary between two lithospheric plates, where one plate (usually an oceanic plate) is sliding beneath the other and plunging at an angle into the mantle

synchronous orbit radius The orbital radius at which the satellite's orbital period is equal to the rotational period of the planet; contrast with synchronous rotation

synchronous rotation When the same face of a moon is always toward its planet, caused by the period of the moon's rotation about its axis being the same as the period of the moon's orbit around its planet; most moons rotate synchronously due to tidal locking

tacholine The region in the Sun where differential rotation gives way to solid-body rotation, creating a shear zone and perhaps the body's magnetic field as well; is at the depth of about one-third of the Sun's radius

terrestrial planet A planet similar to the Earth—rocky and metallic and in the inner solar system; includes Mercury, Venus, Earth, and Mars

thermosphere The atmospheric layer between the mesosphere and the exosphere

tidal locking The tidal (gravitational) pull between two closely orbiting bodies that causes the bodies to settle into stable orbits with the same faces toward each other at all times; this final stable state is called synchronous rotation

tomography The technique of creating images of the interior of the Earth using the slightly different speeds of earthquake waves that have traveled along different paths through the Earth

tropopause The point in the atmosphere of any planet where the temperature reaches a minimum; both above and below this height, temperatures rise

troposphere The lower regions of a planetary atmosphere, where convection keeps the gas mixed, and there is a steady decrease in temperature with height above the surface

viscosity A liquid's resistance to flowing; honey has higher viscosity than water

visual magnitude The brightness of a celestial body as seen from Earth categorized on a numerical scale; the brightest star has magnitude −1.4 and the faintest visible star has magnitude 6; a decrease of one unit represents an increase in brightness by a factor of 2.512; system begun by Ptolemy in the second century B.C.E.; see also apparent magnitude

volatile An element that moves into a liquid or gas state at relatively low temperatures; compare with refractory

x-wind Magnetic fields that either pull material into the protostar or push it into the outer disk; these are thought to form at the inner edge of the disk where the protostar's magnetic field crosses the disk's magnetic field (also called "disk wind")

Further Resources

Abdrakhimov, A. M., and A. T. Basilevsky. "Geology of the Venera and Vega Landing-Site Regions." *Solar System Research* 36 (2002): 136–159. Accessible scientific paper on the impressive achievements of the Soviet Venus program.

Beatty, J. K., C. C. Petersen, and A. Chaikin. *The New Solar System*. Cambridge: Sky Publishing and Cambridge University Press, 1999. The most commonly used textbook on the solar system, with comprehensive and scholarly articles written in accessible language.

Booth, N. *Exploring the Solar System*. Cambridge: Cambridge University Press, 1995. Well-written and accurate volume on solar system exploration.

Comins, Neil F., and William J. Kaufmann. *Discovering the Universe*. New York: W. H. Freeman, 2008. The best-selling text for astronomy courses that use no mathematics. Presents concepts clearly and stresses the process of science.

Dickin, A. P. *Radiogenic Isotope Geology*. Cambridge: Cambridge University Press, 1995. Clear and complete textbook on the study of isotopes in geological sciences.

Fradin, Dennis Brindell. *The Planet Hunters: The Search for Other Worlds*. New York: Simon and Schuster, 1997. Stories of the people who through time have hunted for and found the planets.

Harmon, J. K., and M. A. Slade. "Radar Mapping of Mercury: Full-Disk Images and Polar Anomalies." *Science* 258 (1992): 640–642. Short scientific article on Mercury's surface before the advent of *MESSENGER*.

Kleine, T., C. Munker, K. Mezger, and H. Palme. "Rapid Accretion and Early Core Formation on Asteroids and the Terrestrial Planets from Hf-W Chronometry." *Nature* 418 (2002): 952–955. The science of dating the time of core formation, early in solar system history.

Krimgis, S. M., R. B. Decker, M. E. Hill, T. P. Armstrong, G. Gloeck-
    ler, D. C. Hamilton, L. J. Lanzerotti, and E. C. Roelof. "*Voyager 1*
    Exited the Solar Wind at the Distance of Similar to 85 AU from
    the Sun." *Nature* 426 (2003): 45–48. Announcement of the exit
    of *Voyager 1* from the solar system, making it the first man-made
    object to do so.

Lang, K. *Cambridge Encyclopedia of the Sun*. Cambridge: Cambridge
    University Press, 2001. Comprehensive resource on the Sun.

Nelson, Robert A. "Guide for Metric Practice." *Physics Today*
    (August 2003): BG15–BG16. Easily readable, complete discussion
    of the use of the metric system for scientists and engineers.

Norton, R. O. *Cambridge Encyclopedia of Meteorites*. Cambridge:
    Cambridge University Press, 2002. Beautifully illustrated and up-
    to-date book on meteorites.

Paul, Nigel. *The Solar System*. Seacaucus, N.J.: Chartwell Books, 2008.
    Begins with the origin of the universe and moves through the
    planets. Includes history of space flight and many color images.

Rees, Martin. *Universe*. London: DK Adult. A team of science writers
    and astronomers wrote this text for high school students and the
    general public.

Solomon, Sean C. "Mercury: The Enigmatic Innermost Planet."
    Earth and Planetary Science Letters 216 (2003): 441–455. Sum-
    mary of the state of knowledge of Mercury before the launch of
    MESSENGER.

Spangenburg, Ray. *A Look at the Sun (Out of This World)*. Danbury,
    Conn.: Children's Press, 2002. Young adult book on the Sun, easy
    to read, clear, and with excellent illustrations.

Sparrow, Giles. *The Planets: A Journey Through the Solar System*.
    Waltham, Mass.: Quercus Press, 2009. Solar system discoveries
    told within the structure of the last 40 years of space missions.

Spence, P. *The Universe Revealed*. Cambridge: Cambridge University
    Press, 1998. Comprehensive textbook on the universe.

Stacey, Frank D. *Physics of the Earth*. Brisbane, Australia: Brook-
    field Press, 1992. Fundamental geophysics text on an upper-level
    undergraduate college level.

Stevenson, D. J. "Planetary magnetic fields." *Earth and Planetary Sci-
    ence Letters* 208 (2003): 1–11. Comparisons and calculations about
    the planetary magnetic fields of many bodies in our solar system.

Wetherill, G. W. "Provenance of the Terrestrial Planets." *Geochimica
    et Cosmochimica Acta* 58 (1994): 4,513–4,520.

INTERNET RESOURCES

Angrum, Andrea. "Voyager: The Interstellar Mission." Jet Propulsion Laboratory. Available online. URL: http://voyager.jpl.nasa.gov/. Accessed August 24, 2009. Complete information on the Voyager space missions.

Arnett, Bill. "The 8 Planets: A Multimedia Tour of the Solar System." Available online. URL: http://nineplanets.org. First accessed September 21, 2009. An accessible overview of the history and science of the nine planets and their moons.

Blue, Jennifer, and the Working Group for Planetary System Nomenclature. "Gazetteer of Planetary Nomenclature." United States Geological Survey. Available online. URL: http://planetarynames.wr.usgs.gov/. Accessed August 24, 2009. Complete and official rules for naming planetary features, along with list of all named planetary features and downloadable images.

Dunn, James A., and Eric Burgess. "The Voyage of Mariner 10: Mission to Venus and Mercury." NASA History Office. Available online. URL: http://history.nasa.gov/SP-424/sp424.htm. Accessed August 24, 2009. Complete history of the mission as compiled by NASA and JPL.

Hurlburt, Neal. "Transition Region and Coronal Explorer." Lockheed Martin Missiles and Space. Available online. URL: http://vestige.lmsal.com/TRACE/. Accessed August 24, 2009. Home page of the TRACE space mission to study the Sun.

LaVoie, Sue, Myche McAuley, and Elizabeth Duxbury Rye. "Planetary Photojournal." Jet Propulsion Laboratory and NASA. Available online. URL: http://photojournal.jpl.nasa.gov/index.html. Accessed August 24, 2009. Large database of public-domain images from space missions.

O'Connor, John J., and Edmund F. Robertson. "The MacTutor History of Mathematics Archive." University of St. Andrews, Scotland. Available online. URL: http://www-gap.dcs.st-and.ac.uk/~history/index.html. Accessed August 24, 2009. A scholarly, precise, and eminently accessible compilation of biographies and accomplishments of mathematicians and scientists through the ages.

Rowlett, Russ. "How Many? A Dictionary of Units of Measurement." University of North Carolina at Chapel Hill. Available online. URL: http://www.unc.edu/~rowlett/units. Accessed August 24, 2009. A comprehensive dictionary of units of measurement, from the metric and English systems to the most obscure usages.

Williams, David. "Planetary Fact Sheets." NASA. Available online. URL: http://nssdc.gsfc.nasa.gov/planetary/planetfact.html. Accessed September 21, 2009. Detailed measurements and data on the planets, asteroids, and comets in simple tables.

Williams, David, and Dr. Ed Grayzeck. "Lunar and Planetary Science." NASA. Available online. URL: http://nssdc.gsfc.nasa.gov/planetary/planetary_home.html. First accessed September 21, 2009. NASA's deep archive and general distribution center for lunar and planetary data and images.

ORGANIZATIONS OF INTEREST

American Geophysical Union (AGU)
2000 Florida Avenue N.W.
Washington, D.C. 20009-1277
USA, www.agu.org
AGU is a worldwide scientific community that advances, through unselfish cooperation in research, the understanding of Earth and space for the benefit of humanity. AGU is an individual membership society open to those professionally engaged in or associated with the Earth and space sciences. Membership has increased steadily each year, doubling during the 1980s. Membership currently exceeds 41,000, of which about 20 percent are students. Membership in AGU entitles members and associates to receive Eos, AGU's weekly newspaper, and Physics Today, a magazine produced by the American Institute of Physics. In addition they are entitled to special member rates for AGU publications and meetings.

Association of Space Explorers
1150 Gemini Avenue
Houston, Texas 77058
http://www.space-explorers.org/
This association is expressly for people who have flown in space. They include 320 individuals from 34 nations, and their goal is to support space science and education. Their outreach activities include a speakers program, astronaut school visits, and observer status with the United Nations.

European Space Agency (ESA)
8-10 rue Mario Nikis
75738 Paris, Cedex 15
France
http://www.esa.int/esaCP/index.html

The European Space Agency has 18 member states, which together create a unified European space program and carry out missions in parallel and in cooperation with NASA, JAXA, and other space agencies. Its member countries are Austria, Belgium, Czech Republic, Denmark, Finland, France, Germany, Greece, Ireland, Italy, Luxembourg, the Netherlands, Norway, Portugal, Spain, Sweden, and Switzerland. The United Kingdom, Hungary, Romania, Poland, and Slovenia are cooperating partners.

International Astronomical Union (IAU)
98 bis, bd Arago
75014, Paris
France
www.iau.org
The International Astronomical Union was founded in 1919. Its mission is to promote and safeguard the science of astronomy in all its aspects through international cooperation. Its individual members are professional astronomers from all over the world, at the Ph.D. level or beyond and active in professional research and education in astronomy. However, the IAU also maintains friendly relations with organizations that include amateur astronomers. National members are generally those with a significant level of professional astronomy. With now more than 9,100 individual members and 65 national members worldwide, the IAU plays a pivotal role in promoting and coordinating worldwide cooperation in astronomy. The IAU also serves as the internationally recognized authority for assigning designations to celestial bodies and any surface features on them.

Jet Propulsion Laboratory (JPL)
4800 Oak Grove Drive
Pasadena, Calif. 91109
USA
www.jpl.nasa.gov
The Jet Propulsion Laboratory is managed by the California Institute of Technology for NASA. JPL manages many of NASA's space missions, including the Mars Rovers and Cassini, and also conducts fundamental research in planetary and space science.

Meteoritical Society: The International Society for Meteoritics and Planetary Science, www.meteoriticalsociety.org. The Meteoritical Society is a nonprofit scholarly organization founded in 1933 to promote the study of extraterrestrial materials and their history. The membership of the society includes 950 scientists and amateur enthusiasts from over 33 countries who are interested in a wide range of planetary science. Members' interests include meteorites, cosmic dust, asteroids and comets, natural satellites, planets, impacts, and the origins of the solar system.

National Aeronautics and Space Administration (NASA)
300 E Street S.W.
Washington D.C. 20002
USA
www.nasa.gov
NASA, an agency of the United States government, manages space flight centers, research centers, and other organizations including the National Aerospace Museum. NASA scientists and engineers conduct basic research on planetary and space topics, plan and execute space missions, oversee Earth satellites and data collection, and many other space- and flight-related projects.

Planetary Society
65 North Catalina Avenue
Pasadena, Calif. 91106-2301
USA
http://www.planetary.org/home/
This is a society of lay individuals, scientists, organizations, and businesses dedicated to involving the world's public in space exploration through advocacy, projects, and exploration. The Planetary Society was founded in 1980 by Carl Saga, Bruce Murray, and Louis Friedman. They are particularly dedicated to searching for life outside of Earth.

Index